BUILDING A SOCIAL CONTRACT

In the series *Urban Life, Landscape, and Policy,* edited by David Stradling, Larry Bennett, and Davarian Baldwin. Founding editor, Zane L. Miller.

ALSO IN THIS SERIES:

Stephanie Ryberg-Webster, *Preserving the Vanishing City: Historic Preservation amid Urban Decline in Cleveland, Ohio*
Matthew Smith, *The Spires Still Point to Heaven: Cincinnati's Religious Landscape, 1788–1873*
Roger Biles and Mark H. Rose, *A Good Place to Do Business: The Politics of Downtown Renewal since 1945*
Larry Bennett, John D. Fairfield, and Patricia Mooney-Melvin, eds., *Bringing the Civic Back In: Zane L. Miller and American Urban History*
Henry C. Binford, *From Improvement to City Planning: Spatial Management in Cincinnati from the Early Republic through the Civil War Decade*
Dennis E. Gale, *The Misunderstood History of Gentrification: People, Planning, Preservation, and Urban Renewal, 1915–2020*
Amy D. Finstein, *Modern Mobility Aloft: Elevated Highways, Architecture, and Urban Change in Pre-Interstate America*
Mark Shiel, ed., *Architectures of Revolt: The Cinematic City circa 1968*
Maureen Donaghy, *Democratizing Urban Development: Community Organizations for Housing across the United States and Brazil*
Maureen A. Flanagan, *Constructing the Patriarchal City: Gender and the Built Environments of London, Dublin, Toronto, and Chicago, 1870s into the 1940s*
Harold L. Platt, *Sinking Chicago: Climate Change and the Remaking of a Flood-Prone Environment*
Pamela Wilcox, Francis T. Cullen, and Ben Feldmeyer, *Communities and Crime: An Enduring American Challenge*
J. Mark Souther, *Believing in Cleveland: Managing Decline in "The Best Location in the Nation"*
Nathanael Lauster, *The Death and Life of the Single-Family House: Lessons from Vancouver on Building a Livable City*
Aaron Cowan, *A Nice Place to Visit: Tourism and Urban Revitalization in the Postwar Rustbelt*
Carolyn Gallaher, *The Politics of Staying Put: Condo Conversion and Tenant Right-to-Buy in Washington, DC*
Evrick Brown and Timothy Shortell, eds., *Walking in Cities: Quotidian Mobility as Urban Theory, Method, and Practice*
Michael T. Maly and Heather Dalmage, *Vanishing Eden: White Construction of Memory, Meaning, and Identity in a Racially Changing City*
Harold L. Platt, *Building the Urban Environment: Visions of the Organic City in the United States, Europe, and Latin America*

A list of additional titles in this series appears at the back of this book.

Michael McCulloch

BUILDING A SOCIAL CONTRACT

Modern Workers' Houses in
Early Twentieth-Century Detroit

TEMPLE UNIVERSITY PRESS
Philadelphia • *Rome* • *Tokyo*

TEMPLE UNIVERSITY PRESS
Philadelphia, Pennsylvania 19122
tupress.temple.edu

Copyright © 2023 by Temple University—Of The Commonwealth System
  of Higher Education
All rights reserved
Published 2023

Library of Congress Cataloging-in-Publication Data

Names: McCulloch, Michael, 1979– author.
Title: Building a social contract : modern workers' houses in early
  twentieth-century Detroit / Michael McCulloch.
Other titles: Urban life, landscape, and policy.
Description: Philadelphia : Temple University Press, 2023. | Series: Urban
  life, landscape, and policy | Includes bibliographical references and
  index. | Summary: "Explores developments in Detroit's early
  twentieth-century workers' housing as a significant moment in global
  architectural history. Argues that the city's workers and employers
  negotiated an implicit social contract in which the work of mass
  production was rewarded with access to modern housing"— Provided by
  publisher.
Identifiers: LCCN 2023006419 (print) | LCCN 2023006420 (ebook) | ISBN
  9781439923917 (cloth) | ISBN 9781439923924 (paperback) | ISBN
  9781439923931 (pdf)
Subjects: LCSH: Working class—Dwellings—Michigan—Detroit—History—20th
  century. | Architecture, Domestic—Michigan—Detroit—History—20th
  century. | Housing—Michigan—Detroit—History—20th century. | Cost and
  standard of living—Michigan—Detroit—History—20th century. | Detroit
  (Mich.)—Social conditions—20th century.
Classification: LCC HD7304.D6 M34 2023 (print) | LCC HD7304.D6 (ebook) |
  DDC 305.5/620977434—dc23/eng/20230605
LC record available at https://lccn.loc.gov/2023006419
LC ebook record available at https://lccn.loc.gov/2023006420

9 8 7 6 5 4 3 2 1

For Carrie, Joe, and Matthew

CONTENTS

Acknowledgments   ix

Introduction   1

PART I: MIGRATION

1 Passages: Moving to and through Houses in an Industrial City   19

2 American Houses: Architecture of the Melting Pot Project   31

PART II: MODERNIZATION

3 Forms of Modern Housing: Alternative Models from Dessau to Detroit   55

4 Modern Housebuilding: Policy, Products, and Labor   75

5 Detroit's Other Industry: Real Estate and the Culture of Elusive Security   97

6 Better Lives: Making Do in Modern Houses   123

PART III: STRUGGLE

7 Glass and Stones: Materials of Race and Neighborhood Violence   145

8 Social Contract in Crisis: Welfare, Eviction, and Activism in the Depression   163

Conclusion   183

Notes   189

Index   223

ACKNOWLEDGMENTS

This project, ten years in the making, has benefitted from the generosity of many people and institutions. It began as a dissertation at the University of Michigan's Taubman College of Architecture and Urban Planning, under the guidance of Committee Chair Robert Fishman. Robert always knows the right book to recommend, and as a teacher I often find myself "paying forward" the wisdom I've gained from him. Dissertation advisers Will Glover, June Manning Thomas, and Claire Zimmerman taught me much of what I know about the craft of writing with their feedback on seminar papers and dissertation chapter drafts. Scott Campbell, Matt Lassiter, and Andrew Herscher each taught me new ways to look at buildings and cities. The latter introduced me to Charlie Chaplin's *Modern Times*, which provides the opening scene for this book. I'm appreciative to Matt Biro and Milton Curry for their leadership of the Michigan-Mellon Project on Egalitarianism and the Metropolis, in which I served as a postdoctoral Humanities Fellow in 2015–2016. It was in that role that I began to transform this project from a dissertation into a book.

Many scholars have provided suggestions and encouragement as I tested ideas in conference papers and manuscript drafts, including Joseph Bigott, Nicholas Bloom, Bob Bruegmann, Gabrielle Esperdy, Owen Gutfreund, Marta Gutman, Richard Harris, Thomas Hubka, Brad Hunt, Michael Jen, and Amanda Seligman. The Charles H. Wright Museum of African American History, the Chicago History Seminar, and the University of Michigan's Institute for the Humanities provided opportunities to share this work in progress with public audiences. Anonymous peer reviewers offered timely insights that made the project better. I am grateful to Aaron Javsicas, editor-in-chief at Temple University Press, for championing this book, and to Larry Bennett, editor of the *Urban Life, Landscape, and Policy* series, for his thorough and insightful feedback. Thank you to the staff of Temple University Press, including Ann-Marie Anderson, William Forrest, Gary Kramer, and Ashley Petrucci. Susan Deeks's skillful copyediting made a big difference.

Archivists and librarians from around Metro Detroit and Ann Arbor provided valuable advice and assistance. Thank you to the staffs of the Burton Historical Collection of the Detroit Public Library; the Cranbrook Center for Collections and Research; the Detroit Historical Museum; The Henry Ford; the University of Michigan Libraries, including the Bentley Historical Library; and the Walter P. Reuther Library's Archives of Labor and Urban Affairs at Wayne State University. Thanks also to Justyna Zdunek-Wielgolaska, who translated Polish-language advertisements for the project that appear in Chapter 5.

The American Council of Learned Societies and Andrew W. Mellon Foundation provided crucial financial support and workshop opportunities during this project's dissertation phase, as did the University of Michigan's Institute for the Humanities, the Rackham Graduate School, and Taubman College. Thank you to them and to the many generous scholars who I met in those workshops. Over the past six years, Kendall College of Art and Design at Ferris State University has provided faculty development funding, a network of supportive colleagues, and the opportunity to teach design and architectural history to insightful, ambitious students. If they tire of hearing my stories about Detroit, they have kindly not let on.

In closing, I want to acknowledge my family. Thank you to my parents, Anna and Kevin McCulloch, and my parents-in-law, Mary and the late Matt Walsh, for their support. Thanks also to my extended family, past and present. Writing this book has made me more conscious of the ways that my opportunities build on the hard work of earlier generations, including in Detroit's automobile industry. I am grateful to my late grandfather Frank Stahl, a longtime Ford employee, who taught me to appreciate art and history from a young age. Finally, I dedicate this book to my wife, Carrie, who has done more than anyone to help make the project a reality, and to our wonderful sons, Joe and Matthew.

BUILDING A SOCIAL CONTRACT

INTRODUCTION

> I'll do it! We'll get a home, even if I have to work for it.
> —Factory Worker (Charlie Chaplin), *Modern Times*

The kitchen is bright and spacious. Chaplin's protagonists from *Modern Times*—a down-on-his-luck factory worker and a young woman who befriends him—sit down for dinner. Beyond them, at the sink below the window, light plays off the bridge-style faucet. The curtains are parted decoratively, and the tiled countertop is mostly clean. Napkins adjusted, the pair eagerly begin to cut their steak, as if to have just one bite before the scene fades out and they awake from their daydream.[1]

Their dream is that of the modern worker's house—one that emerged in the early twentieth century as wage earners in American cities gained access to new types of larger and better-equipped dwellings and navigated new representations of those dwellings. Domestic comforts such as indoor bathrooms and electric lighting became widespread in American workers' houses for the first time. Yet Chaplin, like other Depression-era cultural critics, was skeptical of the dream and of the larger project of modernization that gave rise to it. Many of the best laughs in *Modern Times*, after all, are found as his "Tramp" character tries and fails to conform to the rigors of work in a factory and a department store, pursuing the wages a house would require. More tragically, the young woman played by Paulette Goddard becomes homeless in the Depression and is forced to steal to survive. Yet these two, like many workers on the actual streets and shop floors of U.S. cities, were undeterred in their house dreaming.

This book is a history of the houses those workers dreamed of and labored for. It traces the efforts of early twentieth-century employers, government agencies, and the building industry who, along with workers themselves, produced a then unprecedented boom in housing construction that peaked in the mid-1920s. Given its scope and significance, this period in American housing history has gone understudied. As a proportional expansion of the national housing stock, it was nearly as large as the post–World War II boom but has received far less attention in scholarship and popular culture.[2] The early twentieth century was a time of rapid outward expansion in American cities and a historical inflection point in which the design, financing, technology, and marketing of workers' houses were all modernized. In this context, as wage earners sought better houses on the urban periphery, they navigated a shifting landscape of power within American society.

Social Contract

More seemed possible for American workers than ever before in the early twentieth century. Wage earners made substantial gains in the growth years of the 1910s and 1920s, despite the infamous difficulty of some of the work, and began to rent and buy new houses and to improve older ones. Their bungalows, duplex flats, and upgraded cottages, though often far from the ideal, were part of an extraordinary rise in living standards. Yet they were also sites of unease and conflict, where working-class households struggled to maintain their tenuous gains, often living from one pay envelope to the next amid mercurial swings in the economy. Early twentieth-century modernization, in other words, heightened both the promises and the perils of American working-class life. One hundred years later, this history of ambition and struggle echoes in the present as workers continue to struggle for security amid cycles of economic growth and crisis.

Encountering new opportunities and risks in the early twentieth century, workers participated in a rewriting of the American *social contract*. The term, borrowed from political philosophy, is used here to emphasize that power is renegotiated within a democratic society on an ongoing basis and that workers are a party to those negotiations. As employers, government, and workers struggled to maximize their gains amid rapid economic growth, they staked out new social positions, rearticulating their responsibilities to one another. Workers' bargaining power increased in this period, with employers hungry for labor to fuel their expanding industries and fearful of labor unrest. In response, powerful corporations such as the Ford Motor Company, and government agencies at the local, state, and national level, began to take more responsibility for the quality and availability of workers' houses. Employers raised wages in the 1910s while at the same time promoting modern housing construction and worker homeownership. City governments expanded utilities at the urban periphery, priming these areas for development, and rolled out new housing regulations. The federal government partnered with the building industry to increase its production and, with its "own your own home" campaign, lent an authoritative voice to the idea that workers could aspire to own modern houses.

Corporate employers and policy makers expected that workers, if invested in modern houses, furniture, and even automobiles, would be motivated to accept difficult jobs, maintain them steadily, and avoid labor conflicts. Workers navigated this offer—its promises and pitfalls—in a diversity of ways. Their dedicated labor was borne out in the extraordinary economic growth of the 1910s and 1920s, and their promised rewards are evidenced in the period's many newly developed residential neighborhoods. However modest, most workers' early twentieth-century dwellings were the best they had ever lived in, a rising material prosperity that changed the American working-class experience. In the process, however, workers became increasingly vulnerable, disempowered in relation to their employers, who retained economic control and could lay off employees at will during slow periods.

The implicit contract of the 1910s and 1920s, workers understood, did not offer modern housing as a social right. Rather, it was an opportunity that workers were encouraged to pursue and was within the reach of many as long as the economy continued to grow. With economic downturns in 1914 and 1920–1921, and annual shutdowns in many industries, workers were regularly reminded of the uncertainty that loomed over their employment. Nevertheless, through tangibly improved day-to-day living conditions, and rising social prestige, workers learned to demand more in the early twentieth century. When the Depression threatened the security of their houses in the early 1930s, they rose up. Workers protested unemployment, eviction, and foreclosure; pushed for change at the ballot box; and struggled for the right to bargain collectively.[3] They changed America with their activism and New Deal industrial unionism. Workers demanded that their position within the American social contract be strengthened, with social insurance and greater working-class economic control. Pressing government to take a stronger role in the economy and to provide legal protections for labor, they helped to change the course of American capitalism for decades.

Figure I.1. Geographic expansion of Detroit, 1910–1930. The dark-gray area at the right was rapidly developed in these two decades, in Detroit and in the enclaves of Highland Park and Hamtramck, which Detroit grew to surround.

Source: Illustration by the author. Areas of development are derived from Constantinos A. Doxiadis, *Emergence and Growth of an Urban Region: The Developing Urban Detroit Area* (Detroit: Detroit Edison, 1966), 69; Sanborn Map Company, *Insurance Maps of Detroit, Michigan*, vols. 5–8, 1910, University of Michigan, Ann Arbor.

In popular culture, Detroit has long been associated with labor's position in the American social contract. The city attracted outsize attention and symbolic importance in the early twentieth century, when the Ford Motor Company introduced its moving assembly line in 1913 and soon after raised wages and shortened working hours. Detroit's fast-growing automobile industry supercharged the city's physical growth: its population more than tripled in the 1910s and 1920s, to more than 1.5 million residents. Its land area grew by more than three times as well, reaching 138 square miles through outward growth and annexation (Figure I.1). The city's building industry produced more than 150,000 units of new housing in single-family and duplex configurations between 1915 and 1930, introducing the new standard of larger and better-equipped workers' houses.[4]

Early twentieth-century observers saw Detroit's rising culture of industrial work and mass-market consumerism as the purest example of U.S. national trends. European critics coined the terms *Fordism* and *Detroitism* in their analyses of these cultural shifts.[5] Detroit remains a revealing place to explore that transformative period in America's cultural history and is the focus of this book. Though many U.S. cities grew rapidly in the 1910s and 1920s and participated in the period's housebuilding boom, Detroit was among the fastest growing and most transformed. Many urban places contributed to the new working-class politics of the 1930s, when the gains of the growth years were threatened, but Detroit's autoworkers were among the most active. The Motor

City remains associated with the beleaguered but still potent cultural ideal that it helped to construct in the early twentieth century: that in America, hard work should be respected and well rewarded.

Workers and Houses

The American working class was diverse and competitive in the early twentieth century, and the urban world they navigated was profoundly unequal. Even as wage earners made gains in the 1910s and 1920s, salaried professionals benefited more. In industrial work, employers often favored young white men, including immigrants, whom they accepted into whiteness, while discriminating against older workers and Black workers. The latter were often given the most difficult and undesirable jobs.[6] Skilled workers outearned the unskilled, and female workers were routinely paid less than men for the same positions. In 1922, for example, a national study of wages in the automobile industry showed that a semiskilled drill press operator earned an average of $32 per week, $1,660 per year, or about one-third less if the operator was female. A skilled toolmaker earned an average of $38 per week, or $2,000 per year. Around the same time in Detroit, the "cost of maintaining a fair minimum standard of living" for a family of five in a five-room house was about $1,700.[7] A household that lived on the income of a male drill press operator alone, in other words, would struggle to meet the rising standard of living, even if he avoided injury or seasonal layoffs that could cut into the household's income. Amid these economic challenges, as well as the opportunities of working-class life in the early twentieth century, the two-income household became more common.[8]

Even in the Motor City, not everyone worked in a factory. For this reason, individuals from across the working-class landscape appear in the book, including not only industrial workers but also municipal workers such as a firefighter and a water department employee; building industry workers such as carpenters, painters, and masons; a barber, a peddler, and a waiter; and those who washed the clothes and kept the houses of the professional class. Their household budgets and strategies varied, and their prospects in the housing realm reflected their place in the city's employment hierarchy.

One's job, however, was not the only factor that affected one's housing prospects. The growing city beyond the workplace was divided by lines of residential segregation. White Christian workers enjoyed increasing access to modern houses, while restrictive covenants excluded racial and religious minorities, and especially African Americans, from most new subdivisions. These restrictions were backed by law and by realty practices and reinforced by white workers themselves, who perpetrated violent attacks on Black Detroiters who dared to cross racial lines. The working-class experience in early twentieth-century America was thus one of gains for a privileged cohort, but also of deepening inequality, which fell hardest on Black workers, who had few opportunities to translate their labor into modern houses. Tracing the interconnected stories of Black and white workers' houses, this book illustrates how housing segregation was constructed, and how Black workers struggled, in a bitterly racist society, to be included in the American social contract.

Working-class bungalows and other U.S. national plan-book models of the early twentieth century are important and overlooked artifacts in the global history of housing. After World War I, European and Soviet policy makers faced conditions that were broadly similar to those of their American peers: urban housing shortages, new technological possibilities, and rising working-class political clout. Yet while their policies called for centrally planned housing estates in cities such as Frankfurt and Moscow, the U.S. government and America's large employers chose to reinforce the private, speculative housebuilding industry. For all of its faults, this approach did prove capable of developing houses at a mass scale, changing the shape of cities such as Los Angeles, Chicago, and Detroit.[9] American builders did not take up "mass-production" building methods or reinforced concrete structures like their European peers, but they did modernize their practices in the interwar period, adopting new material standards and using new construction machines—not least, gasoline-powered trucks. The productivity of its housebuilding industry allowed Detroit to absorb an extraordinary boom in population—to house and integrate hundreds of thousands of new arrivals into its urban culture in the 1910s and 1920s.

The white walls and flat roofs of European modernism are highly visible symbols of early twentieth-century cultural shifts. Yet American bungalows, quaint though their gabled roofs may seem, were just as transformative, or more so, given how widely they proliferated (Figure I.2). These wood-framed structures were modern in important yet subtle ways and distinct from the nineteenth-century workers' cottages that preceded them. Their most astounding aspects related to infrastructure: the gas and sewer lines underground and the electric wires overhead that brought new services into the house, supporting the popularization of

Figure I.2. "Houses in the Polish District." Photograph of modern bungalows in Detroit's north-of-Hamtramck district by the Office of War Information photographer John Vachon, 1942.
Source: U.S. Farm Security Administration/Office of War Information Collection, Library of Congress, Washington, DC.

the three-fixture bathroom. Bedrooms became more private relative to the active rooms of the house and began to include closets where residents could store their growing number of possessions.[10] Most visibly and recognizably, modern bungalows and duplexes often had broad and deep street-facing porches. The working-class house was becoming a site of leisure as never before.

Employers, government, and the building industry all idealized worker homeownership in the early twentieth century, and amid its rapid tripling in size, Detroit did manage to increase its overall homeownership rate slightly, to 41.3 percent—a notable achievement.[11] American workers had established a prior homeownership culture in the late nineteenth century, as the historians Elaine Lewinnek and Olivier Zunz have shown.[12] Yet the issue became more complicated as standards of living increased in the 1910s and 1920s. Consumer credit was becoming more available, but housing costs rose at the same time, and new possible expenses, such as installment payments for refrigerators, furniture, and automobiles, could crowd out the kind of saving that a down payment on a house would require.

Skilled workers had more capacity to save than the unskilled and were more likely to achieve the ideal of modern homeownership. In the working-class north-of-Hamtramck section of Detroit, for example, Home Owners Loan Corporation (HOLC) data from the late 1930s shows one neighborhood occupied by "laborers," where 30 percent of detached houses were occupied by their owners, right next to one occupied by "skilled mechanics," where owner-occupancy was at 65 percent. An International Labor Office (ILO) survey from 1929 found that 32 percent of Ford workers at the bottom of the company's pay scale owned their houses—a significant minority but also an illustration of the popularity of renting.[13] Some unskilled workers navigated the affordability dilemma by delaying the comforts of a modern house and instead bought lots at the unimproved urban periphery, as the urban historians Richard Harris and Becky Nicolaides have shown. In Detroit, workers could pursue a version of this strategy in B. E. Taylor's Brightmoor development, where residential lots, with or without small houses on them and lacking most modern amenities, were available at low cost. For all of its limitations, Brightmoor had a striking 95 percent owner-occupancy rate in the HOLC survey.

While homeownership among Detroit's lower-paid workers ran below the city's general average, the ILO survey of unskilled Ford workers illustrates that this group did make significant gains in living standards.[14] By 1929, the one hundred households surveyed were living in relatively spacious dwellings in Detroit with four to five rooms, mostly in detached houses such as bungalows or in duplex flats. All of their houses were wired for electricity, and 72 percent were plumbed with indoor bathrooms. In a further indication of Detroit workers' material gains, 47 percent of the surveyed households had acquired a used or new automobile by the end of the 1920s, many having bought them, and other consumer durables, on an installment plan.[15]

Theory, Agency, and Experience

Detroit's early twentieth-century neighborhoods were shaped by many private developers and house builders. They purchased land at the urban periphery, amid newly emerging factories, and worked cheek by jowl to lay out a gridiron of streets, alleys, and salable lots and dwellings. Their profit-seeking motivation, and the consistency of the resulting houses and blocks, has served as a foil for urban theorists. Voices from the Garden City movement and the subsequent Modern movement criticized the kind of uncoordinated, for-profit development that Detroit

Figure I.3. Aerial view of Detroit cited in José Luis Sert, *Can Our Cities Survive? An ABC of Urban Problems, Their Analysis, Their Solutions* (Cambridge, MA: Harvard University Press, 1942). The northwestern Detroit neighborhood in the foreground was home to a relatively affluent group of "merchants, jr. executives, clerks, [and] salesmen" in the late 1930s, according to a description by the Home Owners Loan Corporation. It was a growing center of Detroit's Jewish community. For Sert, it represented the gridiron pattern of speculative development that dominated in Detroit and in most American cities.

Source: *Detroit News* photograph, Archives of Labor and Urban Affairs, Walter P. Reuther Library, Wayne State University, Detroit.

represents for its lack of centralized planning. Without planning, they argued, based on environmental, social, and aesthetic goals, developers over-consumed land, created unnecessary conflicts between pedestrians and vehicles, and treated houses as mere consumer products. José Luis Sert, a leading voice for the Congrès Internationaux d'Architecture Moderne (CIAM), framed modern architecture and planning in opposition to what had been built in the Motor City. In 1941, referring to an aerial view of Detroit's northwestern section (Figure I.3), he urged that "a city should be something more than a monotonous and unending series of real estate developments."[16]

The urban theorist Jane Jacobs, writing in a postwar context, shared Sert's disdain for Detroit's urban form, even as she introduced a radically new perspective. Jacobs was alarmed by the vast scale of demolition and redevelopment that had been normalized under the banner of modernist urban renewal, and in response she argued the merits of dense, diverse urban neighborhoods such as Greenwich Village. Jacobs described the life of her own street in the Village, where neighbors and shopkeepers looked out for one another, with extraordinary sensitivity. She proved to be a powerful critic of Modernist urbanism. Yet when discussing Detroit's form of development in *The Death and Life of Great American Cities*, she became dismissive, adopting a more distanced view than she had brought to Greenwich Village. She criticized the low density and "endless" quality of the Motor City's block structure, and subsequent observers have offered similar assessments.[17]

Sert and Jacobs offered sweeping condemnations of early twentieth-century Detroit, and Marxist scholars have offered their own critique, coining the term *Fordism* to describe the political transformation that accompanied the rise of mass production.[18] They point out, rightly, that industrial workers' consumer gains in the period were no substitute for political power. Access to modern houses or automobiles carried the risk of diminished power, as they made workers more dependent on regular wages and less free to challenge employers. Yet Marxist observers go on to interpret this as the rise of a "false consciousness": a failure on the part of workers to realize, as they made consumer gains, that they were still workers and were vulnerable within the power dynamics of modern capitalism. This reading leaves little room to explore workers' political agency within capitalism, just as planning theorists' criticisms of "endless" subdivisions leave little room to see workers' cultural agency in their houses and neighborhoods. What unites these diverse theorists is the top-down view that they direct at Detroit's urban form and its labor politics. Given the outsize social and cultural influence of figures such as Henry Ford in this period, historians have also tended to favor narratives in which Detroit's early twentieth-century culture and built environment were shaped from above by the powerful.[19]

In response to the limits of top-down readings, this book seeks to engage with workers' voices and their agency in negotiating the terms of early twentieth-century urbanization. It finds that workers saw their so-called monotonous houses in Detroit very differently from Sert and Jacobs. They were hard-earned and intensely personal spaces—full of rewards for the difficult labor of the modern workplace. Workers constructed their houses' specific meanings through the intimate channels of sensory and psychological experience, and the ephemeral nature of such phenomena presents a methodological challenge to the historian.

Building a Social Contract addresses this by engaging with the oral histories of those who grew up in early twentieth-century Detroit, seeking a nuanced understanding of what made its modern houses worth working for and fighting for. It also engages with period fiction and poetry and with reformers' notes and photographs. Historians have rightly pointed out the biases and limitations in middle-class authors' and reformers' records, but this study finds great value in returning to such materials and reading them with a critical eye that is attentive to both what is presented and what is obscured.[20]

Drawing inspiration from Gaston Bachelard's *The Poetics of Space*, this book explores the working-class experience of modern houses and finds a detail-rich world in early twentieth-century Detroit that urban and political theorists have often overlooked.[21] It traces the hardships of working-class life in this period, from risky migration journeys and fears about finances to rising early and returning home exhausted. Rather than adopting a superficial critique of workers' consumerism, this book illustrates how identities were constructed, and pride and agency were found, in even banal-seeming aspects of workers' houses. Wage earners constructed whole worlds of private meanings in choosing, modifying, and outfitting their houses, and because of this there is nothing frivolous about a new stove or hot water heater, a paint or wallpaper choice, a garden planting or a religious icon, or the curtains in a front window. They index the rituals by which residents shaped and maintained their houses, and the relationships within them, as they pursued self-defined better lives.

Workers were not passive receivers of a modern culture that was imprinted on them from above. Rather, they "made do," to borrow Michel de Certeau's apt term, within the constraining order of modern capitalism.[22] Workers outfitted their houses in ways that exceeded and at times resisted the imperatives of powerful institutions, from employers and government agencies to advertisers and real estate brokers, creating a diversity of subcultures and ways of living in modern houses. Their own words illustrate that they were not naïve about the precariousness of their social position. Instead, they were pragmatic actors within an imperfect system, taking risks and working hard to get ahead. Lizabeth Cohen has shown that workers' encounter with mass culture in the 1920s—in film and radio and on company baseball teams, for example—provided common cultural ground that supported their drive for unionization in the 1930s.[23] This book explores what workers were fighting for at that crucial moment. It advances housing, where the quality-of-life gains of the 1910s and 1920s were experienced, as an understudied but essential motivator for workers' collective struggle. From amid their diversity, and with individual household economies on the line, American workers collaborated when their houses were threatened in the 1930s. They struggled against capitalism from within it, as Mario Tronti has pointed out, to extraordinary effect.[24]

In recent decades, urban historians have begun to write wage earners and factories into the story of U.S. suburbanization, building on the middle class–focused narratives that preceded them, such as Kenneth Jackson's *Crabgrass Frontier* and Robert Fishman's *Bourgeois Utopias*.[25] Lewinnek and Zunz, along with Margaret Garb and Joseph Bigott, have contributed in-depth studies that center on late nineteenth-century working-class homeownership and point to the early twentieth century as a period of change in American housing.[26] Nicolaides and Harris have traced the self-building practices of early twentieth-century workers in the little-regulated outskirts of Los Angeles and Toronto. Thomas Hubka has studied the new spatial arrangements of early twentieth-century houses, such as the bungalow plan and the three-fixture bath, showing how these elements made workers' houses modern in an architectural sense.[27]

This book engages with modern workers' houses in a new way. It draws out wage earners' agency and lived experience in this context, as mentioned previously, and emphasizes that the U.S. speculative development model was not the only one available, comparing Detroit's housing with concurrent, centrally planned developments in Europe. Drawing methodological inspiration from the work of the Aggregate Architectural History Collaborative, this project treats workers' housing not only as architecture but also as real estate, emphasizing its role in a changing economy, in the politics of governance, and in the construction of racial identities and segregation.[28] As N. B. D. Connolly has illustrated in his study of Miami real estate, housing segregation reflected both the ideology of white supremacy and the practices of developers and landlords who profited from racial, spatial divides.[29] *Building a Social Contract* shows that housing, then as now, distributes economic risk within society, spatializes race and class relations, and is central to workers' struggle for security.

Roadmap

This book begins on the road, so to speak, as early twentieth-century workers made their way to Detroit from abroad and from many U.S. points of origin, seeking work and new possibilities. It draws to a close on a road, as well, at the border between Detroit and adjacent Dearborn. There, in 1932, those same workers marched toward the Ford Motor Company's gates to protest unemployment and housing insecurity. They, and the city itself, had been thoroughly transformed in the meantime.

Chapter 1 traces workers' migration experiences, on ships and trains and in the back of trucks. As their letters and oral histories show, this mobile workforce endured many uncertainties but also made choices in their travels, not least in choosing whether to return home or to stay and invest long-term in a place like Detroit. It explores the transitory experiences of boardinghouses, where many of the newly arrived found a foothold in the city. It argues that these, and the risks and contingencies of migration, shaped the meaning of workers' modern houses in the years to come. Chapter 2 engages with the project of "Americanization," which immigrant workers encountered on arrival in the city. In night-school manuals and employee handbooks, it finds business leaders and government, eager to secure the workforce, framing the modern house and homeownership as markers of American identity that were available to new arrivals. The Ford Motor Company and others presented "carrots and sticks" to employees. Offering assistance with modern house seeking to workers, and penalties for those who refused, they established the principle that modern employers took a measure of responsibility for the quality and security of employees' houses.

With Chapter 3, the focus begins to shift from the experiences of the newly arrived to the development policies and practices that shaped Detroit in the early twentieth century. It begins with paths not taken, examining centrally planned housing policy and projects from the period in London and Berlin and two largely unbuilt planned housing proposals for Detroit itself. Though unplanned, speculative housing won the day in the United States, the chapter underscores that urban development in America, and the social distribution of risk, might have proceeded very differently. Chapter 4 takes a closer look at the speculative housebuilding industry that proved so productive in early twentieth-century America, exploring builders' efforts to modernize their practices. Supported by employers and government, and seeking to capitalize on booming demand, the construction industry began to modernize itself. Contractors adopted new machines, methods, and schedules and responded to new building codes. Material suppliers increasingly standardized the dimensions and grades of their lumber products and circulated plan books that aided the proliferation of new house types such as bungalows and duplexes. Though many small builders continued to operate, larger-scale speculative developers emerged as a more significant force, leveraging enough capital to develop dozens of speculative houses at a time. The chapter features the experiences of building industry workers in this context—an often overlooked cohort among Detroit wage earners—as they navigated new working methods and shifting labor politics.

Chapter 5 follows the real estate agents who helped to connect builders with house-buying workers and investors. They, too, modernized their practices in the early twentieth century, becoming organized through the National Association of Realtors, adopting the posture of fiduciary advisers, and collaborating with the federal government. Leveraging their increased authority within culture, agents spoke to workers' concerns in their sales discourse. They presented modern houses, in restricted peripheral subdivisions, as a way to raise one's social prestige and increase children's future prospects. Homeownership, they added, would allow workers to face the daunting process of aging with security. Amid Detroit's extraordinary early twentieth-century growth, real estate boosters predicted economic expansion on a fantastical scale, giving a false sense that the period's speculative development model could be sustained indefinitely.

Through their houses, workers built complex modern identities, and their practices and experiences are the focus of Chapter 6. Within the corridors of their residential blocks, wage earners performed their ethnic identities and minded one another's children. Those children went on to record oral histories. They illustrate the distance between the period's bourgeois ideals, projected by advertisers, poets, and home economics instructors, and the lived experiences of households that inevitably had to make compromises. The boys in one such family, for example, shared a bed in the cold attic above an otherwise finished house. Yet these former children of early twentieth-century Detroit also recall their parents' pride—pride in proprietorship, in well-tended gardens, and in ethnic and racial identities. They describe the interrelationships between work and household priorities in this period, recalling their parents' exhaustion and determination as they labored, in part, to give the next generation more choices and greater ease.

As the book turns from the theme of housing modernization to that of workers' struggle, Chapter 7 focuses on Detroit's racial conflicts of 1925, which followed the violent Red Summer, in Chicago and other cities, in 1919. Black migrants sought a fair share in Detroit's white-dominated social contract but encountered a growing culture of segregation and violence in the city's new neighborhoods. White Detroiters created a "storm" of mob attacks to enforce racial boundaries, seeking to defend against perceived threats to their social standing and to the economic value of their houses. The well-known violence at the Black physician Ossian Sweet's residence was just one of several such incidents in the city, and the chapter focuses on the little-known case of another household: working-class Black residents who refused to leave their duplex flat in a white-dominated neighborhood. A member of that household recalled the attacks they suffered in a local memory book, allowing for a detailed reconstruction of the violence. It shows that the assailants leveraged the particular conditions of the modern house to create maximum terror and that the family under attack leveraged the house, as well, in their struggle to resist.

Detroit's racial conflicts of 1925 played out against a backdrop of relative prosperity in the national economy. Nevertheless, workers' gains were precarious throughout the early twentieth century. When the ILO studied unskilled Ford workers' budgets in 1929, before the Depression began, it found that only 37 percent of those surveyed earned more than they spent. The rest ran deficits. This made each payday essential, and unlike in Europe, U.S. workers had no access to social insurance in unemployment or advanced age.[30] As Chapter 8 shows, the good economic times that built modern Detroit did not last. By the early 1930s, workers' pursuit of domestic security was in tatters as mass layoffs created a crisis of evictions and foreclosures. Installment-purchased furniture was repossessed. With the modern social contract in crisis, and in the absence of federal support, mayors such as Detroit's Frank Murphy scrambled to provide local relief to stave off unrest. To simulate work and its rewards, Detroit's city government created relief gardens, and for a time workers grew food staples and ethnic specialties on vacant lots and undeveloped tracts amid the city's newly built subdivisions. But as workers' losses mounted, they began to demand that employers, government, and the larger society insure the social contract they had established in better times. Some resisted eviction, in acts of civil disobedience, and many joined communist-led marches, demanding that government and employers restore the security of workers' houses. After marchers crossed into Dearborn in 1932, Ford Motor Company agents and police opened fire, causing five deaths and scores of injuries, which only amplified workers' demands for change.

The Conclusion returns to present-day Detroit, where the interstate highways of a long-decentralized metropolis cut through early twentieth-century neighborhoods. There, as in other "shrinking city" contexts, the demolition of abandoned structures has been an urban policy priority for years. The rising standard of living and working-class political power these houses once represented seems consigned to a bygone era, following half a century of labor declines and rising inequality. Yet within the present-day social contract, workers retain profound benefits from early twentieth-century struggle, not least in the social security and unemployment insurance programs that now help to secure workers' hard-earned gains. However, in an echo of early twentieth-century culture, the Great Recession and coronavirus crisis of the early twenty-first century have made economic uncertainty feel like the norm, even as workers' wages have begun to rise amid a recovery and a tightening labor market.[31] Detroit's history attests, however, that higher wages in the absence of power will not be enough. Seeking a measure of economic control, American service-sector workers have begun to challenge giant corporations such as Amazon and Starbucks with their organizing. In the present-day social contract, these workers benefit from the social insurance programs and labor laws earned in the past, but unlike their early twentieth-century predecessors, they do not live in a society focused on creating affordable housing, making it difficult to translate today's economic gains into quality-of-life gains.

Policy and building practice in recent decades have made affordable housing more and more scarce. In this context, early twentieth-century workers' houses serve as a timely historical precedent. Despite their limitations, debated in urban theory and explored in this book, these understudied houses do represent a moment when "all hands were on deck" in American cities to produce more and better housing. In this sense, they might inspire present-day employers, policy makers, and designers to reimagine houses and their production anew, creating visions of a better life worth working for. As in the past, the success of future housing will be found, to a significant degree, in human experiences—in dinners at kitchen tables—which cannot be understood from the distance of an aerial view.

PART I

MIGRATION

1

PASSAGES

*Moving to and through Houses
in an Industrial City*

> An entire past comes to dwell in a new house.
> —Gaston Bachelard, *The Poetics of Space*

Though millions of workers migrated to U.S. manufacturing centers in the early twentieth century, the difficulty and uncertainty of each individual's path should not be taken for granted. Their human experiences, as Gaston Bachelard suggests, would be reflected in the modern cities and houses that these new arrivals helped to create. In large numbers, immigrants from Europe, Canada, and the Middle East, as well as migrants from the American South and upper Midwest, made their way to Detroit. Their passage, whether on ships and trains or in the back of a truck, involved a range of costs and risks. New challenges emerged on arrival. In search of stable work and housing, in an increasingly crowded city, many lived as boarders for a time and relocated from place to place. Some left Detroit to seek opportunities elsewhere, but the majority stayed, betting that they could build a better life in the Motor City.

Tracing workers' difficult and uncertain paths to and through Detroit, this chapter illustrates how hard-earned their later, modern houses were. The uncertainty of the migration process and the sacrifices made along the way would live on in those future houses for years to come, in spatial memories and in meaningful objects. Though access to the fleeting experiences of migration is limited, important work has been done to preserve the oral histories of workers who made their way to the city. Middle-class reformers and authors, too, have left a complex and important record of migration experiences. Their hopeful, exasperated, and romantic descriptions, read against the grain, illuminate the choices faced by workers seeking to establish themselves in the city. Even in scornful descriptions of the lives of the newly arrived, these authors show how human relationships, cultural rituals, and the hopeful possibilities of a booming city could provide new arrivals with a measure of comfort during a vulnerable period of transition.

The Contingencies of Migration

Passing through Ellis Island and other points of entry, the immigrants who made their way to Detroit transformed the face of the city. In 1910, three-quarters of Detroit's residents were foreign-born or first-generation Americans, with more arriving daily on inbound trains. They included many so-called "new immigrants" from places in southern and eastern Europe, such as Italy, Poland, Hungary, and Russia. As David Roediger shows, Americans of nativist sentiment viewed these groups as racially distinct from the northern European immigrants of the past and stereotyped new immigrant cultures as inferior and incompatible with an industrializing society. This construction of race—while not as severe or punishing as that which African Americans experienced—was one of the many challenges these new arrivals faced in Detroit. New immigrants had powerful and varied reasons for accepting these challenges, however. In addition to bettering their economic prospects, Poles, for example, saw opportunities to develop their Polish and Catholic identities in America, free from the imperial repression they faced in Europe. Many Jews fled the violent pogroms of czarist Russia in this period when they migrated to America.[1]

Some never made it past Ellis Island. Illness could cause death aboard a ship, for example, or provoke rejection on arrival—rejection that could divide families. These cases illustrate that much could be lost, even as much might be gained, leaving home for industrial America. The sociologist Edward Steiner traveled with immigrants at the turn of the twentieth century, and his magazine articles and books presented their experiences in a sympathetic light for a U.S. audience. He describes the difficulty of a sixteen-day voyage in the crowded steerage compartment of a ship, where as many as nine hundred passengers endured being "packed like cattle."[2] As Alfred Stieglitz showed in his 1907 photo *The Steerage*, first-class passengers enjoyed relative comfort on the upper decks of these ships and were able to peer down on the steerage deck below. Steiner recalls one case in which a boy traveling in steerage, "in the last stages of consumption [tuberculosis]," was brought out to the lower deck for fresher air but whose relief was short-lived. Upon request from first-class passengers on the upper deck, who were upset by the sight of him, the boy was driven back downstairs, out of sight.[3]

At Ellis Island, American officials assessed each traveler independently, and those found unfit were forced to return home in the next available transatlantic steerage. Only about 1 percent of arrivals were turned away, but this nonetheless infused the process with uncertainty and the possibility of painful separations.[4] In one case, Steiner describes the experience of a Jewish tailor and his son, migrating from Russia. The former was "a pitiable looking object" with a "small, emaciated body," and the latter, "stalwart" and "neatly attired in the uniform of a Russian college student."[5] The father had supported his son's education; forced to leave home, they had traveled to the United States hoping to work and to join the father's brother. The inspector looked unfavorably on the father, however, and asked whether he and his son were willing to be separated. The father replied, as Steiner recalls:

> "Of course." And the son sa[id], after casting his eyes to the ground, ashamed to look his father in the face, "Of course," [after which the inspector ruled,] "The one shall be taken and the other left."[6]

Letters sent between those who moved to America and their families back home illustrate the work of maintaining relationships and cultural connections over great distance. The sociologist William Thomas collected and translated many such letters in the early twentieth century. He framed the challenge faced by these immigrants, as Eli Zaretsky explains, as that of "leaving behind a close-knit, family based, traditional culture and seeking to adapt to a more individualistic and competitive world."[7] His collection reveals a robust transatlantic exchange—of stories, photographic portraits, prayer cards, name-day gifts, tobacco, cash, and advice—that kept homeland commitments alive for many. Parents back home sought to protect and advise their children from a distance. A Polish immigrant's parents, for example, urged their son to "economize as much as you can," perhaps fearing that he would fail to save for the future. Another's parents feared the influence of American materialism and secularism and advised their son, when looking for a marriage partner, not to "look at her dresses, but esteem only whether she loves our Lord Jesus."[8]

The economic risks and opportunities of migration were felt on both sides of the Atlantic. Many undertook their voyage with little cash in hand and owed a substantial debt for their travel costs to a creditor back home. There was no guarantee that they would succeed in America, and it was not uncommon for immigrants to move from city to city until they found acceptable work and housing conditions. One Russian Jewish immigrant had lived in New York on arrival in America, working nights and sleeping on a park bench. After moving to Detroit in 1913, on the advice of a cousin, he began to have better economic success. After two years working as a peddler, he recalled, "I saved enough money to bring my wife and three children from Russia."[9] Other immigrants worked to send money home in support of family members who remained abroad and who faced their own creditors and, in some cases, the threat of hunger. Well-paid work in the United States might generate enough capital to transform conditions back home. One sister, writing from Poland, urged her brother in America to send investment money, saying, "If your health favors you, earn whatever you can and send [it to] us; it won't be lost for you here."[10]

Thirty percent of Poles who traveled to America returned home after some time, difficult choices that are illustrated in the correspondence of the Markiewicz brothers and their parents back in Poland.[11] The brothers' father offered one of them, Wacław, a financial incentive to return to Poland: if he returned with just "a few hundred rubles," his father would add his own money to help the young man buy a farm of his own.[12] Wacław declined the offer, causing his mother to try a different tack: guilt. She had received his message of intent to stay in the United States, she wrote, "But I don't think it true, because I believe that you love your parents and your country."[13] By contrast, Wacław's brother Stanisław, also in America for a time, returned willingly in 1914. With the U.S. economy in recession, he explained that America "is a golden land as long as there is work, but when there is none, then it is worth nothing."[14] He was perhaps fortunate to leave when he did. In the winter of 1914–1915, a Detroit sociologist found that unemployed workers who might otherwise leave could not, as returning to Europe was "impossible this winter on account of the present War."[15] When they could, many did leave Detroit, yet larger numbers continued to arrive. The city's Board of Commerce noted that while 5,404 immigrants had left the city in 1914, 24,819 had entered.[16]

When World War I dampened the flow of immigrant workers, employers in cities such as Detroit increasingly looked to the American South and Appalachia. Black and white southerners moved northward in large numbers, and while white migration from the South was numerically greater, newly arrived Blacks were more transformative of northern cities' racial landscapes. Detroit's Black community grew precipitously, from fewer than six thousand to forty-one thousand in the 1910s, part of an extraordinary demographic shift that we have come to know as the Great Migration.[17] Relocations to northern cities, as Richard Thomas argues, must be read in terms of southern migrants' choices, and not only as the result of external forces. Many Black migrants moved northward to find better-paying work, distance from Jim Crow segregation, and a "way off the farm."[18] Labor agents encouraged this by offering complimentary transportation, and word of the Ford Motor Company's profit-sharing plan, the "Five Dollar Day," certainly enticed workers. At the same time, there were countervailing efforts in the South. Elites such as business owners, clergy, and the press worked to dissuade Black workers from leaving. As James Gregory shows, the white press warned its southern readership that recruiters were "Taking away Our Labor" and described recruiters as tricksters who were "fooling" the Black workers they drew north with their promises.[19] In the end—like their European peers—southern Blacks *chose* the path of urbanization and industrialization for themselves, despite the risks and the separation from family that this required.

Oral histories collected by the Detroit Urban League shed light on the choices made and challenges faced by Black migrants during these journeys. Oscar Lee, for example, was seventeen when he "hoboed" from Alabama seeking factory work. He bought a new and expensive suit of clothes before leaving and gave the rest of the cash he had saved to his young spouse, who stayed behind. Resolved not to spend money on the trip, Lee snuck free rides on trains and in the back of a Detroit-bound truck before finally jumping off as it passed through downtown.[20] M. Kelly Fritz took a more circuitous path. He left a small town in Alabama at fourteen, without his parents, and worked in Birmingham, Alabama, then Sharon and Washington, Pennsylvania, before finally moving to Detroit. After a few years working as a waiter in Detroit, he returned to Pennsylvania to study mortuary science, before finally returning to the Motor City for good.[21] As with their European peers, African Americans' movements to and through Detroit were contingent on economic conditions and personal choices. While many stayed, some would move on again. Facing unemployment in the 1920–1921 recession, some left the city. Others saved their wages to make extended trips back south when they could.[22]

In a city where segregation and a housing shortage limited the available options, cash-poor immigrants' and migrants' first dwellings often left much to be desired. Katherine E. Reid, in an oral history, recalled moving as a child from Arkansas to Detroit, along with her parents and brother. The family "rented a room" east of downtown in one of the few districts that did not exclude African American residents, and she remembers being frightened to hear "voices talking loud during the night and early mornings."[23] This densely occupied urban neighborhood was very different from the small town they had come from. Dissatisfied, her father, a Ford worker, moved the family twice on the east side of the city seeking better accommodations, and later they moved to the west side.

The Life of a Room

Residential blocks at the edge of Detroit's central business district were a prominent gateway for newly arrived workers in the early twentieth century, as were the blocks near Ford's Highland Park Plant, six miles north of downtown.[24] Many lived in rooming houses—environments that alarmed the city's social reformers. Detroit's rooming-house architecture differed from that of the New York tenements, made infamous by the housing reformer and photographer Jacob Riis.[25] To the secretary of the Detroit Welfare Managers' Association, these houses were not only overcrowded but deceptively so:

> We have no large tenements, therefore the general public has blindly labored under the impression that Detroit is a city of homes. As a matter of fact . . . , there is less danger from a tenement house which outwardly shows its character than from small houses of a story or two which may be crammed with boarders, but escape the municipal inspector because of their innocent exterior.[26]

New York was an outlier in America, with its heavy concentration of four- to five-story tenement structures. Detroit's "housing problem" was more typical: detached single-family houses converted to accommodate many boarders within.[27] The crowded interior sleeping rooms, therefore, of innocuous-looking one- and two-story frame houses became the central focus of the city's reform discourse. Agents of the Ford Motor Company visited many of these rooms, documenting them and encouraging employees to move to modern houses with more sunlight, ventilation, and privacy. These agents' photographs and descriptions represent the views of a powerful and paternalistic corporation, but they are also an archive of the social, spatial, and material practices of new arrivals of little means.[28] They provide a retrospective portal to the

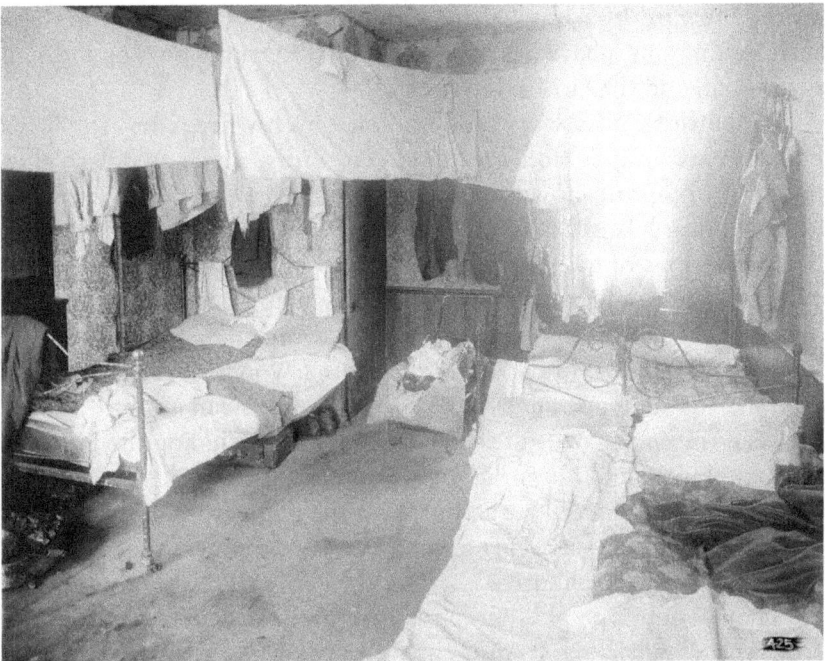

Figure 1.1. Sleeping room for seven at 778 Woodbridge, photographed by the Ford Motor Company's Sociological Department.
Source: Image from the Collections of The Henry Ford, Dearborn, MI.

rooms where immigrant and migrant workers, with little capital and few social connections, engaged the opportunities and challenges of a crowded industrial city.

The two-story, nineteenth-century frame residence at 778 Woodbridge was an anonymous rooming house near the east riverfront before corporate reformers made it a symbol of Detroit's housing problem in the 1910s. A photo of a sleeping room that investigators found there came to represent, for many, the ills of boarding in Detroit (Figure 1.1). The image was used to illustrate "unhealthy living conditions" in the Ford Motor Company internal report *Fifty-one Human Interest Stories* and was circulated in at least three publications: the company's *Factory Facts at Ford* (1915), the Detroit Housing Association pamphlet *Homes of Today and Citizens of Tomorrow* (1915), and the *Michigan Housing Commission Report* (1918).[29] Ford Motor Company inspectors described the scene as "typical of the crowded foreign boarding houses of Detroit."[30] Reflecting their faith in environmental determinism, these Progressive-era reform agents argued that such rooms would spread disease and corrupt their residents morally. "Imagine the view and the attitude toward life," they wrote, "that the child brought up in these surroundings must have. . . . Isn't it enough to start the boys on the high road to jail and the girls to the streets?"[31]

Ford investigators' work followed some twenty-five years after Riis's book of photographs *How the Other Half Lives*, which used flash photography to capture crowds of sleepers inside New York tenements and lodging houses. While Riis had emphasized the faces and something of the interactions of those he photographed—often posing them as sympathetic figures—Ford agents took a different approach.[32] Visiting during daylight hours, they let empty beds do the work of illustrating crowded conditions. In the often reproduced Woodbridge photo, however, there is an important exception: an infant lying in its pram, placed between the empty beds of the child's parents (including the father, a Ford employee), and four other beds that belonged to other residents of the room. This infant likely accounts for the popularity of the image in reform discourse, as it seems to reinforce the argument that boarding conditions threaten children.

The Woodbridge photograph is carefully constructed. It suggests crowding with the many closely spaced beds while also implying that the infant, lying alone, is neglected in this context. But this is unlikely. By the child's age, we can assume that one of its parents or some caretaker was indeed present and kept behind camera, perhaps at the request of the photographer. In another photo from this same visit, an adult's leg is partially visible in the lower right corner of the frame—perhaps the child's caretaker.[33] One cannot see the interactions of this room's residents in the photographs, and in this way the social aspects of their domestic life together are suppressed. If a parent or another adult were there beside the pram, caring for the child, it would undermine the photograph's rhetoric. Its message about the vulnerability of childhood in the context of boarding might be lost to a more empathetic reading. The material artifacts captured in this and similar photographs, and in reformers' descriptions of them, begin to sketch the life of such rooms.

Suitcases are stored beneath a bedframe; sheets and shirts are washed and hung overhead; and a small assortment of dishes are left out on the table. Some of the possessions observed in the Woodbridge sleeping room may have been carried over great distances, bearing associations from elsewhere to the city. A Russian family of four, for example, was documented in 1917, "just as they stepped from the train in Detroit," with the kinds of items that would support their domestic lives in America.[34] Among their few belongings were a fringed blanket tied around what appears to be a bundle of clothes, a decorative pitcher, and a locked case.

Ford Motor Company agents described boarders' few material possessions and multiuse rooms—used for sleeping, eating, and washing and drying clothes—as evidence of social disorder. They also, perhaps unwittingly, humanize these residents. Publishing several such photographs in their 1997 *Muddy Boots and Ragged Aprons*, Kevin Boyle and Victoria Getis point out, for example, one boarder's practice of keeping a portrait of two women over his bed.[35] Despite wall space being at a premium in the densely occupied room, this resident saw that their clothes were hung carefully so as not to obscure their view of the portrait. In a similar way, another Ford Motor Company photograph intends to illustrate a shabby kitchen but also includes a framed picture of a haloed figure, apparently a Christian saint, hung at the far left and nearly excluded from the image.[36]

Investigators' reports interpreted boarders' religious and social practices, as well. One agent noted that Mustafa, an immigrant from Turkey, practiced his Muslim faith by washing his hands and feet in the yard behind a "squalid" downtown boardinghouse three times per day, before prayer.[37] By juxtaposing this washing practice with a description of the house's unclean environment, the writer apparently intended to show the corrupting quality of the "slums." From another perspective, however, the passage reads as proof of the normalcy of the daily life of boarding, or even the capacity of religious faith to ennoble modest environs. Another Ford agent decried the communal meal of a group of boarders, saying, "Empty beer-boxes [were] used as tables in the so-called dining room. . . . I was often present when the people had their dinner or supper—I will never forget it. Knives and forks were objects of luxury; the same opinion was held of plates. The meal was put in a big plate, and everyone ladled the soup out of the plate. Only spoons and fingers were in use."[38] What disturbed the investigator might instead be seen as "making do" in Michel de Certeau's sense. It could even be seen as a meaningful ritual of community for a group of people with few material possessions in Detroit who were, perhaps, still deciding whether to stay in the city or to move on.

A domestic life involving few belongings and little space encouraged a different relationship to the city from that of a spacious modern house. For those who used their dwelling as little more than a place to sleep, the city's shops, theaters, and bars complemented a simple domestic life by providing sustenance and recreation. A review of Sanborn Fire Insurance Maps, which describe each building in the district surrounding 778 Woodbridge, shows the area's vibrancy. Residents of the house could walk to a city recreation center with pools and ball fields, an Italian

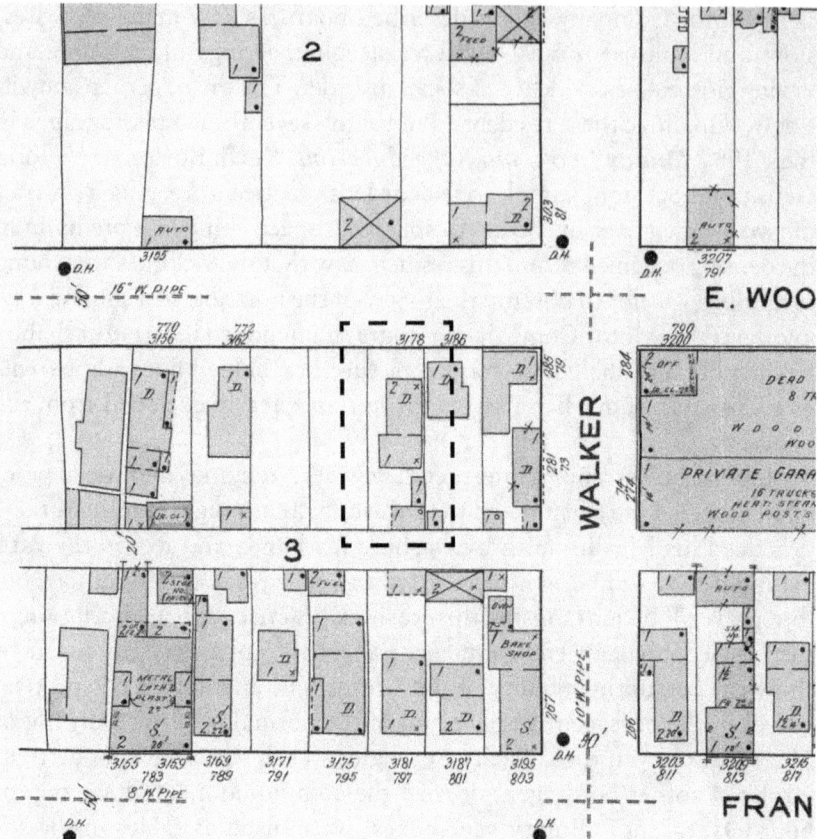

Figure 1.2. The house at 778 Woodbridge (later renumbered 3178 Woodbridge) and context. This neighborhood of nineteenth-century frame dwellings and small industrial shops was located a mile and a half east of the city center. On the drawing, *D*s indicate dwellings and *S*s indicate shops. The rooming house is identified with a dashed outline, and a bake shop appears around the corner from it.

Source: Sanborn Map Company, *Insurance Maps of Detroit, Michigan*, vol. 4, sheet 84, 1922, Library of Congress, Washington, DC, http://hdl.loc.gov/loc.gmd/g4114dm.g03985192204.

Social Center, a motion picture house, and many small industrial shops. There was a bakery just around the corner (Figure 1.2). From such a residence, one might live to a large extent in the city itself, eschewing the bourgeois ideal of the "home" as a refuge from urban congestion.[39] Others, however, were willing to trade a measure of their freedom for the benefits that a reform institution could provide in a subsidized and regulated boarding environment.

The Young Woman's Home Association provided room and board to newly arrived women in a four-story Romanesque building in downtown Detroit, constructed in the 1880s.[40] In the 1910s, as the city's population boomed and the available housing stock dwindled, the facility accommodated just a fraction of those who applied, serving long-term residents for up to two years and short-term "transient" guests. Many residents originated from Michigan, but other midwestern and southern states were represented, as were Canada, England, and Russia. To qualify, applicants had to be unmarried, younger than thirty, and earning a modest income. Residents' work ranged from stenography and telephone operating to laundry and tailoring. At the association, residents enjoyed on-site library and laundry facilities, hot water, and rug-covered floors but were held accountable to an eleven-point list of house rules. Bedrooms were to be clean and ready for inspection at any time, and in contrast to the Woodbridge sleeping room, no laundry was to be washed or dried within bedrooms at the association. Silence and darkness were required after 10:30 P.M., and residents were "earnestly requested to be present" for Christian services on Thursday evenings and Sunday mornings. In its annual report for 1917, the Young Woman's Home Association noted that "a subject for congratulation is the growing tendency of our young women to spend their evenings at home, occupied with their sewing, music or dancing, rather than finding their entertainment outside." This measured statement illustrates both the influence of the association's rules and the opportunities to push their margins by enjoying city life in the evenings.[41]

Conclusion

Moving to and through industrial cities, workers faced a range of uncertainties and challenges. Immigrants had to stay healthy enough to be accepted at the border. All new arrivals faced the fear they might not find good work or a place to live. What would happen if they ran out of money? What might happen to family left behind in their absence? Adding to the complexity, "new immigrants" and Blacks faced stereotyping and discrimination as they traveled and when they arrived in a city dominated by its white American elite. Workers pursued self-defined better lives in this context, struggling for a share of the benefits of a modernizing city. As they did, moving from one house to another, the improvements they managed in their everyday lives were given greater meaning by the uncertainties and indignities they had faced during their migration. These were hard-won gains.

Of course, in a modern city, no one's achievements are simply a reflection of their own hard work and perseverance. Where one stood relative to powerful employers and government policies could make all the difference in Detroit and elsewhere in the early twentieth century. In the 1910s, "new immigrants" were embraced by Detroit's business interests as modern Americans in the making, even as Black workers were further marginalized. Chapter 2 discusses the efforts of employers and government to "Americanize" new arrivals from abroad, which centered on the improvement of their houses. These efforts illustrate that even as newly arrived workers sought a precarious foothold in a new city, their labor was increasingly in demand, and employers were willing to make investments to secure it.

2

AMERICAN HOUSES

Architecture of the Melting Pot Project

> There is something sacred about wages—
> they represent homes and families and
> domestic destinies.
> —Henry Ford, *My Life and Work*

Detroit's industrial employers modernized and expanded their operations in the early twentieth century, creating opportunities that drew workers to the city. Immigrants and migrants arrived in such large numbers that the city's population doubled in the 1910s, to nearly one million. Detroit jumped from ninth to fourth largest among U.S. cities.[1] The villages of Highland Park and Hamtramck each gained a major auto plant, becoming surrounded by Detroit as it expanded northward, and recorded a combined ninety-five thousand residents by 1920. Detroit's business leaders, including Henry Ford in Highland Park and the Dodge brothers in Hamtramck, were eager to grow their businesses by hiring newly arrived workers, but this proved to be challenging. Turnover rates were high for strenuous modern factory work, and an increasing housing shortage raised the question of where the city's fast-growing workforce would live.[2]

Worse, fearsome stories were coming in from outside of Detroit. Labor organizations had launched strikes in Lawrence, Massachusetts, in 1912 and in Akron, Ohio, in 1913. This unrest and the Soviet Revolution of 1917 showed that traditional authorities were vulnerable to working-class revolt.[3] Employers believed that, to gain workers' loyalty on the shop floor, they needed to increase their cultural influence beyond the gates of the factory by providing more and better housing for workers. Employers wagered, as a cartoonist for the business journal *The Detroiter* vividly illustrated (Figure 2.1), that new workers' housing

Figure 2.1. "The Sure Way to Snuff It Out." Cartoon by Tom May for the business journal *The Detroiter*.
Source: Detroit Board of Commerce, *The Detroiter*, vol. 10, no. 39, 1919, 4.

development would allow them to "snuff out" the flame of potential unrest, and overcome the toxic the influence of "Bolshevism."

Concerned about high turnover rates and the threat of unrest, Detroit's business leaders opened an implicit negotiation with the city's workforce in the 1910s. They raised wages but expected workers to make commitments in return: commitments to remain in Detroit and at their jobs, despite their difficulty. Employers developed a program of "Americanization" for immigrant workers, pushing them to achieve English-language fluency and U.S. citizenship while, at the same time, encouraging new arrivals to aspire to a higher, "American" standard of living. Toward this end, they wove the new standard of living into language and citizenship courses and employee manuals, encouraging workers to raise their social status with better houses and household practices and with homeownership. Their efforts suggested that corporations were beginning to take some responsibility for workers' housing—a significant change to the social contract. This helped to establish a cultural ideal: that in a modern city such as Detroit, steady, hard work would be rewarded with upward mobility in modern houses.

Americanization addressed employers' desires for better communication on the shop floor and increased workers' loyalty, but it also reflected broader cultural themes of the 1910s. In this period, nativist contempt for "new immigrant" identities ran strong in U.S. culture, and among the middle class so did a Progressive-era desire to "uplift" the less fortunate, especially immigrants.[4] In this context, Detroit's business elite invited immigrant workers to enter a cultural "melting pot," be transformed, and join them in a shared American identity. This was famously dramatized in the graduation ceremony of the English School at the Ford Motor Company. At commencement, as a reward for their efforts studying English, graduates would enter a stage-set pot dressed in clothes that represented their former ethnic identities. After the pot was stirred, they would emerge from it wearing "their best American clothes and waving American flags."[5]

Employers valued English-language skills, but they believed that a deeper Americanization could be achieved by engaging with workers' housing. E. W. Lewis, an executive with the Timken-Detroit Axle Company, wrote in 1913 that "a more undesirable class of labor" was growing in Detroit, "a class which 'live in suitcases.'" Workers' suitcases represented their tenuous relationship with the city and its employers, and to American identity itself. Instead, Lewis added, "We want the class of workmen to come to Detroit who will attach themselves to our city in a permanent way as home-builders."[6] With the Ford Motor Company and the Board of Commerce in leading roles, Detroit's business leaders encouraged immigrants to put away their suitcases and become American by committing to work, a modern house, and homeownership in Detroit.

Night School Social Transformation

Cities across the United States adopted Americanization efforts during World War I, but Detroit was an early leader in the use of night schools to teach the English language, citizenship, and "American" standards of living. The New York–based National Americanization Committee publicized the Detroit program in the book *Americanizing a City* (1915) and argued that the Motor City's approach could be followed "in every city or town that has an unassimilated foreign population." In 1916, proud of its influence, the Detroit Board of Commerce took note of the fact that hundreds of cities had "follow[ed] Detroit's example" and begun their own night school Americanization programs.[7]

The Detroit Board of Commerce framed workers' housing as essential to the city's progress and promised employers that at night school, workers would "learn how to make their homes real American homes," places that reinforced stable and disciplined work.[8] For industrialists, modern housing promised improvement to workers' health, morality, and dependability. Charles Paull, a researcher and staff member at Harvard's Bureau of Vocational Guidance, championed this idea. He advised that when a worker "understand[s] that he can improve the conditions under which he is living" and is "taught the elements of household hygiene[,] there should be a change in his attitude toward his work. He will grow to understand that the relation between capital and labor is one of reciprocal advantages, and that each should be of economic advantage to the other."[9] Despite these enticing possibilities, starting a night school program was no simple task. It required reaching workers where they were, often in ethnic communities and in crowded boarding conditions, and convincing them to spend their evenings in a classroom.

The Ford Motor Company initiated night school Americanization at its new Highland Park plant in 1914, compelling non–English-speaking employees to attend. The curriculum included language instruction, as well as lessons on "domestic" and "industrial relations."[10] As one Ford manager explained, "In [the Ford English School] the men are taught first of all English. Later on the lessons deal with personal hygiene, the care of the home and the right relations therein. . . . [L]ast but not least must be mentioned our professor of table manners, who, with grammatic art, teaches the use of the napkin, knife and fork, and spoon."[11] Drawings were used to illustrate lessons, and the importance of the detached house in classroom conversation is revealed at the edge of a company photograph: as a Ford English School instructor addresses his students, he refers to a chalkboard drawing of a gabled, detached house and its residents (Figure 2.2). Drawings and physical gestures were favored in night school education, where spoken language alone might be misunderstood. Ford instructors used what they called a "dramatic" method for greater clarity and impact. "For instance," the company sociologist Samuel Marquis explained, "a teacher says 'I wash myself,' and goes through the correct action while saying the sentence."[12]

In the fall of 1915, the Detroit Board of Commerce followed the Ford Motor Company's lead, coordinating with the municipal school administration to create a citywide night school Americanization program. The board used its journal, *The Detroiter*, to promote the program among employers, who in turn strongly encouraged workers to participate.[13] The Packard Motor Car Company pushed its employees to attend by instituting an "Americans First" policy in 1916, explicitly barring non-Americans from "promotions to positions of importance"

Figure 2.2. Ford English School at the Highland Park plant. The weaving of American standards of living into English language instruction is reflected in the drawing of a detached house and its residents on the blackboard at the far right.
Source: Image from the Collections of The Henry Ford, Dearborn, MI.

in the plant. Further, the company warned that all employees would "be required to explain why they do not [attend night school] if they cannot show that they are taking other means of learning the language."[14] Packard's support for the night school program was facilitated by Alvan Macauley, who served the automaker as both a company vice-president and a member of the Detroit Board of Commerce's Committee on Education in 1917. A majority of the committee's members were employers, and they were joined by social reform advocates and Detroit's mayor Oscar B. Marx in their work.[15] To the board's delight, Packard's "Americans First" policy drove a noticeable increase in night school participation and inspired similar policies at other factories.[16]

In further outreach efforts, the board asked ethnic community leaders such as priests and editors of foreign-language newspapers to promote the night schools. Its agents "penetrated into every nook and corner of the foreign sections of Detroit. In the saloons, the coffee houses, the meat shops and stores," spreading the word that fall classes were available.[17] The board also operated a "Free Information Bureau for Aliens" on the ground floor of its headquarters and advertised night

Figure 2.3. Detroit night schools map, 1916. The small stars indicate municipal night schools, and the larger star indicates the Ford English School at the company's Highland Park plant. Large concentrations of "new immigrants" within Detroit are noted with gray circles: (1) Hungarian; (2–3) Polish; (4) Italian, Russian, Syrian, and other nationalities.

Source: Illustration by the author, with reference to Steve Babson, *Working Detroit: The Making of a Union Town* (New York: Adama, 1984), 26; Detroit Board of Commerce, "Evening School Map of Detroit," *The Detroiter*, September 11, 1916; Jerome Thomas, "The City of Detroit: A Study in Urban Geography" (Ph.D. diss., University of Michigan, Ann Arbor, 1928), fig. 6.

school in public libraries and pools. At playgrounds within the city's ethnic enclaves, the committee distributed handbills to children that read, "Can Your Mother and Father Speak English Well? Take this card home, it will tell them where to go to learn English."[18]

As demand grew, the city increased its appropriations for the public night school program. By the fall of 1916, the number of participating schools had doubled, to twenty-six, and enrollment had reached seven thousand for the season. Most of the schools were located within or near the bounds of Grand Boulevard, which encircled old Detroit about three miles from the city's center (Figure 2.3), making them accessible to large communities of immigrants from Poland, Italy, Hungary, and elsewhere. The number of facilities had expanded to meet the growing interest, but the board reported that attendance in the fall of 1916, as the evenings grew cooler and the classrooms grew more comfortable, rose to the point that "students were sitting upon the windowsills and even upon the floor."[19]

The Ford Motor Company and the public night schools taught the "American" standard of living. They also encouraged workers to pursue homeownership as the ultimate emblem of American identity. The night schools' official textbook, the *Manual of American Citizenship*, was written by the Detroit Board of Commerce. It framed Detroit as "A City of Homes," arguing:

> To buy a home, save rent, have a flower garden and vegetable patch, should be the worthy ambition of every man in this beautiful city. Nothing will add so much to the prestige of a citizen than to be able to say, "I own my home."[20]

The Board of Commerce was by no means the first to see the value of worker homeownership. On Detroit's Polish- and German-dominated near-east side, for example, workers had already achieved city-leading high levels of homeownership in the late nineteenth century. Scholars have also found strong cultures of late nineteenth-century worker homeownership near Chicago's stockyards and in the Calumet region. But homeownership meant something different to that earlier generation of workers than it did to early twentieth-century employers. In the nineteenth century, workers often owned relatively inexpensive small frame cottages with few amenities. They often built these houses themselves and were more likely to own them outright.[21] In the early twentieth century, Detroit's business leaders sought to extend and modernize worker homeownership, encouraging engagement with the city's formal real-estate and credit markets, which could put a new, higher standard of living within newly arrived workers' reach.

Helpful Hints and Advice: Ford Motor Company Housing Reform

Ford, like many other industrial firms, adopted "scientific management" principles in the 1910s, carefully observing and coordinating workers' physical movements throughout the production process. Under this paradigm, many employees were asked to focus on narrow and physically strenuous tasks, at a machine or along a moving assembly line, and to repeat those tasks at great speed for long periods of time. The difficulty of this kind of labor tested workers' commitment, and it did not go well at first. The historian Steven Meyer has shown that Ford had a staggering turnover rate of 370 percent in 1913, meaning the company had to hire more than fifty-two thousand workers that year to maintain a workforce of fewer than fourteen thousand.[22] Like many employers in the period, Ford sought to win workers' loyalty by instituting "corporate welfare" programs. The company offered extras such as recreational facilities, a band, and a discounted company store, as well as a savings-and-loan association and an in-house medical department. Most significant, though, was Ford's profit-sharing plan, launched in 1914 and known as the "Five Dollar Day." The program effectively doubled an unskilled worker's income, from about $2.50 to an unprecedented $5 per day, and reduced working hours from nine to eight per day. Earned wages remained about $2.50; the rest of the $5 wage came in the form of shared profits. This was the catch. As Meyer explains, "All Ford workers received their wages, but only those who met Ford standards received their profits."[23] This gave the company a great deal of leverage, and workers were subtly reminded of that leverage in their pay envelopes, where earned wages and shared profits were separated out.[24]

Profit sharing was so attractive that it ended the company's crisis of attrition.[25] It also forced other Detroit industrialists to compete for labor, and the average wage citywide rose to $5.30 a day by 1919.[26] Ford leveraged its profit sharing to encourage a new American standard of living. The company laid out its expectations in the manual *Helpful Hints and Advice to Employes*, using a now uncommon form of the word *employees*.[27] Samuel Marquis, Ford's head sociologist, described profit sharing as a tool to shape workers' commercial desires outside of the plant and thereby to provide greater motivation for steady work and earning. "The Ford idea," he wrote, "is to increase a man's capacity for happiness and at the same time to increase his efficiency, his earning capacity, his worth to society, so that he may have access to the things he has been taught to enjoy."[28] The pamphlet encouraged workers to move to a better house without delay but also to keep up the goal of eventually owning their house: "[i]t is the hope of this company that every one of its married employes will own his own home as soon as conditions, consistent with comfortable and clean living, will permit."[29]

The Ford Motor Company's Sociological Department was responsible for the profit-sharing program and for ensuring that profit-sharing employees complied with its terms. It recruited investigators from among the literate members of the company's workforce and tasked them with investigating the conditions of their colleagues' houses to ensure that they were working toward "comfortable and clean living." These investigators assessed conditions, took photographs, and wrote reports.

When needed, they could offer advice to help a colleague make changes to meet company expectations. But the program also had teeth. If a worker failed to comply with the investigators' requests, profit-sharing privileges would be taken away. With so much at stake, most employees tolerated these investigators' intrusions and found ways to navigate the company's prescriptions.[30] Many workers turned their profits into better rental houses, and a growing minority achieved homeownership. Two years after the Five Dollar Day was instituted, more than one-ninth of the company's workers were homeowners, a near-doubling from earlier levels and rising.[31]

When workers accepted house inspections, they were also accepting company scrutiny of their household relationships. Marriage was the gold standard. Ford sought to incentivize marriage, and the sexual propriety and stability that it implied, with the lever of profit sharing. Under the Five Dollar Day, married men of any age "who can qualify as to sobriety, industry and cleanliness" could receive profit sharing if they lived with their family. Unmarried men younger than twenty-two were excluded. Rather than leaving so much money "on the table," some young men married hastily, while others reportedly hired women and children to pose as family members to qualify for profit sharing—a practice that company investigators attempted to discover and penalize.[32] The company's marriage requirement reflected a fear that surplus cash in the hands of independent young men would be squandered in the pool hall or saloon or on inappropriately fine clothing. It also discouraged the strategy of living lightly and cheaply—by boarding in someone else's house for example, to send money home to a family living abroad to whom a worker might eventually return. The program, in effect, offered newly arrived employees a deal: they could double their income if they began putting down the roots of family life in Detroit.

At the Highland Park plant, the company sharply limited women's role in this deal in its early years. There, Ford employed fewer than three hundred women in 1914, a little more than 2 percent of the workforce. The company withheld profit sharing from female workers unless they proved they were the sole provider to dependents. This suppression of women's income reinforced the company's ideal of the male sole breadwinner and reflected a discriminatory management culture that perceived women's employment as less significant and more provisional. General Manager James Couzens, for example, suggested that female employees were less committed and likely to "make sudden announcement of their marriage and leave."[33] As the company continued to grow, however, its need for female workers was reflected in the decision to

Figure 2.4. "A Good, Clean Room with Plenty of Light and Air." Photograph taken by the Ford Motor Company Sociological Department.
Source: Image from the Collections of The Henry Ford, Dearborn, MI.

extend the Five Dollar Day to women in 1916. By 1922, a survey of auto industry workers showed that many more factory jobs were open to female employees, who worked as assemblers, for example, and operated drill presses, grinding machines, and lathes. Women's wages, however, reflected persistent discrimination and, on average, were two-thirds what men were paid for the same work.[34]

Moving from the family to the house itself, the Five Dollar Day program reinforced a central theme of Americanization curricula: cleanliness. To share in profits, workers' houses and family members needed to be clean, and more than money was at stake. The company argued that cleanliness was a sign of upward social mobility and American identity. "Employes," the *Helpful Hints* manual advised, "should use plenty of soap and water in the home, and upon their children, bathing frequently. Nothing makes for right living and health so much as cleanliness. Notice that the most advanced people are the cleanest."[35] By way of illustration, the manual presented a tidy bedroom, with white linens on made beds and decorative wallpaper (Figure 2.4). Its wood floor was clean and accented with a rug, on which the viewer could imagine standing while selecting clothes from the dresser and checking their appearance in the mirror. For emphasis, on the same page the company juxtaposed its infamous photo of the "unhealthy" 778 Woodbridge sleeping room discussed in Chapter 1, with its unmade beds, clothes hung throughout the room, and suitcases stashed under the bed.

The three-fixture bathroom, perhaps the most important modernizing feature of an early twentieth-century house, made the practices of cleanliness outlined in Ford's *Helpful Hints* easier to achieve. At its sink, a Ford worker's family members were to brush their teeth. The manual illustrated the need for brushing with a photo of a worker, jaw pried open by an inspector's hand, revealing his missing front teeth, next to a white-collared figure, with a full gleaming smile, who "always uses a toothbrush."[36] One's appearance, a Ford investigator warned, would not go unnoticed in Detroit. "Dirt," he explained, "lowers one in the opinion of his community, making it harder to get a job."[37] Moreover, the journalist Ida Tarbell implied, to be clean was to transcend one's foreign identity. In praising Ford's program, she illustrated the nativist stereotyping that immigrants from southern and eastern Europe faced in early twentieth-century Detroit. Having met a Ford worker, she wrote that she would "never forget the spotlessly shining face, and neck and arms of a foreigner of the type that I never before have seen clean either in America or Europe. He looked as unfamiliar as the façade of an ancient church which had been put under the grinder."[38]

With half of their income on the line, most workers did what they needed to in order to meet investigators' demands, and the number who were disqualified from profit sharing plummeted from 23 percent to 1.5 percent of the workforce in seven months.[39] The Sociological Department celebrated this by collecting reports of its investigators' work under the title *Fifty-one Human Interest Stories*, which illustrated the extent to which the company would go for housing reform. These reports underscore the complex nature of Progressive-era "uplift," which could be disturbingly paternalistic and earnestly humanitarian at the same time.

One "human interest story" describes the help given to the Kostruba family, immigrants from Russia, after the father, Joe, landed a job at the Ford Motor Company. The Kostrubas lived on Detroit's near-east side, a gateway district for new arrivals, and the investigator described their dwelling as "an old, tumble-down, one and a half story frame house." This house was partitioned into four apartments, and the Kostrubas lived in the attic. Their apartment had low headroom, and the investigator found it unacceptably small and unclean. His report noted that another apartment within the same house was occupied by "a negro family," perhaps registering his disapproval of racial mixing.[40]

The Ford investigator observed the Kostruba children, who ranged in age from an infant to a fourteen-year-old, to be "half-clad, thin, pale and hungry looking" and considered the case an urgent one. Rather than waiting for conditions to improve due to Joe's enhanced income, he ordered a basket of provisions that was delivered to the family that same evening. The company, at the investigator's request, provided a $50 advance on Joe's future earnings, which was used to help the Kostrubas settle past-due bills with the landlord and grocer and establish rent in a private five-room house a few blocks away. The same $50 also bought basic furniture, a set of kitchen utensils and provisions, a supply of coal for warmth, and inexpensive clothing. The investigator gave the family "a liberal amount of soap . . . , with instructions to use freely." In an almost ritualistic act, he had the family's "dirty, old, junk furniture" piled in the yard and set aflame, noting, "It went up in smoke."[41]

In addition to stories of exceptional need, investigators recorded cases of extraordinary success. One human interest story centered on a family who became the owners of a modern house within just fourteen months. The company photographed their newly built semi-bungalow, north of Detroit in Greenfield Township (present-day Ferndale), to illustrate what was possible with profit sharing (Figure 2.5). The family—two parents and one child—acquired a residential lot with $40 down and built a one-room shack for themselves at the rear of the lot, which they lived in cheaply while the semi-bungalow was constructed. Leveraging credit, they had quickly become the owners of a house valued at $2,600.[42] Opting to be pioneers on the urban fringe, and eschewing central city services and community amenities for a time, they were well positioned to profit as Detroit's outward growth led to rising real estate values.

The Ford Motor Company was proud of its housing reform work and shared it with a global audience at the Panama-Pacific Exposition in San Francisco in 1915, where the company also mocked up a display of its new moving assembly line. The housing exhibit included a sequence of physical models of workers' dwellings, described in the *Ford Times* as showing "the evolution of a Ford workman's home and surroundings, from a sordid boarding house to the comfortable home of the profit sharing employee" (Figure 2.6).[43] Frank Vivian, who worked for Ford in San Francisco and oversaw the displays at the exposition, recalled that the housing evolution model contained "miniature people . . . in slum condi-

Figure 2.5. The newly built semi-bungalow of a profit-sharing employee, photographed by the Ford Motor Company Sociological Department. The temporary dwelling that the employee's family occupied prior to the house's completion is visible behind it.

Source: Image from the Collections of The Henry Ford, Dearborn, MI.

tions" to show "how the department operated by taking care of and watching the employees."[44] The most advanced house in the sequence was a true "American" house, with an American flag planted on a pole in the front yard. Though the company's moving assembly line exhibit likely drew larger crowds, the housing display showed the extent to which the company embraced its role as a responsible partner in providing modern houses for workers. Vivian recalled that his team "showed practically 20,000,000 people around [the Ford] exhibits" during the exposition, giving the company an extraordinary opportunity to influence early twentieth-century American culture.

The American house from Ford's San Francisco exhibition resembles a real house the company had featured in *Helpful Hints* (Figure 2.7).[45] It was two stories tall, with a front-facing gable and wood siding. Though this particular house type would not prove as popular as the single-story bungalow in Detroit, it did illustrate important modern features.

Figure 2.6. "The Evolution of a Ford Workman's Home and Surroundings." Photograph of a model created by the Ford Motor Company for the Panama-Pacific Exposition in San Francisco in 1915 and displayed afterward at the Detroit Board of Commerce's building.

Source: Detroit Board of Commerce, *The Detroiter*, vol. 7, no. 21, 1916, Burton Historical Collection, Detroit Public Library.

Figure 2.7. "A Good Representative Home Owned by a Ford Employe." Photograph from the company's 1915 employee manual *Helpful Hints and Advice to Employes*.

Source: Image from the Collections of The Henry Ford, Dearborn, MI.

The house's small front porch left room for leisurely sitting, perhaps in the extra hour that the shortened workday had opened up. Its large front window suggests a modern living room within, and subtly but importantly, a vent pipe protrudes from the roof, signaling indoor plumbing and perhaps a modern three-fixture bath.[46] After the exposition, the model was returned to Detroit and placed on long-term public display at the city's Board of Commerce building, where this and other innovative forms of "corporate welfare" were displayed. They included the "elaborate" workers' washrooms at the Pierce-Arrow Motor Car Company, the vast cafeteria of Cleveland's National Lamp Works, and the "unusual and successful" milk depots inside the Cadillac Motor Car Company's plant, "where the men are allowed to leave their work to get a pint."[47]

The Challenge of Worker Homeownership

In Detroit as elsewhere, lenders injected a great deal of credit into the housing market in the early twentieth century, making the period's housebuilding boom possible.[48] The overall percentage of metropolitan Detroit houses that were owned on credit, as opposed to outright, jumped from 39 percent in 1900 to 59 percent in 1920 and rose more slowly thereafter.[49] Yet for house buyers of modest means, buying on credit remained challenging and relatively risky prior to the 1930s, when federal mortgage insurance was introduced. Nationwide, building-and-loan organizations offered some of the most attractive terms for working-class buyers during the 1910s and 1920s, offering larger, longer-term, amortized loans. But these were less prominent in Detroit than in other cities.[50] In Detroit, a larger proportion of house buyers' loans came from commercial banks.[51] A study of the city's money market explained that Detroit had an exceptionally dense network of commercial banks, because across its expanding periphery ethnic communities preferred to work with their own local bankers. These banks also focused on real estate to what the study called an "exceedingly high" degree, accounting for 38.2 percent of all lent funds in 1931, as opposed to a 15.7 percent average among other large U.S. cities' banks.[52] For many buyers, a primary loan, however, was just the beginning.

A primary commercial loan might cover half the cost of a house. That, plus a cash down payment, would still leave many buyers seeking a secondary or "junior" lien to cover the remaining cost. This could mean a second mortgage, at higher interest, or, as a Depression-era study of Detroit lending explains, the seller of the property might finance the remaining balance with a "land contract." Under such an arrangement, the seller would withhold the deed to the property until the land contract was paid off, with interest. This arrangement came with a significant downside: it was relatively easy for a seller to cancel a land contract, repossess a house, and keep the buyers' invested equity if they missed payments.[53] In a period of strong employment and rising house values, a land contract could succeed, but these conditions were not assured. Dramatizing what could go wrong, the protagonists of Upton Sinclair's novel *The Jungle* (1906) lost their house, and years of accumulated equity, when the family fell two months behind on their payments and the seller repossessed the property.[54]

In the 1910s, business groups, employers, and government worked to bolster lending, helping to drive the period's boom in consumer credit.[55] The Detroit Board of Commerce worked with manufacturing employers and the real estate industry to expand financing options for workers. A cartoon published in the board's journal *The Detroiter* in 1919 illustrated their frustration: it depicted a banker, happily working in his office, while outside his window, workers trudged about a peripheral tent city, where they lived for lack of available houses. The board's remedy was to develop two limited-dividend lending institutions of its own: the Detroit Society for Savings in 1916 and the Detroit House Finance Corporation in 1919. No simple philanthropy, these institutions were a calculated investment. The directors of the Society for Savings had much to gain from growth in housing: nearly every member was a prominent figure in real estate, building materials, fuel, or housebuilding. Workers who received a "helping hand" in the form of a board-financed loan would become the directors' customers.[56]

The House Finance Corporation made loans to housebuilding contractors and to house buyers while also developing some housing itself.[57] The corporation was led by E. W. Lewis of the Timken-Detroit Axle Company, quoted earlier on the subject of workers' "suitcases," who attested to the potential creditworthiness of newly arrived workers. "Our investments will be based on character," he explained. "The man with only a few hundred dollars with which to start a home may be just as good a risk as the multimillionaire. It will be our mission to assist such men with their banking problems and thus enable them to secure a home."[58] The Board of Commerce agreed, calling on its members from the manufacturing sector to "roll up their sleeves" and fund these lending institutions, to make the "desert" of undeveloped speculative subdivisions at the periphery "bloom" with new housing.[59] The board urged that "the greatest need . . . is that [financial] assistance be given to the wage earner in building his home," adding, "There are many men or families who have from $100 to $500 with which to build."⁶⁰ To keep their lending institutions capitalized, the board reported on their successes and urged further investments, noting in 1920 that the Detroit House Finance Corporation had "built seven hundred homes in its first eight months, tying up all of its available capital."⁶¹

Industrial employers created their own direct programs to support worker homeownership, as well. The American Blower Company's program allowed one of its workers, who had purchased a vacant parcel with $800 cash, to build a $2,500 house on it financed completely on credit. This was made possible by pairing a Society for Savings loan for 60 percent of the cost with a special employer-sponsored second mortgage to cover the balance. The worker would be responsible for making on-time monthly payments of 1 percent of the loan, or $25, plus insurance, taxes, and other costs, until the balance was paid.⁶² This kind of arrangement stands in contrast to the worker home-buying practices of the late nineteenth century, when incremental self-building was used to overcome cash shortages. Such efforts made formal house buying, which, as Sam Bass Warner has noted, was "by definition" a middle-class activity in the nineteenth century, available to a growing number of early twentieth-century workers.⁶³ American Blower emphasized that its loans were not charity—they bore interest and supported the company's desire to "make its employes permanent as far as possible."⁶⁴

In 1919, *The Detroiter* noted that several companies were developing special departments tasked with "furnishing their workmen with funds in reasonable amounts to help them build [houses]," listing the Solvay Process Company, Gemmer Manufacturing Company, and General Motors Corporation along with American Blower.⁶⁵ General Motors, which built and sold workers' houses on a large scale in Flint and Pontiac though its subsidiary Modern Housing Corporation, allowed its employees to have their house payments deducted directly from their wages or from their account at the company's Savings and Investment Fund, "considerably eas[ing] the lot of thrifty employees in their progress toward house ownership."⁶⁶

After World War I, the federal government joined local business leaders in promoting homeownership.⁶⁷ It created a multimedia campaign that included the 1923 U.S. Commerce Department pamphlet *How to Own Your Home*. Secretary of Commerce Herbert Hoover wrote the foreword and reinforced the notion that homeownership elevated a family's social prestige in America—allowing them to enjoy the "cultivating influences of our modern civilization."⁶⁸ *How to Own Your Home* acknowledged the culture shift that a formal credit market represented for many buyers, given the long-standing nineteenth-century culture of unencumbered ownership among workers. "Borrowing money to buy a home is no disgrace," the pamphlet explained. Rather, it was a normal practice and "a step toward financial independence."[69] If prospective buyers were anxious or confused about the process of financing a house purchase, this pamphlet could help. Local Detroit employers and lenders, however, understood that more hands-on assistance was likely needed, and made staff available to offer legal and technical advice to workers contemplating a purchase.[70]

Workers took real risks with modern homeownership, even as the credit market grew at an unprecedented rate in the 1920s.[71] Despite the longer loan terms and amortization that savings-and-loan organizations offered, commercial loans remained shorter term, and their renewal every few years depended on an owner's house retaining a steady or growing value. Moreover, house payments required steady income, and illness or injury could unexpectedly disrupt a worker's ability to earn and to pay, putting a mortgage or land contract at risk. Given the challenges of homeownership in this context, it is remarkable that nearly one in three unskilled Ford workers owned a house by the end of the 1920s. The larger number continued to rent, and while they avoided the risk of losing sunk equity to foreclosure, they remained vulnerable in other ways. To see one's family evicted from a modern rental house, and to have one's installment-purchased furniture and appliances repossessed, was a fearsome prospect. Owners and renters were regularly reminded of the risks they faced. Annual production stoppages for retooling, common in early twentieth-century Detroit, created regular pinch points in household budgets.[72] Cyclical economic crises were another threat, and they triggered industrial layoffs in 1914, 1920, and 1929.[73] Yet despite these risks, workers—white workers—were privileged to be able to translate their wages into modern houses. Black workers, no matter how hard they labored in early twentieth-century Detroit, seldom could.

The Great Migration and the Segregated City

Migration from Europe was interrupted by World War I, even as the war increased demand for industrial labor. Seizing the opportunity, many African Americans moved northward to cities in what is known as the first "Great Migration."[74] Detroit's African American community grew especially quickly, with only Gary, Indiana, seeing a greater proportional growth of its Black community in the 1910s. These migrants hoped to escape segregation, agricultural peonage, violence, and the biased legal system they had endured in the rural South. What they found in Detroit was a rapidly urbanizing society, and one in which many whites, including immigrants who had only recently achieved whiteness through Americanization, refused to receive Black Americans as neighbors.[75]

There were jobs available, however, and the Detroit Urban League helped to steer many newly arrived African Americans into industrial work. The Ford Motor Company hired Black workers in exceptionally large numbers beginning in 1919, when as many as 1,700 hires were recorded. By 1926, 10 percent of Ford's Detroit workforce was Black—accounting for ten thousand jobs—and while unskilled Black workers received the same compensation as their white peers, they were often confined to the most difficult and dangerous jobs in the plant, such as foundry work.[76] African Americans made some inroads in employment, but their opportunities for social advancement outside of the plant were delimited by increasingly hostile white communities that were intent on maintaining racial segregation in the city's neighborhoods.[77]

In fact, the "melting pot" project to expand whiteness in Detroit was paradoxically achieved by redoubling efforts to exclude another "other"—Black Detroiters—from the city's new neighborhoods and modern houses. Detroit's early twentieth-century race lines were drawn by developers, who placed restrictive covenants on properties within their subdivisions as an "asset" to their future owners. The covenants often included a racial restriction that barred Black residents from living in new subdivisions and sometimes included a religious restriction against Jewish residents, as well. Discrimination, in realty practice and in the mortgage market, reinforced housing segregation.[78] Olivier Zunz has pointed out that Black Detroiters "lived history in reverse," becoming increasingly segregated from the benefits of a white-dominated urban modernization even as many "new immigrants" were assimilated into those benefits. Black migrants, having few other options, moved in large numbers to the neighborhood of Black Bottom, east of downtown and long a gateway district for new arrivals from Europe. It had been named in the nineteenth century for the quality of the area's soil.

The Detroit Board of Commerce's Americanization Committee took an interest in the housing conditions of newly arrived African Americans in Black Bottom, suggesting its members perceived Black migrants as foreign to Detroit even though they were already U.S. citizens. The committee reported "deplorable" conditions in Black Bottom and claimed that the district had become a center for vice and immorality in the form of gambling, prostitution, and rum running.[79] *The Detroiter* featured the committee's report on its first page:

> Here, we see whole blocks, yes, streets, filled with mean, ramshackle, rickety, wheezy shacks; down at the heel in every sense of the word. The only condition that keeps them from tumbling down is their proximity to each other. These, with rare exceptions, are *sans* plumbing equipment of any kind, and are totally unfit for decent habitation.[80]

The area east of downtown was socially and culturally diverse and included finer houses and businesses, but the committee focused on the district's problems, illustrating its findings with a photograph that featured a debris pile in a yard and a dwelling with a crudely constructed wooden roof (Figure 2.8). The biggest problems the district had, however, were the crowding and exploitation caused by racial segregation. Because Black Detroiters were locked out of most other neighborhoods, there was an artificial scarcity of housing in Black Bottom. Under these conditions, property owners could charge sky-high rents for antiquated

Figure 2.8. "Where Many Detroit Negroes Are Forced to Live." Photograph used by the Detroit Board of Commerce's Americanization Committee to illustrate the poor housing conditions that racial segregation was causing in the Black Bottom neighborhood.

Source: Detroit Board of Commerce, *The Detroiter*, vol. 11, no. 11, 1919.

dwellings, such that "the dirtiest dilapidated shack, facing an alley, will bring the landlord at least $60 per month," more than white workers paid for modern houses elsewhere in the city.[81]

While it emphasized the poor housing conditions in Black Bottom, the Americanization Committee stopped short of condemning racial segregation. It observed that housing integration might ultimately reduce the chance of racial violence in the city but added that whether integration "is an ideal condition from many points of view is a question."[82] The committee's proposed solution reflected this ambivalence: it called for philanthropic investors to construct race-specified rental houses on a limited-dividend basis, "for Negro men and women," while adding that such developments must "be done tactfully and carefully" to avoid reinforcing "segregated colonies."[83] Despite acknowledging the injustice its investigation found, as the historian Beth Tompkins Bates notes, the committee "ultimately declared that its organization was not concerned or responsible for the crisis in housing Black Americans." It dropped the issue, apparently taking refuge in a return to its work on the assimilation of white immigrants.[84]

The city's business leaders needed and accepted the labor of Black workers but did little to address their housing needs, allowing segregation to force many of them into a material poverty that belied their hard-earned industrial wages. In Black Bottom, many workers lived in substandard houses and enjoyed less access to homeownership and to the social networks of the larger city than their white colleagues. Black workers, in short, were treated as less fully American than the city's newly arrived, Americanized white immigrants.[85] Yet Black workers would push back, as discussed in Chapters 5 and 7, asserting their right to participate in the evolving American social contract. They would establish new, Black-dominated neighborhoods at the city's periphery and challenge racial boundaries, despite threats of violence.

Conclusion

In the 1910s, seeking to grow and modernize their operations, Detroit's employers engaged in an implicit negotiation with the city's workforce, and especially its many newly arrived immigrants. They raised wages and offered other benefits but expected workers to use those wages to commit to the United States, to Detroit, and to their work. The Ford Motor Company and Detroit Board of Commerce developed a night school Americanization program that taught the English language and American citizenship while also promoting the modern worker's house and its ownership. The house was to be the means by which employees would plant roots in the city. Ford used the lever of profit sharing to further encourage modern houses, while other employers offered loans and technical advice to assist with workers' house purchases. Detroit's Americanization programs and Ford's Five Dollar Day were intrusive and coercive, but many newly arrived workers saw them as an opportunity worth navigating. They leveraged their rising wages to live in better houses, on Detroit's growing periphery, and despite the rhetoric of the melting pot, they created distinct Polish, Black, Jewish, Italian, and other communities within it.

Whether renters or owners of modern houses, workers took risks as they spent their wages and extended themselves with credit-based purchases, adapting to a new, higher standard of living. The mercurial economy continued to threaten their gains. Designers and planners, the protagonists of Chapter 3, understood the economic risks of a speculative housing market such as Detroit's. They also criticized the environmental and social limitations of a conventional grid of blocks, lots, and detached dwellings—the model that Ford's *Helpful Hints* had assumed would solve the city's housing problem. Instead, designers created visions of centrally planned housing integrated with large shared greenspaces—in Detroit, across the United States, and in Europe. While their impact on early twentieth-century Detroit was ultimately limited, these advocates for housing design and planning illustrated that there was more than one way to develop the periphery of an industrial city, and more than one way to imagine workers' modern domestic lives.

PART II

MODERNIZATION

3

FORMS OF MODERN HOUSING

Alternative Models from Dessau to Detroit

> A great era has just begun. . . . [T]he problem of the house is a problem of the era.
> —Le Corbusier, *Toward an Architecture*

The United States was one of many countries that struggled to house workers amid early twentieth-century urbanization.* The Swiss-born French architect Le Corbusier, in his landmark book *Toward an Architecture*, argued that this housing problem was an urgent political imperative, that the industrialized world faced a choice: "Architecture or Revolution." Workers were suffering a "great disaccord," he explained. They could see the potentials of modernization, buildings graced by "sun, heat, clean air, and clean floors," and yet they returned home to dismal, antiquated houses at the end of each day.[1] Le Corbusier's basic formula, modern housing as a hedge against unrest, was already well understood by policy makers on both sides of the Atlantic. The Detroit Board of Commerce, for its part, had framed housing as the key to "snuffing out Bolshevism" four years earlier. The revolutions in Russia and Germany loomed large on both sides of the Atlantic. Yet housing promised more than social stability. Many governments embraced it as a physical manifestation of a new social contract, an opportunity to reset the relationship between the state and its citizenry. In Russia, the Soviets developed residential projects designed to support the transition to communism, while policy makers and planners in the

---

* An earlier version of this chapter appeared as Michael McCulloch, "Workers' Housing and Houses: Interwar Planning from Dessau to Detroit," *Journal of Planning History*, Vol. 19, No. 4, (November 2020): 314–35, https://doi.org/10.1177/1538513 220922626.

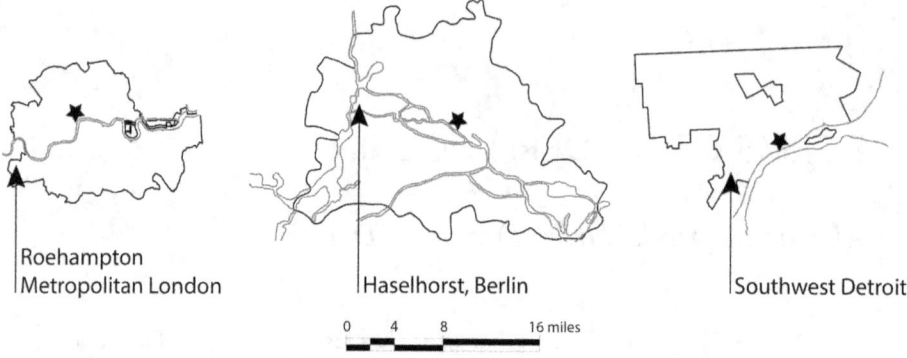

Figure 3.1. The London, Berlin, and Detroit housing developments examined in this chapter were each located at the periphery of a growing city. Stars indicate city centers.
Source: Illustration by the author, with assistance from Andrew Dancer.

industrial West offered their own vision: a higher quality of life for the working class, achieved without the radical dismantling of capitalism.[2]

Housing histories often view the European and American cases separately, but this chapter offers a comparative, transatlantic view.[3] It explores a range of early twentieth-century housing policies and designs by juxtaposing case studies from Berlin, London, and Detroit. In each of these contexts, policy makers, planners, and architects saw the urban periphery, where open land was readily available, as the best setting for new housing development (Figure 3.1). Given the distinct economic and cultural contexts, though, modern housing took different forms in each of these cities, reflecting different social visions and affording different kinds of domestic experiences.

In transatlantic comparison, America's post–World War I housing policy stands out for its embrace of speculative private-sector subdivision building as the primary method of development. By contrast, European policy makers supported large-scale planned housing estates and emphasized research through institutions such as the Bauhaus, encouraging experimentation in housing design. The American focus on speculative development is partly explained by the strength of the U.S. economy, which was less disrupted by the war. The United States became the world's leading industrial power in the post–World War I era and had more reason to believe that its private sector could solve the housing shortage without direct federal investment.[4] Ultimately, though, the differences in housing policy on each side of the Atlantic were primarily driven by different political ideologies.

In interwar England and Germany, social democratic policy makers envisioned a larger role for government in ensuring that the benefits of modernization were shared broadly, especially in housing.[5] The new Weimar Constitution gave each German citizen the right to a decent dwelling, something the U.S. Constitution did not afford. Many American architects, planners, and reformers, however, were sympathetic to the European approach. They argued for government-sponsored housing in the United States, pointing out that centralized planning could improve the quality of new developments. With planning, urban greenspace would be better preserved, and community amenities would be better integrated with housing. While speculative subdivisions emphasized the individual consumer's choices and risks, government-supported housing estates could, as one reformer put it, reflect "the doctrine of community responsibility for the housing of the people."[6] In the United States and in Detroit, clearly, the emphasis on speculative subdivisions was not a foregone conclusion. It was a social choice among known alternatives, and a high stakes one at that.

Government-Supported Developments in Interwar Europe

Post–World War I political shifts created an extraordinary opportunity for European architects and planners, who embraced housing as a central disciplinary concern as never before.[7] Building on Ebenezer Howard's Garden City concept, the architect Raymond Unwin rose to prominence in the early twentieth century, helping to establish broadly influential design principles for housing. With his books and designs for Letchworth Garden City and Hampstead Garden Suburb, Unwin illustrated the value of common green space and integrated community facilities in housing developments. In 1919, with the passing of the British Housing and Town Planning Act, Unwin's principles gained powerful government backing. Ultimately, 30 percent of interwar housing in England was developed by government.[8]

The first state-led housing development in post–World War I London was Roehampton. It was designed by the Architect's Department of the London County Council and took the form of two-story row houses along the perimeter of each block. This method reserved the open centers of residential blocks for garden allotments and other community amenities. Despite its benefits, the kind of public investment that Roehampton represented did not come easily. British housing policy went through much debate and compromise as it proceeded through the 1920s, driven by policy makers' concerns about costs. Roehampton's development, and England's larger state-led housing effort, were halted in 1922 before being revived two years later. In the second phase of work at Roehampton, its steeply pitched roofs, detailed brick facades, and generous unit sizes were replaced with lower-cost alternatives.[9] Nevertheless, Roehampton brought new experiences within the reach of its residents—a way of life transformed by plumbed bathtubs and greater indoor illumination and ventilation, along with convenient access to green spaces and community facilities.

German architects and planners found their own opportunities in government-sponsored housing development, especially as their country's war-ravaged economy gained steam in 1924. The most innovative of their projects joined British-inspired Garden City principles with an emerging modernist design agenda. Ernst May, who had previously worked for Unwin, oversaw the design and construction of many new housing estates at the periphery of Frankfurt am Main. They were recognizably modernist, with flat roofs, unornamented white walls, and long horizontal bands of windows. But modernism was more than these aesthetic cues. It was also an embrace of rational and efficient spaces and production processes, drawing inspiration from American industry and Detroit's automakers in particular. Margarete Schütte-Lihotzky, the only female architect on May's team, developed one of the era's most iconic modernist designs: the Frankfurt Kitchen. Prefabricated in a factory and modular in their dimensions, these kitchens could be transported to the construction site and installed with relative ease. Finished in easily washable metal, tile, and linoleum, they were designed to reduce the physical effort of meal preparation. At May's Bruchfeldstrasse Estate in Frankfurt, residents relaxed on roof terraces, chatting with neighbors or reading newspapers while watching the passing of other neighbors in the courtyard below.[10] New ways of building brought new pleasures within residents' reach.

About 5 percent of German interwar housing was designed in the modernist, or Neues Bauen, style, with its advocates concentrated in Weimar, Dessau, Frankfurt, and Berlin. Historians have noted that, while modernists theorized their projects around workers' needs for housing, the benefits of modernism were often priced out of reach for unskilled workers in the early twentieth-century period.[11] More commonly, new developments reflected what the historian Adelheid von Saldern describes as a "moderate modern" approach.[12] They combined traditional formal cues, such as exposed brick walls and gabled roofs, with a modernizing social agenda. Like the modernists' projects, these developments increased residents' access to sunlight, ventilation, and green space and introduced modern technologies such as hot water, private bathrooms, and, in some cases, central heating.[13] Between 1919 and 1936, 15 percent of all German housing construction was subsidized by municipalities, with 26.2 percent more financed by public utilities and cooperatives.[14] By the end of this period, between public- and private-sector construction, every seventh housing unit in the country was new.[15]

Walter Gropius was a leading figure in modernist housing experimentation. Beginning in 1926, from his position as director of the Dessau Bauhaus, he designed a system of site-cast concrete beams and floors for the nearby Törten housing estate. Three years later, when the German Government Research Institute sought designs for three thousand low-cost apartments at Berlin's Haselhorst—the largest such development in the city—Gropius won. His proposal included long, narrow, twelve-story apartment slabs in parallel rows. The height of these buildings was particularly innovative, prefiguring the future popularity of high-rise housing. Haselhorst's design, however, was modified on the path to realization. Following disputes, the state-supported developer of the project worked with other modernist architects, who largely kept Gropius's site-planning approach but replaced his high-rise elevator buildings with four-story walk-ups.[16]

In the rationalizing spirit of modernism, Haselhorst's units were designed to eliminate waste or perceived excess. The British housing advocate Elizabeth Denby criticized the modernist theory of the minimal dwelling applied in the development, noting that it was "common to most of Europe."[17] While this approach may have saved money, she argued, and provided intellectual pleasure to architects, Haselhorst's "rooms were often so small that families had been obliged to discard their furniture on moving into their new homes and, poor though they were, to buy new."[18] Her concern about furniture replacement may have been overstated, however. To the chagrin of Germany's interwar reformers, many families made do with their existing furniture and unfashionable decorative objects. Some even "misused" a room in their minimal flats, treating it as a traditional parlor and reserving it for special occasions instead of using it to meet everyday needs. Tolerating the gaze and the intrusions of reformers was a price that residents paid to live in the large Weimar-era housing estates, whose administrative offices enforced rules, published newsletters on domestic hygiene, and monitored residents' adherence with inspectors.[19]

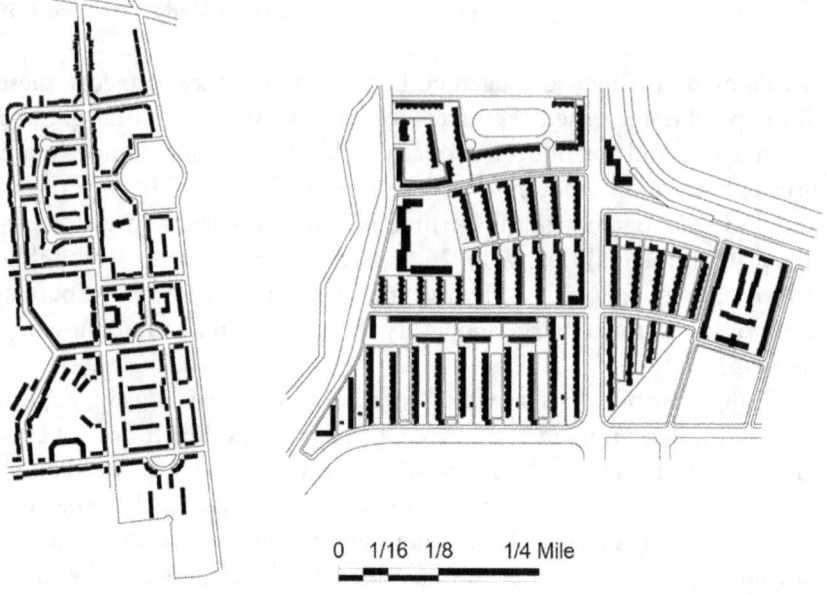

Figure 3.2. Site plans of London's Roehampton (*left*) and Berlin's Haselhorst (*right*) housing developments.

Source: Illustration by the author, with assistance from Andrew Dancer and Zada Harris, and with reference to Elizabeth Denby, *Europe Rehoused* (New York: W. W. Norton, 1938); Mark Swenarton, *Homes Fit for Heroes: The Politics and Architecture of Early State Housing in Britain* (Portsmouth, NH: Heinemann Educational Books, 1981).

Living in a planned environment certainly came with benefits, however. With control over a large, 111 acre site, Haselhorst's designers were able to define the size and shape the development's blocks. Using large blocks, they reserved pedestrian-oriented recreational space between the buildings, where, as Denby noted, "the common garden, grass, and flowers, [are] open to all."[20] The plan integrated a town hall, schools, washhouses, a church, and a cinema amid the housing. The community laundry, as Denby noted, was "particularly well planned and equipped."[21] With its four-story apartment buildings, Haselhorst combined accessible open space with higher residential density than was achieved with the two-story row house approach used at Roehampton (Figures 3.2–3.3).

Though different in their site plans and architectural forms, Roehampton and Haselhorst shared the basic principle of planning. Coordinating landscape and architecture over a large area, they were able to concentrate development in selected locations and restrict building elsewhere, preserving open spaces. Careful planning could reduce unnecessary conflicts between vehicles and pedestrians and provide residents with easier access to daily needs. Planning also had a visual effect. The consistent architectural forms and materials used at Roehampton and Haselhorst reflect something of their social context, signaling that the whole of

Figure 3.3.
A contemporary street view of London's Roehampton (*top*) and a contemporary aerial view of Berlin's Haselhorst (*bottom*).

Source: Photo taken by the author (*top*); Google Earth and GeoBasis-DE/BKG (*bottom*).

the development is greater than the sum of its parts. They manifested the ideal that housing was a matter of common interest, managed by government. In the United States, meanwhile, advocates of planned housing faced a less favorable political context. This did not deter them from their work, but ultimately they would face significant disappointment.

A Path Not Taken: Planned Workers' Housing in Post–World War I Detroit

After the armistice, the U.S. government withdrew from its wartime investments in direct housing production, undercutting the hopes of many housing reformers. Nevertheless, there was still cause for hope. Powerful employers seemed poised to step forward where government had stepped back and began to commission large-scale investments in workers' housing. The corporate social influence that this implied was a far cry from the publicly led paradigm of Europe: employer-controlled housing did not necessarily advance democratic principles. Nevertheless, American planners and designers seized the opportunity and designed

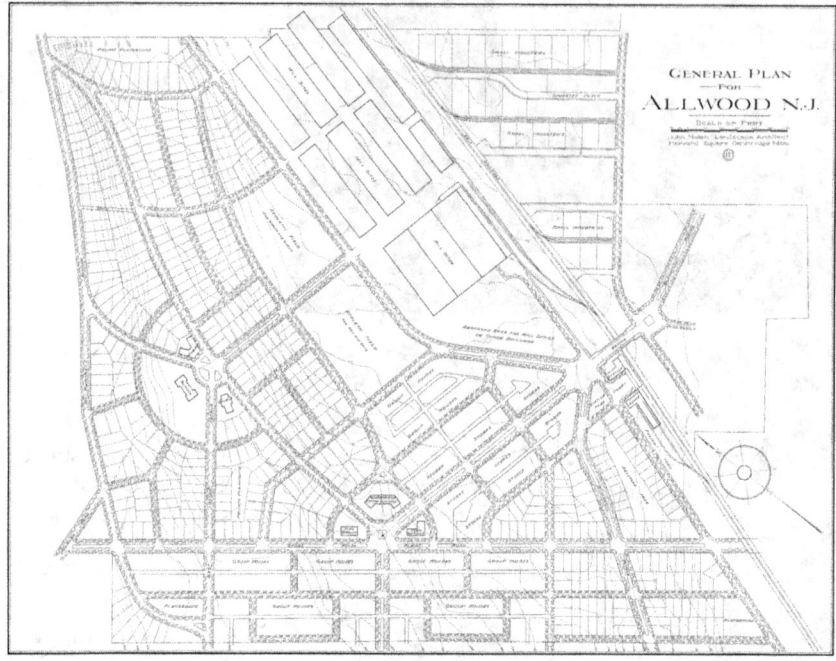

Figure 3.4. General plan for Allwood, New Jersey, prepared by John Nolen for the Brighton Mills company.
Source: Division of Rare and Manuscript Collections, Carl A. Kroch Library, Cornell University, Ithaca, NY.

many "company town" developments in the post–World War I period. They often reflected the influence of British Garden City precedents, with their picturesque, curving streets and formal civic centers. Goodyear Heights in Ohio, Kistler Industrial Village in Pennsylvania, and Allwood in New Jersey all followed these principles (Figure 3.4).[22] In Detroit, the Solvay Process Company and Ford Motor Company both initiated planned workers' housing developments around 1918 (Figure 3.5). The war had halted private-sector housing construction, even as it drew more workers to Detroit, and the city's growing shortage of dwellings prompted employers to take the housing question into their own hands.

The Solvay Process Company produced carbonate of soda and coke at a riverside plant in southwestern Detroit's Delray neighborhood.[23] In Delray, the plant's management embraced the role of corporate social reformer among the neighborhood's many working-class immigrants from Hungary. The company operated a Guild Hall, providing educational and recreational programs to area residents.[24] Concerned about the crowding and poor hygiene they observed in Delray, the Solvay plant commissioned a small housing development circa 1918 called Jefferson

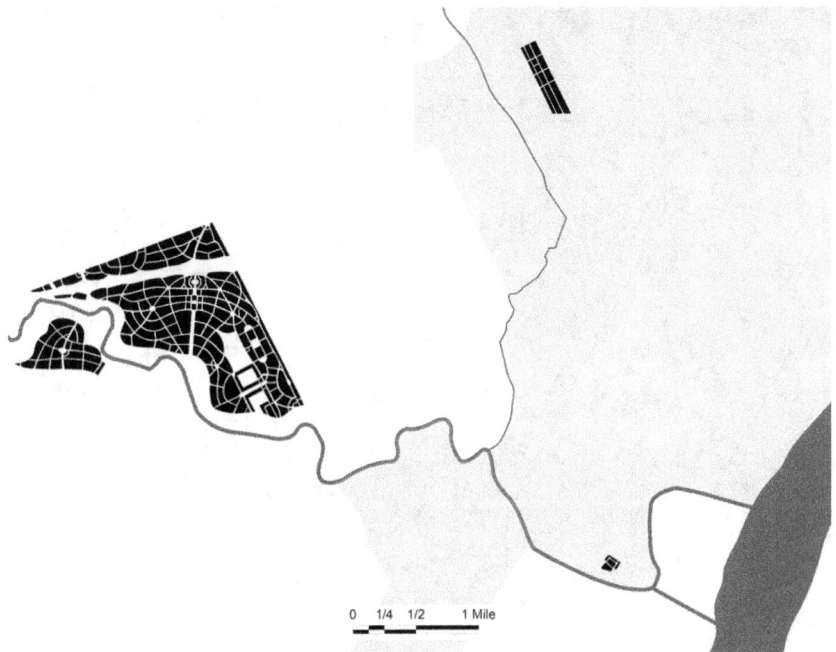

Figure 3.5. Three housing development models in southwest Detroit. Solvay's small Jefferson Rouge development (*lower right*) and Ford's Fordson Village (*left*) were professionally designed, but went largely unbuilt, while Burton's Michigan Avenue Subdivision (*upper right*) was built, and epitomizes the unplanned speculative development that dominated Detroit's interwar growth. The light gray area indicates the city of Detroit.

Source: Illustration by the author.

Rouge. It hired New York's Mann and MacNeille, housing specialists with a "company town" résumé that included Goodyear Heights and Kistler Industrial Village. Though modest in scale at 186 units, Jefferson Rouge received good press in a U.S. planning and architecture culture that was hungry for housing innovations. It was featured in *Architectural Forum*'s 1918 issue on "Workingmen's Houses" as a model of affordable development.[25]

Mann and MacNeille's cost-reduction efforts began with site planning. They reserved the prominent Jefferson Avenue frontage for future commercial development to subsidize the dwellings tucked behind (Figure 3.6). The architects included two-story row houses, four-family structures, and company-regulated boardinghouses, bringing the efficiency of higher housing density to the site. They also designed the buildings to be clad in surplus brick that Solvay already owned (Figure 3.6). As at Roehampton, Jefferson Rouge's dwellings aligned to the perimeter of each block, reserving the centers for community greens, one of which would serve as a playground.

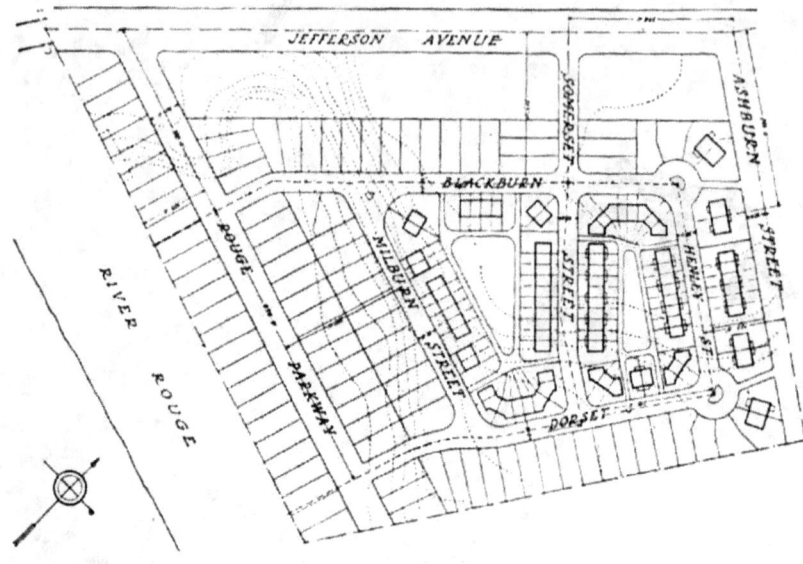

Figure 3.6. Site plan (*top*) and street view of Jefferson Rouge (*bottom*), designed by Mann and MacNeille for the Solvay Process Company.
Source: Architectural Forum, April 1918, 121.

Planning brought consistency to the development: each dwelling had an indoor three-fixture bath, as well as modern heating and hot water systems—comforts that were available but not ensured in the city's speculatively built houses. Jefferson Rouge's shingled roofs, in dull red, and the brick veneers of each building, tied the ensemble together visually. Common gable angles and a regular rhythm of chimneys added to this sense of cohesion.[26] This aesthetic unity reflected not only the company's stake in improving workers' quality of life, but also the measure of leverage that bought them. Company-sponsored construction created an opportunity to exert influence on the lives of workers outside the gates of the plant. The architect Charles May, writing in *Architectural Forum*, urged institutions to take that opportunity. He argued that a housing plan was not complete without a program of oversight and education. This, he explained, would ensure that residents used their modern domestic spaces as designed, and were not keeping livestock on the green spaces.[27]

The Ford Motor Company commissioned its own large workers' housing estate after the war. The company had grown rapidly and was developing what would become its new flagship plant on the Rouge River, just west of Detroit, in Dearborn. Understanding the significance of this future plant, Ford had also purchased a great deal of land nearby. It was there, adjacent to the emerging Rouge Plant, that the company decided to build "a model city for employees" called Fordson Village. At 3,500–4,000 housing units, it was to be even larger than Berlin's Haselhorst and would have been a landmark achievement for planned housing in the United States.[28] As news of the company's intent spread, Ford received a number of proposals from builders and designers, ranging from the pragmatic to the utopian.[29] A concrete housing company reached out, arguing the merits of its novel construction system. The reform-minded journalist Ida Tarbell also wrote, offering to introduce the automaker to Grosvenor Atterbury, designer of the celebrated, British-inspired Forest Hills Gardens development in Queens.[30] Intriguingly, an agent for Peter Roveda, a designer from Milan and New York, sent drawings for what he called the "City of the Sun" (Figure 3.7).[31]

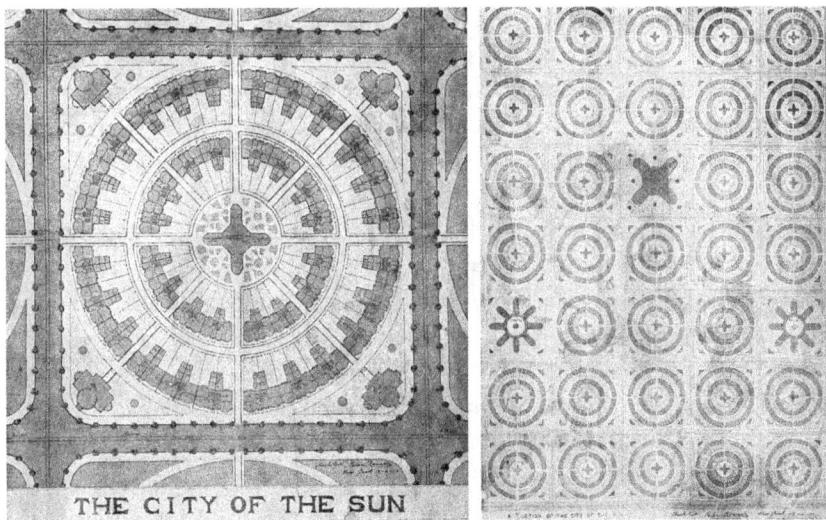

Figure 3.7. Peter Roveda's "City of the Sun" proposal, illustrated with a single block plan (*left*) and a city plan composed of many such blocks (*right*).
Source: Image from the Collections of The Henry Ford, Dearborn, MI, acc. 47, box 5.

Roveda had publicized his utopian city concept as early as 1910, when it was featured in *American Homes and Gardens*. Hearing of Ford's plans to build, Roveda's agent sent drawings to the automaker's office, urging that the proposal "ought to be of great interest to mister Ford."[32] The City of the Sun appears to have been inspired by the Renaissance philosopher Tommaso Campanella's utopia of the same name and by the concentric circular form of Ebenezer Howard's Garden City diagrams.[33] Roveda, like Howard, imagined bands of housing encircling central civic spaces. Echoing the attitudes toward housing of many Detroit business interests, Roveda also argued for homeownership within the plan, proposing modest duplexes that workers might purchase. In becoming homeowners, as he had explained in *American Homes and Gardens*, employees would become thrifty and adopt the "noble sentiment of love for country."[34] There is no indication that Ford seriously considered the City of the Sun, but it does illustrate how wide open Detroit's housing future was at that moment through the eyes of an ambitious designer.

The actual contract to design Fordson Village went to a local architect, Leonard Willeke, who had studied industrial housing developments in Germany and England.[35] In Detroit, he had worked for Eleanor and Edsel Ford on a house addition in 1916, and it was Edsel, Henry Ford's son, who advocated for his hire.[36] Willeke looked at Mann and MacNeille's nearby Jefferson Rouge project as he designed Fordson Village, and as they had, he introduced a diversity of dwelling types to meet a range of budgets.[37] In size, however, there was no comparison. Jefferson Rouge's designers were limited to two small blocks, while the Fordson Village's large scale offered the opportunity to more fully show the environmental and social benefits of planned housing. Where the Rouge River cuts through Fordson Village, Willeke introduced a chain of lagoons, and reserved the lands around the watercourse for recreation and a "virgin timber reserve." Where a rail line passes through, he designed a grade separation to protect the adjacent houses from the noise and disruption of passing trains. As was favored in Garden City planning, he created curving, naturalistic streets, and composed them in a legible hierarchy. His minor streets converge in subcenters, with churches, schools, and shops, and these lead to the central municipal and business center (Figure 3.8).

The residential density at Fordson Village was lower than in the other projects explored here. Its single-family, duplex, and row-house structures were set apart from one another and from the street, with reference to the suburban ideal of a dwelling set in a natural landscape. It imagined a different transportation model, as well—one that Ford was working to achieve—in which most residents would drive automobiles

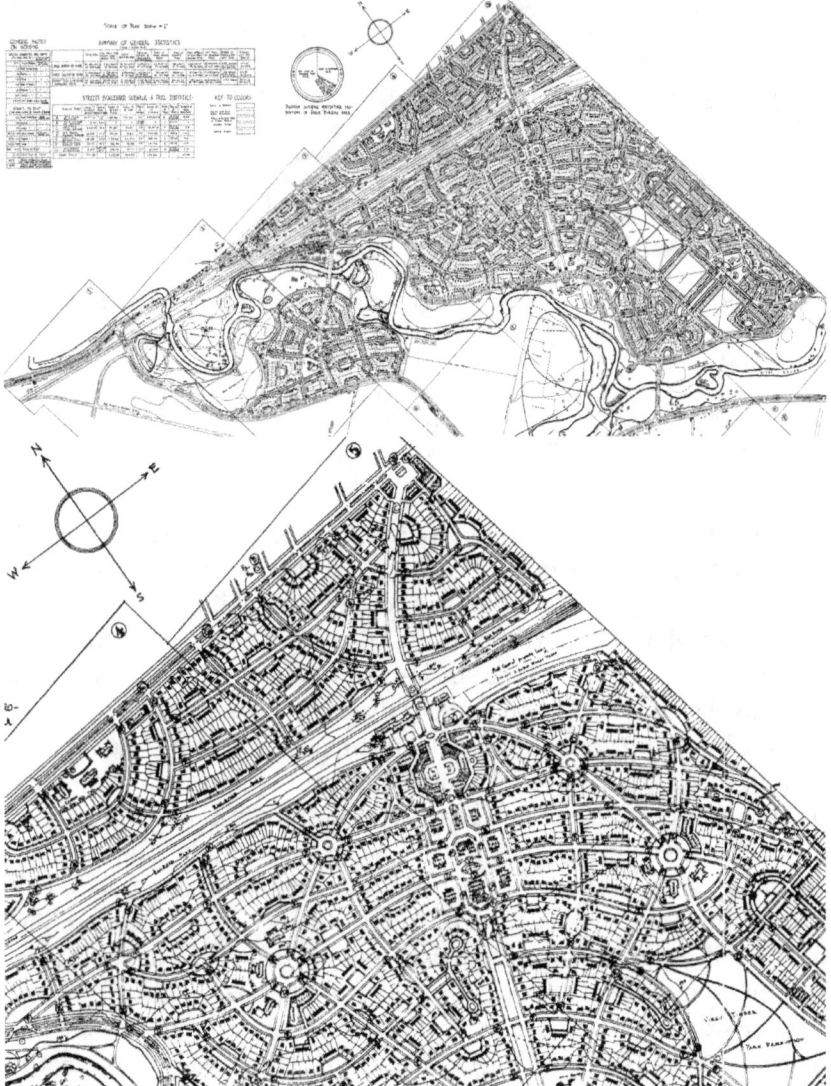

Figure 3.8. Fordson Village, designed by Leonard Willeke for the Ford Motor Company, full site plan above and detail view below.
Source: Leonard B. Willeke Papers, Bentley Historical Library, University of Michigan, Ann Arbor, tube 26.

and park in shared garages behind the houses. Rather than giving the blocks' interiors over to community green spaces, as at London's Roehampton and the nearby Jefferson Rouge, Fordson Village staged neighborly cooperation at a smaller scale, in semicircular greens at the street, and gave the blocks' centers to neighbors' shared driveways and garages.

Willeke balanced aesthetic unity and variety with Fordson Village, using a spare, unornamented language that referenced English vernacu-

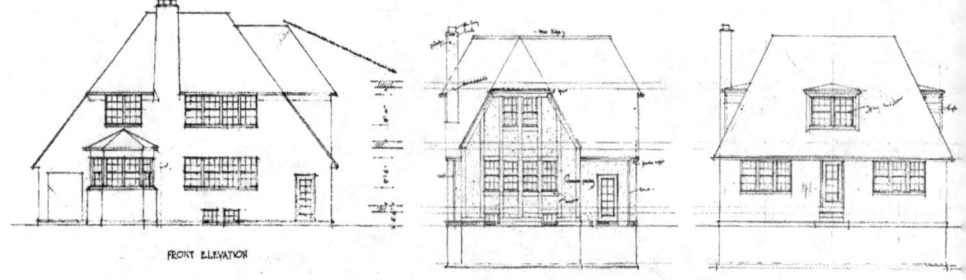

Figure 3.9. Three Fordson Village housing types in elevation view, including a boardinghouse (*left*) and two variations on the detached single residence (*center* and *right*).

Source: Leonard B. Willeke Papers, Bentley Historical Library, University of Michigan, Ann Arbor, drawer 7, folder 47. Also see Thomas Brunk, *Leonard B. Willeke: Excellence in Architecture and Design* (Detroit: Wayne State University Press, 1986).

lar and a mix of brick cladding, stucco, and, occasionally, half-timbering. Amid the diversity of house types in the development, he used horizontal regulating lines that served to tie the buildings together as a perceptible whole. Across three distinct types, for example—a boardinghouse and two versions of the single-family house—the windows fall at the same height in elevation and use the same six-pane glazing pattern (Figure 3.9). The varying roof gables distinguish each unit, but in places their hips end at the same horizontal lines, quietly attesting to their coordinated design. The same tapered chimney profile is used throughout.

Each household at Fordson Village had access to the same modern amenities, such as three-fixture baths and common green spaces. Further, Willeke's unit plans, from the single-family types to the boardinghouses, all center on living room pianos—an artifact of household pleasure and sociability that he clearly valued. In the boardinghouse, twelve of the Ford Motor Company's workers would share a dining room and living room, and could gather on Sundays to play music—an alternative to the unregulated entertainment that corporate reformers feared in the city beyond (Figure 3.10).

While Europe's government-supported housing estates often leased their units, most American employers favored worker homeownership in their planned developments of the 1910s. This was partly a response to events in Pullman, Illinois, where a disastrous strike in 1894 erupted when the employer, who rented houses to workers, cut jobs without offering rent relief.[38] Presumably, if Pullman's employees had owned their own houses, the company would not be held so directly responsible for ensuring their housing security amid an economic downturn. The Ford Motor Company promoted worker homeownership with its Five Dollar Day program, and Willeke integrated that same value into Fordson Vil-

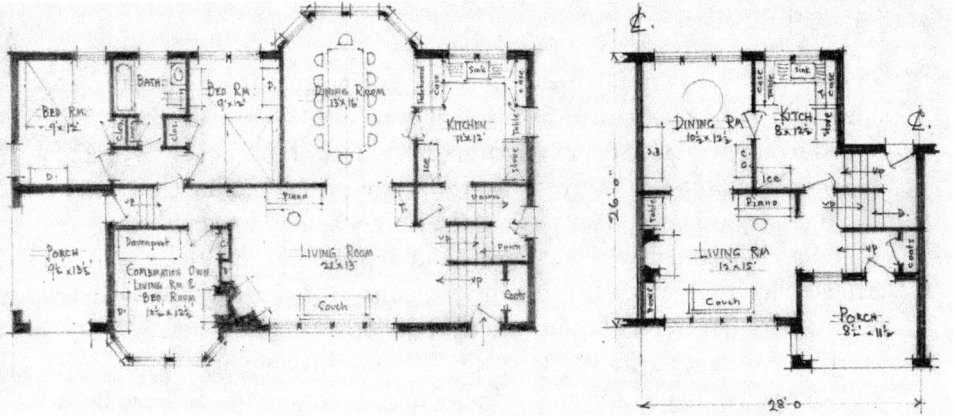

Figure 3.10. First-floor plans of the "Large Boarding House Type" (*left*) and a "2 & 4 Family House Unit" (*right*), designed by Leonard Willeke for the Fordson Village development.

Source: Leonard B. Willeke Papers, Bentley Historical Library, University of Michigan, Ann Arbor, drawer 7, folder 46.

lage, where 65 percent of the units were intended to be owner-occupied, not counting the more itinerant boardinghouse beds, which were not included in the tally.[39]

Yet even if Ford planned to sell the units within Fordson Village to workers and other investors, the company still faced risks. Construction would require a large, up-front capital investment, and more subtly, a large workers' housing estate built by Ford would reinforce an implicit message that was introduced by the Five Dollar Day program: that the company was taking responsibility for the domestic security of its employees. Ford would be putting its name, through architecture, on the development's long-term success. By decade's end, both Solvay and Ford had scaled back their development plans, allowing the risks of housing production to fall to others. These decisions were part of a larger national withdrawal from corporate housing development: of the twenty-five designs that John Nolen prepared for U.S. companies between 1914 and 1920, only seven were ultimately realized. The Allwood plan he created for Brighton Mills was among the unrealized.[40]

American Houses

In Detroit and nationwide, the progressive housing reform ambitions of the 1910s began to wane by decade's end. Government agencies and corporate employers increasingly relinquished responsibility for housing and looked to private builders to address the shortage. Herbert Hoover, the U.S. Secretary of Commerce through most of the 1920s, was an outspoken opponent of social housing, fearing that it would stifle an idealized American culture of private and individual enterprise. He failed to acknowledge the environmental and social benefits of planned housing, but Hoover's faith in the productive capacity of the U.S. building industry was not misplaced. Detroit's house builders created more than ten thousand new single-family and duplex units in 1919, a record, after being at a near standstill the previous year. This was consistent with a national trend of increased production.[41]

In the summer of 1919, Henry Ford leveraged company resources to buy out stockholders, diverting funds that might otherwise have been invested in housing.[42] In place of Fordson Village, the company built the much smaller Maloney Subdivision, consisting of 250 detached single-family houses designed for a middle-class budget. They replaced Willeke with another architect, Albert Wood, and disputed Willeke's design fees for the unbuilt Fordson Village.[43] The company sociologist Samuel Marquis, who had overseen the Five Dollar Day housing reform effort, resigned in 1921. He had argued until the end that the company should build housing for workers but was not successful.[44] Instead, Ford turned its efforts at social control inward, focusing more on hard-driving shop-floor discipline than on workers' quality of life outside of the factory.[45]

Solvay's Jefferson Rouge fared little better. It was only half completed when *Architectural Forum* had featured it and was never finished as designed. In 1921, Solvay shut its Detroit plant, causing 1,600 to lose their jobs.[46] The operation would reopen under the name Allied Chemical and go on to survive into the 1960s, but the context of Jefferson Rouge was declining rapidly.[47] Industrial interests transformed the Rouge River into a heavy shipping channel, and the residential district just north of Jefferson Rouge was replaced with a vast sewage treatment plant in 1940.[48] As industry overtook the riverside all around them, the residents of the half-completed Jefferson Rouge faced a risk inherent in place-bound housing developments: to be fixed amid the contingencies of a dynamic, changeful context, in the absence of robust public regulation of development.

Turning away from planned housing estates, American policy makers and employers dispersed the tasks and the economic risks of housing development to private developers, builders, and U.S. households themselves. In this context, most American housing developers—large "Community Builders" such as J. C. Nichols notwithstanding—relied on a risk-averse strategy.[49] They produced tried-and-true orthogonal grids of individual lots, on which builders could construct detached wood-framed houses. Burton's Michigan Avenue Subdivision, estab-

Forms of Modern Housing / 71

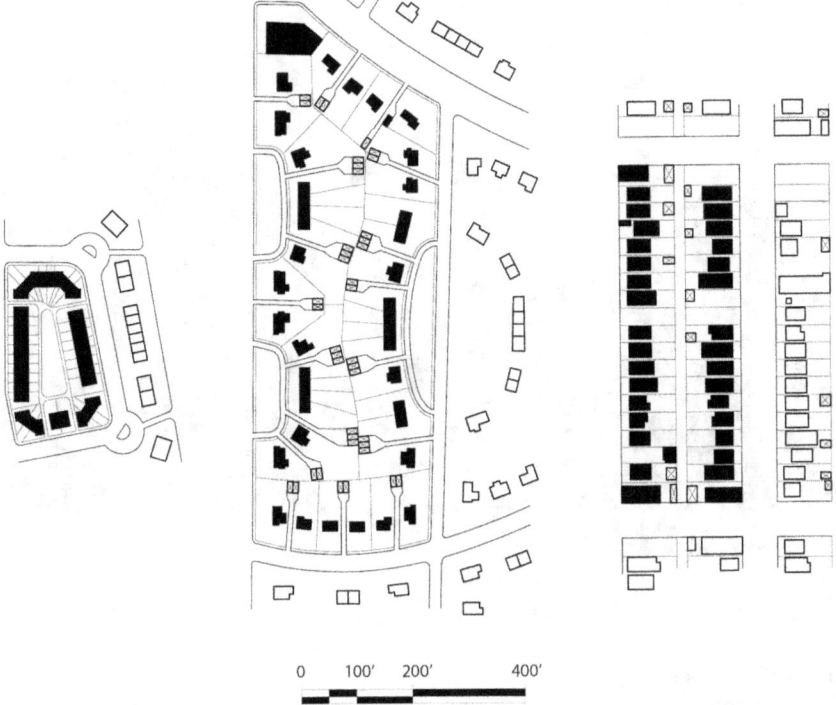

Figure 3.11. A comparison of block plans from southwestern Detroit: Solvay's Jefferson Rouge (*left*), Ford's Fordson Village (*center*), and Burton's Michigan Avenue Subdivision (*right*). Auto garages are marked through with an "X."
Source: Illustration by the author, with assistance from Zada Harris.

lished in 1913 by Second Ward Alderman Charles Burton's realty firm, epitomizes this model.[50]

Burton's subdivision, in west Detroit, consisted of nine rectangular blocks and four half-blocks.[51] Unlike the planned developments discussed here, which featured uniquely shaped, alley-free blocks, the speculative grid of the Michigan Avenue Subdivision was modular and conventional, with thirty-foot-wide lots suited to common national house types such as bungalows and duplexes (Figure 3.11). This allowed flexibility within a system of disaggregated control: house builders large and small could add units to the subdivision, without significant coordination, either working on contract for a future homeowner or investor or building speculatively with the intent to sell.[52] This process, absent the design control of planned development, produced houses with an individuated quality. Most of the structures in the subdivision are bungalows or duplexes, but their aesthetic effect is that of many singular

Figure 3.12. Houses on Chopin Street in Burton's Michigan Avenue Subdivision, illustrating the uncoordinated juxtaposition of different styles (*top*) and the nearly exact duplication of a style (*bottom*).

Source: Photographs by the author.

Figure 3.13. Our Savior on Golgotha Church, located on Chopin Street in Burton's Michigan Avenue Subdivision. This photograph was taken on the occasion of a visit by Bishop Francis Hodur, founder of the Polish National Catholic Church, circa 1923.

Source: Resource no. DPA2023, Digital Collections, Detroit Public Library. Courtesy of Burton Historical Collection, Detroit Public Library.

decisions aggregated: three houses, closely spaced, might have different roof styles, heights, and color palates. Elsewhere, on the same block, another manifestation of speculative development appears: the simple repetition of the same house type on a few adjacent lots—perhaps finished with different paint colors—reflecting the expediency of reproducing common types (Figure 3.12).

Chopin Street runs north and south through Burton's Michigan Avenue Subdivision, and while no planner coordinated its mix of community amenities, it did attract a few. A 1924 Sanborn map of the street shows small shops on many of the corner lots and a combined four-lot property at mid-block developed by an ethnically Polish institution: Our Savior on Golgotha Church.[53] There, a brick basilica stands among the houses, with a clapboard bell tower to one side and an open yard to the other, in street-facing orientation like its residential neighbors. For the special occasion of a bishop's visit to Detroit, the congregants—in the absence of a planned community space—transformed the street itself, with banners and regalia, children in white dresses, and a camera to record the moment for posterity (Figure 3.13). The neighborhood's residents could enact a significant degree of individualism in the selection, modification, and outfitting of their houses, but for those who belonged to the church, the same block afforded opportunities to construct the bonds of community.

Conclusion

Detroit was by no means the only city grappling with a housing shortage in the early twentieth century, and its speculative subdivisions were by no means the only solution. Housing alternatives, from Roehampton and Haselhorst to largely unbuilt projects closer to home, illustrate the environmental, social, and aesthetic benefits of planning and design. Compared with Detroit's speculative development model, they were less prone to sprawl, as planning controls allowed for the concentration of denser housing in specific areas and the preservation of green space in others. They also helped to avoid conflicts among incompatible uses, such as the close proximity of housing, heavy industry, and a sewage treatment facility in Detroit's Delray neighborhood. Yet for all of its flaws, Detroit's housebuilding industry achieved a great deal. As noted in the Introduction, an International Labor Office (ILO) survey in 1929 found that among one hundred unskilled Ford workers, most lived in relatively spacious four- to five-room dwellings in Detroit; all had electricity; and most had plumbed indoor bathrooms.[54] The potential richness of community life in Detroit's subdivisions is illustrated by the celebration at Our Savior Church on Chopin Street, even if it took place in the street for lack of a formalized outdoor gathering space.

For all that it achieved, Detroit's model for early twentieth-century housing came with unique risks—it rested on unsteady economic and social foundations. Even as the ILO acknowledged the Motor City's successes in workers' housing, it hastened to note that Detroit workers' gains were much more precarious than those of their European peers. Detroiters had "no compulsory social insurance of any kind," no way to support themselves and maintain their housing security if struck with illness, injury, or unemployment. By contrast, in "nearly every European town[,] provisions to meet some or all of these contingencies exist."[55] The U.S. housing stock, in other words, was expanding and modernizing faster than the social infrastructure that surrounded it. In this context, industrial workers were not the only ones being pushed to the limit in their work. American house builders were navigating the pressures of modernization, as well, and are the focus of Chapter 4.

4

MODERN HOUSEBUILDING

Policy, Products, and Labor

> Everyone should beware of the carpenter or contractor who claims to be able to do "just as well" without plans, or with pencil sketches. Such claims denote inefficiency, or a desire to "get by" with his own methods of construction, which are never as good.
> —**Standard Homes and Sibley Lumber Company,** ***Better Homes at Lower Cost***

Housebuilding changed in the boom years of the 1920s as the industry scaled up its production following the lull of the World War I era. During the war, construction had fallen to levels not seen since the 1870s, yet urban populations continued to surge.[1] New arrivals were flowing into Detroit and other urban centers, seeking work, but it was by no means certain that these cities could build housing fast enough to receive them. Rental costs rose as the supply dwindled.[2] In 1919, Detroit's Board of Commerce reported that workers' tent encampments were developing at the urban periphery. It implored builders to accelerate their work, chiding that the construction site was "no place for the sleeping sickness."[3] The housebuilding industry did awaken. Seeing opportunity in urban growth, it developed modern products and practices and engaged with local and national government in new ways. Strengthened by these efforts, and a robust economy, the industry's production accelerated from about 118,000 units nationwide in 1918 to 937,000 in 1925, nearly eight times as many.[4] In Detroit, the increase was more extreme. Between single and duplex houses, 1925 saw the production of 18,190 units, more than sixteen times the 1918 rate (Table 4.1).

The building industry achieved its extraordinary growth by modernizing its methods, and at the same time it raised the quality of its products. Factory-made components, new material standards, and power tools all sped up construction. Yet this was not the prefabricated archi-

TABLE 4.1. SINGLE-FAMILY AND DUPLEX HOUSING CONSTRUCTION IN DETROIT

Year	Single	Duplex	Notes
1915	3,139	1,537	
1916	4,266	3,305	
1917	2,466	1,468	United States enters World War I
1918	729	189	
1919	7,191	1,569	
1920	4,007	440	
1921	2,956	605	Post–World War I recession
1922	7,134	1,371	
1923	11,172	2,271	
1924	11,848	3,144	
1925	11,952	3,119	High point of housing production
1926	10,452	3,344	
1927	5,602	2,065	
1928	6,794	2,242	
1929	5,926	1,576	Great Depression begins
1930	2,264	604	
Total	97,898	28,849	

Note: Each duplex provided two units of housing, bringing Detroit's total housing production in single and duplex configurations to 155,596 units for this period.

Source: Housing numbers are from the reports of the Department of Building and Safety Engineering in the *Annual Report for the City of Detroit* series, 1915–1930, most of which are recorded in Matthew Daley, "City of Mass Production: Building, Managing, and Living in Detroit, America's First Automobile Metropolis, 1920–1933" (Ph.D. diss., Bowling Green State University, Bowling Green, OH, 2004), 98–99.

tecture imagined by European modernists. American builders' success in the 1920s was still earned the hard way: on-site in the sun, rain, and, at times, snow. Though muddy, this was indeed a labor of modernization and was subject to an increasingly robust policy framework. Indeed, the behind-the-scenes efforts of reformers and policy makers to support modern housing were as important to its production as masonry and wood.

Reform and Development Policy

Detroit's housing reformers lamented center-city crowding in the 1910s and sought to promote lower-density, decentralized development to ease the congestion. The Detroit Public Health League, for example, hosted the Chicago sanitation official Charles Ball to speak on "Homes of Today and Citizens of Tomorrow" at the Detroit Museum of Art. He spoke of the "bad physical and moral effect upon the whole family of bad air, bad drainage and overcrowded rooms."[5] For children, Ball continued, the lack of privacy in overcrowded slums "causes familiarity and moral indifference, the hardest obstacles to overcome."[6] Business leaders—powerful allies in housing reform—shared these sentiments. The Detroit Board of Commerce came out against a sixty-four-room "lodging house" proposal in 1916, fearing windowless tenement-like conditions, and made public calls for the city to enforce its building codes to prevent the project's construction.[7]

For Frank Blair, president of the Union Trust Bank, such lodging house proposals illustrated the need for stronger building regulations and better enforcement. Toward these ends, he created an offshoot of the Board of Commerce called the Detroit Housing Association (DHA). In 1913, Blair's DHA worked with the city Health Department to improve its effectiveness, publishing the pamphlet *Right Methods in a Housing Bureau*.[8] The DHA also called for legislation that would make crowded and unhealthful residences illegal in Michigan and saw the Housing Law of Michigan passed in 1917. It was based on New York's model law, developed by the leading reformer Lawrence Veiller, and set minimum room sizes and detailed window requirements: living rooms required the largest windows, and bathrooms the smallest.[9] The act called for indoor water closets in each dwelling, "where connection with a public sewer and with public water mains is or becomes reasonably available."[10] In the name of privacy, it required access to each bedroom and to the bathroom without passing through another bedroom. The act set minimum size requirements for rear yards and discouraged alley flat rentals, limiting outbuilding occupancy to the family or employees of the main household.[11] These regulations supported a lower-density model of development at the city's periphery; they also blurred the line between public and private interests. Bankers and other Board of Commerce members stood to profit from urban development and had significant lobbying power to shape state development policy.

Local policy was also overhauled in the 1910s. A coalition of Progressive industrialists, Protestant church leaders, and American-born white voters approved a new Detroit City Charter in 1918. Citing concerns about corruption and the rule of "liquor interests" in immigrant districts, they replaced the city's ward-based council with an at-large City Council. The new council was strongly supportive of housing development and significantly enmeshed in the building industry itself: of the nine at-large councilors, five were personally involved in the property development industry that their public policies would bolster.[12] The city's aggressive expansion of roads, utilities, and schools, in concert with the annexation of outlying land, supported the rapid development of subdivisions at the expanding urban periphery.[13] These efforts grew Detroit's land area by more than 50 percent in fewer than ten years, to 138 square miles, before its outward expansion was finally halted by independent suburbs in 1926.[14]

Transportation policy also supported new developments. James Couzens, a former Ford executive, spearheaded an improvement to the city's streetcar system beginning in 1919. After achieving a public takeover of the streetcars in 1921, he announced, "We will now start building." By 1931, the system boasted fifty-three new miles of track, increased speed, and 548 buses to connect outlying districts to the streetcars.[15] This helped to meet the demand created by the city's rapid population growth—an increase of about 80 percent—in the same period. Expanded public transportation connected workers with the new industrial plants emerging along the city's peripheral belt rail line and empowered developers and house builders as they invested in urban decentralization.

While Couzens, the City Council, and the Detroit Board of Commerce worked locally to promote peripheral housebuilding, the federal government made its own interventions nationwide. At the end of World War I, as mentioned in Chapter 3, the government ended its short-lived effort to develop workers' housing directly, and threw its support behind the private-sector building industry. The U.S. Department of Labor brought leading figures in construction, real estate, and lending on board, a group that included the Detroit-based savings-and-loan representative K. V. Haymaker. They joined in an established effort of the National Association of Real Estate Boards to promote homeownership.[16] Their "Own Your Own Home" campaign appeared in print, film, and radio and was most tangibly present in urban "model home" exhibits coordinated with local real estate agents. The Detroit Real Estate Board urged its members to "Help the 'Own Your Home' Movement" by reaching out to prospective clients and encouraging them to visit the Detroit Builders' Show of 1919. There, future home buyers could see the latest domestic technologies, listen to music, and attend the lecture of "a prominent orator from the Department of Labor at Washington, who [would] talk on the 'Own Your Home' topic."[17]

Herbert Hoover, as Secretary of Commerce beginning in 1921, extended the government's support for housebuilding. He continued the homeownership campaign established by the Department of Labor three years earlier and established a Division of Building and Housing (DBH) within his department.[18] To make the building industry more efficient, the DBH encouraged material suppliers to adopt consistent standards for their products on a voluntary basis, such as common grades and dimensions for lumber. It also developed model building code and zoning regulations, calling for widespread rationalization of urban development.[19] Adoption of these federal recommendations was uneven, but the building industry certainly did accelerate its efforts to make and sell modern houses in the 1920s.

The Bungalow and Other Products

The housebuilding industry, bolstered by supportive policies, created new dwelling types and technologies in the 1910s and 1920s. Urban workers were an important customer base, and their rising consumer clout was acknowledged in the 1920 Detroit Builders' Show. It introduced "Workers' Day" into the week's calendar, inviting blue-collar consumers to peruse realtors', builders', and product suppliers' exhibits and to listen to the Studebaker Company band.[20] There, workers encountered an increasingly standardized national consumer market for houses and domestic technologies. The bungalow rose to prominence in this period as a popular national type, contributing to the higher standard of living to which many workers were gaining access. This standard, as Thomas Hubka and Judith Kenny have described, was "a generic house plan containing five to six rooms with bath, including a living room, dining room, kitchen, [and] two or three bedrooms."[21] Within the growing city, where expanding utilities and a professional building industry were making modern amenities more broadly available, the bungalow plan was a dream that labor and sacrifice might make real.

The proliferation of stock plans and advertisements helped the bungalow rise to national popularity in the 1910s and 1920s. These plans were developed by architects and designers but then distributed by magazines and building material suppliers to a mass market at a much lower cost than that of an architect's direct engagement in a project (Figure 4.1). Still, official plan sets cost something, and pirated drawings and specifications were common enough to prompt a Detroit-based material supplier to urge that "imitators are warned against infringement."[22] Suppliers produced beautifully rendered plan books, as Richard Harris has shown, to be more accessible to potential clients as they

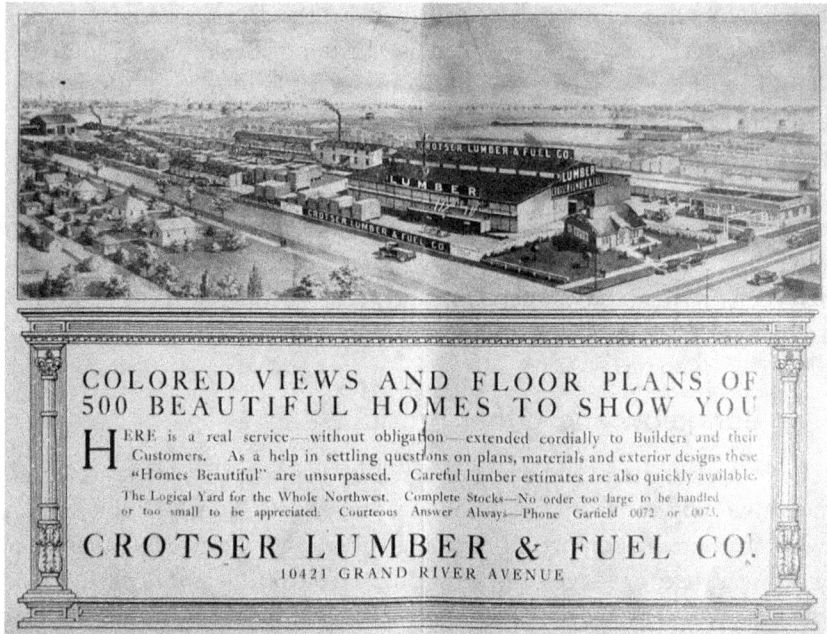

Figure 4.1. An advertisement for stock house plans by the Detroit building material supplier Croster Lumber and Fuel. The company seeks to make the best impression on nonspecialist customers, promising to answer the phone courteously and claiming that no order is "too small to be appreciated."

Source: Detroit Builders' Exhibition Inc., *To Those Who Build: A Valuable Reference Book*, pamphlet, February 1923, 24–25, Real Estate Files, Burton Historical Collection, Detroit Public Library.

faced competition from media-savvy, precut house kit makers such as Sears and Michigan's Aladdin Company.[23] In the same spirit, leading voices in the construction industry urged contractors to make the best impression possible on the public and potential customers, even through small acts such as keeping the sidewalks in front of their job sites clear. The editors of *Building Age* reminded their readers, "You are in the building business, therefore have some pictures on your office walls to give an atmosphere of building to it," including photos of completed houses, "perhaps a year or so [after construction] when the shrubbery has had time to grow around it, making a good looking picture."[24]

Popular housing types, such as the bungalow and duplex, did not succeed solely on the power of advertisement, the availability of plans, or the charm of the builder's office décor. Their forms were also well suited to their purpose. As long, narrow house types, they fit well within the thirty-foot-wide lots that were common in Detroit's working-class neighborhoods. Such narrow lots created a fairly compact development pattern, but these popular house types engaged with the outdoor environment nevertheless, with generous front porches, large living-room windows, and kitchens opening onto the rear yards that the building code required. Advertisers of bungalows and duplexes, of course, consistently overstated this access, representing these houses in a romantic natural setting rather than an urban neighborhood. The Sibley Lumber Company touted the bungalow's proximity to "foliage, trees and flowers" as an experience that would strengthen the homeowner, "whose nature rebels at the thought of crowded halls and tenements."[25]

The bungalow type had many variants, including more elaborate versions produced for the households of middle-class professionals and for the wealthy. The best known were probably Greene and Greene's Arts and Crafts bungalows, such as the Gamble House in Pasadena, California. It engaged the outdoor environment with broad porches on two levels, and its eaves extended out to protect against the sun. It was richly detailed throughout with wood, brick, and stained-glass details and celebrated in architectural journals and popular magazines such as the *Ladies' Home Journal*.[26] Middle-class bungalows, such as those along Detroit's northwesterly Grand River corridor or in Highland Park, featured some Craftsman-style details of their own, in their porch rails and extended eaves. Working-class bungalows, by contrast, were smaller and mostly unornamented. Their distinguishing feature was typically the gable, which could be front-facing, side-facing, hipped, or gambrel-shaped. At the same time, these modern workers' bungalows were more comfortable than the cottages of the nineteenth century, with interior bathrooms, bedroom closets, and porches, even as their basic floor plan, as Joseph Bigott notes, was similar to that of the larger cottages that preceded them (Figure 4.2).[27] The meaning of the front room changed significantly in the transition from cottage to bungalow. The front room of a modern house was a "living room" and was intended to replace the formal, special occasion space of the nineteenth-century parlor. Intended as a light-filled, multiuse space, the living room was a place where modern parents could meet the growing cultural expectation that they actively engage with and nurture their children.[28]

Detroit's Sibley Lumber Company offered stock plans for "The Elwood," a front-gabled, seven hundred-square-foot bungalow that illustrates the common type (Figures 4.3–4.4). Its two bedrooms and bath, separated by a short hall, are aligned to one side of the rectangular plan. The kitchen, dining room, and living room run along the other side, the living room being the largest and most open room in the house, receiving the front entry and featuring large windows on two

Figure 4.2. Extant nineteenth-century cottages in Detroit's Corktown neighborhood.
Source: Photograph by Erin Nelson.

walls. Having many windows, and relatively large ones, was a defining feature of the modern bungalow. Sibley explained this, with reference to "The Elwood," by claiming that "doctors have but few calls from happy new homes that are provided with an abundance of light."[29] The attic, by contrast, could provide a less well-lit but useful additional sleeping room in a one-story bungalow.[30]

"The Lynnhaven," a one-and-a-half-story semi-bungalow with more than one thousand square feet, illustrates a more advanced variation on the type (see Figures 4.3–4.4). In it, two bedrooms and a bath are moved to the private space of the upper story, and living and dining rooms—the most social spaces in the house—are aligned to the street front on the first story. As Hubka and Kenny point out, the back door leading into each bungalow's kitchen provided a place for workers to wash off the day's grime before entering the rest of the house.[31] While Sibley's plans illustrate standard types, the company noted their adaptability, explaining that "any reliable contractor can easily move partition walls, windows or doors to suit the owner."[32] Detroit's bungalows were typically clad with wood siding, as opposed to the brick commonly used in Chicago's "bungalow belt." Wood cladding meant, as the Aladdin precut house kit company put it, that the owner was "privileged to choose any colors of paint or stain . . . for the exterior."[33]

Detroit's other popular workers' house type of 1910s and 1920s was the duplex or two-flat. These were clad with either brick or wood siding and often presented two separate front doors to the street. Inside, the two units would either be stacked one on top of the other or side by side with a central party wall. Sibley's "Olympia" model illustrates the common two-flat: one door leads to the lower-story residence, five rooms plus bath, and the second door leads via stairs to a nearly identical second level residence (see Figures 4.3–4.4).[34] Describing its plan, the company acknowledges the compromise it represents in terms of privacy while emphasizing its potential economic benefits:

> The home that nearest approaches in comforts and conveniences the private residence is the modern two-family. . . . [T]he occupants of such dwellings are denied certain private privileges to be found in the individual home, yet there are many practical and desirable features . . . from a monetary standpoint.

Two-flats were an important source of rental housing. They were less likely to be owner-occupied than detached bungalows, according to a Home Owners Loan Corporation (HOLC) analysis from the late 1930s, but even when the owners' household occupied one of the flats, they could rent the other as an income property. In her oral history, a woman who grew up on the west side of Detroit in the 1920s recalled such a case. Her father, a barber, bought a duplex because he believed it to be "a good investment," and the family moved into the second-floor residence to rent out the ground floor unit.[35]

Modern houses in Detroit were not an all-or-nothing proposition. Instead, they could be incrementally upgraded with new technologies in an à la carte fashion. One resident of Lincoln Park, just southwest of Detroit, for example, sold his house in 1926 with the description: "5 room bungalow with bath, thoroughly modern except heat (stove heat); oak floors, paved street. 1 block to street car and bus."[36] A modern furnace for central heating could be added to such a house, suppliers assured, "on easy payments." And lest anyone doubt the need for such sophisticated equipment, the FarQuar company urged that "VENTILATION in the HOME is as assential [sic] as in the SCHOOLS or HOSPITALS" and "CLEAN, FRESH AIR is as necessary as CLEAN FOOD and PURE WATER."[37] While the integration of electricity, plumbing, and the three-fixture bath were signatures of the period's housing modernization, they were not immediately pursued by all working-class families. As Richard Harris and Becky Nicolaides have shown, workers used incremental,

Figure 4.3.
"Elwood" Bungalow (*top*), "Olympia" Duplex (*center*), and "Lynnhaven" semi-bungalow (*bottom*), from a collection of stock plans sold by the F. M. Sibley Lumber Company, a building material supplier based in Detroit. They reflect the city's typical workers' housing types, though some embellishments seen here, such as roof brackets, decorative columns and trim, or a fireplace, were less common.

Source: Standard Homes Company and F. M. Sibley Lumber Company, *Better Homes at Lower Cost: 101 Modern Homes Standardized* (Washington, DC: Standard Homes Company, 1926), 48, 92, 100.

Figure 4.4. Floor plan comparison of four Detroit workers' housing types. Each includes a porch and an adjacent living room. In the bungalow and duplex, bedrooms and bathrooms are made private by separating them from the rest of the house with a hallway. In the semi-bungalow, two bedrooms and the bath gain privacy from their second-floor location.

Source: Illustration by the author, with reference to Standard Homes Company and F. M. Sibley Lumber Company, *Better Homes at Lower Cost: 101 Modern Homes Standardized* (Washington, DC: Standard Homes Company, 1926), and *Building Age*, August 1924, 84–87.

self-building strategies in the unregulated suburbs of Los Angeles and Toronto to get an affordable foothold in those cities—a practice that occurred outside Detroit, as well.[38]

The largest-scale workers' housing development in interwar Detroit contained both professionally built and incrementally self-built houses. It was B. E. Taylor's Brightmoor, built northwest of Detroit in the early 1920s, years before city regulations and utilities arrived with the area's annexation in 1926. The "Brightmoor Homes" that Taylor's company built in the area were at the low end of the city's market for formal workers' housing. Though advertised as "bungalows," these tiny, four- to six-room (440–600-square-foot) dwellings stretched the definition of the type: they lacked indoor toilets and basements and had smaller and

Figure 4.5. Behind the children at play, the back sides of two of B. E. Taylor's "Brightmoor Homes" are visible. One appears to be in the midst of receiving an addition, with a gabled extension under construction.

Source: *Building Age*, August 1924, 86.

Figure 4.6. "Typical Brightmoor Houses," 1940. A very small, perhaps two-room house (*left*) shares the street with what appears to be one of Taylor's standard bungalows (*right*), illustrating the diversity that resulted from Brightmoor's limited regulations and incremental self-building practices.

Source: Brightmoor Community Center Inc., *Brightmoor: A Community in Action* (Detroit: Brightmoor Community Center, 1940), 60.

fewer windows than typical bungalows (Figures 4.5–4.6). However, they were outfitted with bedroom closets and often with front porches sized for sitting out. Though they were the product of modern, large-scale construction techniques, these houses were spartan, built on provisional cedar posts rather than masonry foundation walls, and therefore uncomfortably cold in winter.[39] Taylor sold vacant lots, as well, to those who preferred to build incrementally while living in "tents, tar paper shacks and . . . garage homes" on their lots.[40] Though provisional shelters were accepted at Brightmoor, the neighborhood touted its restrictiveness in another sense: its lots contained racial deed restrictions that assured buyers the district would remain exclusively white. Perceived by some as "a community of 'shacks,'" Brightmoor was a place where residents made incremental investments in their houses as their budgets allowed, such as digging basements, or adding bathrooms or other additions.[41]

Modern Housebuilding

Like material suppliers, housebuilders changed their practices in the 1920s to meet the opportunities presented by strong demand. Initially, they struggled to ramp up production following the war era's disruption to building and amid postwar inflation in labor and material costs. The editors of *Building Age* magazine were exasperated. Reflecting on the nationwide flood of new house orders and the shortage of skilled tradespeople to fulfill them, they asked, "Can't We Stand Prosperity?" The "We" this question was aimed at was a diverse cohort of both small- and large-scale builders.

The smallest early twentieth-century house builders produced only one or two houses per year, likely in addition to other work, while moderate-scale merchant-builders could produce a few or batches of ten, twenty, or even fifty or more houses at a time.[42] Building was either done speculatively or on contract for the future owner—a homeowner or an investor seeking a rental property. Those seeking a new house could consult the "Building Propositions" section of the *Detroit Free Press* classifieds, where builders offered to work with the client's plans, or to furnish their own, and where some offered to finance the construction "on easy terms."[43] A national survey found more than half of new single-family houses were built on contract in 1928.[44] Speculative builders produced units in small and large numbers with the aim of selling them at a profit. One Detroit builder, for example, produced three duplexes on the east side's Springle Street in 1923 and offered to sell them with financing. The builder sweetened the deal by also offering to accept a vacant lot from elsewhere in the city as the down payment, perhaps convincing buyers to abandon their plans to build on contract and instead to buy ready-made.[45]

Detroit's urban pattern reflects the copresence of owner-contracted and speculative building, as mentioned in the discussion of Burton's Michigan Avenue Subdivision in Chapter 3. The repetition of nearly identical houses is common, reflecting batches of speculatively built houses. However, as noted in Chapter 3, the uncoordinated intermixing of bungalows and two-flats is also very common, produced as residents made their own lot-by-lot decisions about what to contract and build. In the spring of 1923, the *Detroit Free Press* noted that a record 1,000 houses were under construction on the east side, and 90 percent of the projects were owner-led, as opposed to speculatively built, giving the area a "variety of architecture" that was "pleasing to the eye."[46] Whether working speculatively or on contract, modern housebuilding was complex, requiring plans and credit and the specialized knowledge of tradespeople such as plumbers and electricians. The needed components ranged from lumber and masonry to windows, appliances, and landscaping materials.[47] The largest operators of the period—the emerging cohort of "community builders"—began to fold many facets of housebuilding into large corporate building companies.

Community builders such as Kansas City's J. C. Nichols and Detroit's B. E. Taylor leveraged enough capital to buy land, subdivide it into lots, and build and sell hundreds of speculative houses at once.[48] Taylor and General Motors' Modern Housing Corporation in Flint leveraged economies of scale to build houses for Michigan workers.[49] While building the spartan "Brightmoor Homes" mentioned earlier, Taylor pursued an innovative approach to construction that the reform-oriented DHA had called for in 1919: "hundreds of houses under construction at one time," with staggered crews, so that "while one set of contractors is digging cellars, another will be laying foundations, another will be engaged in carpentry work, while others will be painting and doing interior finishing."[50] The speed and scale of production achieved at Brightmoor, and the resulting low cost of the houses produced, won the project a feature in *Building Age*'s housing issue of April 1924, under the headline "Building a Bungalow City in 18 Months."

Operations at Taylor's scale, however, remained in the minority in this period.[51] The Long Island builder Samuel Rosenberg represented the other end of the spectrum. After years as a flooring contractor, he was just getting into the housebuilding game in 1924, "doing a little building of two-family houses on the side, on 'spec!'" but not yet able to able to rely on the business as his main line. Similarly, some carpenters who worked for contractors by the hour also harbored the ambition of striking out independently. This was the case for two brothers featured in *Building Age*, immigrants who at the turn of the twentieth century had found work in the building industry without formal training. They developed their skills in carpentry over five years, working for others, and then began to go out on their own. They did "jobbing" as carpentry subcontractors for other builders before attaining enough experience, capital, and risk tolerance to step into speculative building in their own right. Their independent business began modestly, developing two to four houses at a time, and grew to be a substantial firm by the early 1920s.[52]

The transitional nature of the 1920s, in which the dominance of small builders was beginning to be challenged by larger-scale operations, is captured by the Detroit business magazine *Pipp's Weekly*. It described a flurry of activity in the city's College Park district, noting, "Not only are individuals building homes in almost every part of this vast section, but corporations are already well advanced with building programs in each of which fifty or more houses are being erected," units that would be ready some six to eight months later.[53] The practices of the large-scale Sloan Brothers Development Company suggest the cheek-by-jowl operation of builders large and small in Detroit. In July 1925, the firm reported plans to build fifty houses in a subdivision it owned and had improved with water service and sidewalks. The firm's Construction Department was tasked with spreading the fifty houses across the subdivision, on every third lot.[54] In this way, the firm might profitably sell the other two-thirds of its lots to smaller-scale speculators or to future residents, who, in turn, would contract with their own builders. Even as the industry changed, housebuilding in the 1920s remained relatively slow, imprecise, and skill-intensive in comparison with the city's new manufacturing processes. The Ford Motor Company's moving assembly line, for example, could produce an automobile in one hour and thirty-three minutes. Detroit's contract house builders, by comparison, advertised their ability to finish a house within sixty days.[55]

The labor of housebuilding meant exposure to weather, and modernizing voices in the industry sought to reform builders' relationship with the cold in the 1920s. They criticized seasonal fluctuations in temperate-zone building, where less work was performed in winter, as old fashioned. A spokesperson for the Portland Cement Association argued that the idea of a "spring rush after a winter's rest . . . has been more of a habit than anything else," given the many opportunities to work through the cold. He concluded, "There is no reason why the construction business should be confined to eight months a year."[56] Winter issues of *Building Age* advised contractors on best practices for cold weather work. "Naturally it costs something to protect a job from cold and storm," one commentator noted, "but often the extra cost is small, and our only real reason for not going on with the job is lack of gumption."[57]

The limits of winter work did tend to be human rather than material: even concrete work and painting need not wait for spring if appropriate measures were taken when mixing, but "when a workman is frozen he can of course produce but little work."[58] Canvas windbreaks lashed to scaffolding could increase both the efficiency and the comfort of workers. Concerns for comfort, of course, varied from job to job. The painter Ashmun Kelly preferred to do winter work strategically, repositioning himself throughout the day so that he was always painting on the sunny side, or the less windy side, of the house. Unfortunately, though, he found that "most employers insist on [painting] the building right around regardless of weather conditions," causing workers like him to "run to shelter every little while to knock my frozen fingers to get the blood to going in them."[59]

The greatest benefit of increased winter work was the reduction of seasonal unemployment. Factory workers faced their own seasonal shutdowns, for retooling, but the construction industry's months-long off-season was worse in terms of interrupted income.[60] *Building Age* commentators noted that with winter work, labor could benefit from steadier income, and employers would see less attrition, especially among "common labor." A contractor's core group of skilled tradespeople was unlikely to disappear, but unskilled staff who earned less, and who had not invested years in learning a trade, might well find other work during the off-season, never to return.[61] In the spring rush that followed a winter lull, "the cost of breaking in a new man must be charged to overhead."[62] Growing and maintaining the labor pool was a major concern of the industry in the 1920s in all seasons, as the opportunities for building, and for profit, outstripped the available labor to do the work.

Great demand for labor, and limited supply, gave some skilled tradespeople leverage to earn increased wages, and extreme cases of labor-cost inflation were fodder for employers' complaints. A national business group, the American Construction Council, reported that builders were forced to provide bonuses and to bid for skilled tradespeople, in some cases paying a reported $15–$18 per day. Reflecting their frustration with labor's rising clout, the group warned that if labor costs—and thus building costs—did not come under control soon, workers would lose in the end and see the market for construction cool to the point that they would face unemployment.[63] Plasterers demanding excessive pay, one author predicted, would only hasten the adoption of wallboard as a substitute material.[64] Building industry leaders called for a system of apprentice schools outside the union system to relieve the shortage of labor. One put it bluntly, writing, "I do not feel that this problem will be solved until the open shop principle has been established."[65]

Labor relations varied from city to city. Craft unions affiliated with the American Federation of Labor had made substantial gains during the war, and by 1923 as many as half of the bricklayers nationwide were organized and thus entitled to union wages and work rules. The number was much higher in some strong union markets: nearly 80 percent of Chicago-based bricklayers and more than 95 percent of Boston bricklayers were organized.[66] In Detroit, where the "open shop" reigned in the city's industrial factories, a group of employers—joined by the Michigan Chapter of the American Institute of Architects—banded together in the post–World War I era to suppress the power of the trade unions. The group called themselves the Associated Industries and adopted a position that retains power in Michigan politics today, arguing for each citizen's constitutional "right to work" on any building site, regardless of labor affiliation. Contractors who used nonunion labor and who were willing to undermine union actions by completing work abandoned by striking tradespeople forced the city's unionized construction workers to make concessions.[67]

Labor's weak position in 1920s Detroit allowed contractors to demand exceptionally high levels of output. The British social critic Ramsay Muir, who scrutinized Detroit, noted that the city's unionized trades lacked the clout to set restrictions on output or to resist labor-saving technological advances. "Though the majority of building operatives in Detroit are Union men," he explained, "the rate of construction in Detroit is much higher than in other cities. Elsewhere the number of bricks set per man per day sometimes falls as low as 410. In Detroit the average is said to be 1,400–1,600." He noted that other cities' business leaders were beginning to learn from Detroit, as evidenced in new employers' associations in San Francisco and Cleveland.[68] Detroit's Associated Industries claimed as early as 1920 to have extracted significant concessions from labor and touted the fact that wage scales in Detroit's building trades were lower than those of the labor stronghold of Chicago. Detroit carpenters were bringing home $1 per hour, while their Chicago peers made $1.25. The difference extended to unskilled laborers, who reportedly earned $0.65 per hour in Detroit, compared with $1 in Chicago.[69] The president of another business group, the Associated Building Employers of Detroit, noted in 1922 that the Motor City's construction industry was "going along placidly," without strikes and "with union and nonunion men working in peace and harmony, and with construction costs considerably lower than in other cities."[70]

Nationwide, the relative shortage of skilled tradespeople in the 1920s had construction industry commentators worried. They feared that the rise of the professions, and the prestige associated with office work, were siphoning off prime candidates for the trades.[71] Blaming women, one Louisville builder argued that "mothers don't want their sons to soil their hands" and, instead, "want them all to be preachers, lawyers, salesmen."[72] The architect D. Knickerbacker Boyd felt similarly, writing that the "dear ladies do not want to see their boys, brothers or 'boy friends' dressed in overalls or the clothes of working men, and littered with mortar, plaster, sawdust, metal filings or paint." These women, he complained, "use their persuasion . . . to keep [men] from engaging in this sort of work."[73] The editors of *Building Age* were more sanguine, citing the building industry's high wages and arguing that trades work was a highly desirable path. Tradespeople may not be as well dressed as clerks, they argued, but they were certainly better paid. Illustrating the point, the editors juxtaposed a photo of dapper office workers, striding out of a building, with one of blue-collar workers in overalls leaving a job site. The men on the left, they explained, were "Twenty-Five Dollar a Week Office Clerks Going to Lunch," while those on the right were "Fifty Dollar a Week Building Mechanics" doing the same.[74] The editors even claimed to know of "clergymen leaving their pulpits and professors their desks to take up carpentry, brick-laying or plastering" because of the "universal desire to find more money in the pay envelope at the end of the week, besides congenial work."[75]

While some skilled tradespeople continued to migrate from Europe, *Building Age*'s xenophobic bent reflected a broader American turn against immigration in the 1920s.[76] The magazine argued, "When trained[,] you will find that our young men will make better and more thorough mechanics than the European plodder. There is something about the atmosphere of America which produces a desire to excel."[77] This prejudice, in some cases, was reflected in the hierarchy of the job site. One builder in Syracuse, New York, reported that while nearly all of his skilled employees worked full time, "scarcely 40 per cent of the unskilled labor work steady." He added that "holidays are frequent with them, as we employ Italians and Indians," and that "lack of responsibility is probably the chief reason."[78]

In addition to matters of class, gender, race, and national origin, builders faulted the trade system itself for the shortage of workers, framing it as out of step with modern values. "No kid of today is going to spend a few of his best years learning a part of what some mediocre artisan knows," the builder W. M. Newton argued. Instead, mechanically inclined young people should be taught how to think in the public schools, rather than traditional apprenticeship, so they can contribute to modern construction, where new techniques would replace the old. "This is an age of science, not of skill," he argued. "What need have I for an expert hand jointer at $10 per day when the mill down the street has one tuned up to 4,000 revolutions per minute, which can handle close to a carload of stuff in ten hours?"[79]

The rise of factory-made building components transformed housebuilding in the late nineteenth and early twentieth centuries. Sophisticated new tools empowered millwork factories to produce standard windows, doors, moldings, and other finished components. They could be produced more efficiently in large numbers and made available for easy on-site installation by local builders. Lumber suppliers began to kiln-dry their dimensional lumber in this period and were able to provide reliable sizes within tighter tolerances.[80] They developed new products, such as laminated composite doors, gypsum board, and asphalt shingles. Sibley Lumber boasted that "practically all windows and doors [in its stock plan book] are of standard designs usually carried in stock," and with good reason.[81] A factory-produced window or a standard batch of dimensional lumber, for that matter, promised higher quality and simpler, more predictable construction in the field, which would have appealed to builders and clients alike. Sibley's stock plans and specifications were adapted to use the available standard products efficiently. They would also guide the builder's work with precision, ensuring, for example, the "proper alignment" of windows and doors as they wrap around the four elevations of the house, lending a professional appearance to the finished product.[82]

The emphasis on two major house types in Detroit—the bungalow and duplex—reflects among other things the risk-aversion of housebuilders. For small-scale contractors, the consistent use of a few familiar types would make construction time and salability more predictable, just as they had for the late nineteenth-century builders observed by Sam Bass Warner.[83] Large-scale builders enjoyed the economies of scale provided by repeated use of standard plans and materials. For the same reasons, house builders were consistent in the material systems that they used, embracing light wood framing as the structural basis for housing construction.[84] Framing consisted of milled wood studs and joists sheathed with wood boards, all fastened with machine-made nails to tie the assembly together and give it strength (Figure 4.7). Framing systems became increasingly simple to execute across the late nineteenth and early twentieth century as the accuracy of the sizing of dimensional lumber improved. All this, and the simple butt joints that the nailed system of fastening allowed, "permit[ed] the frame to be rapidly

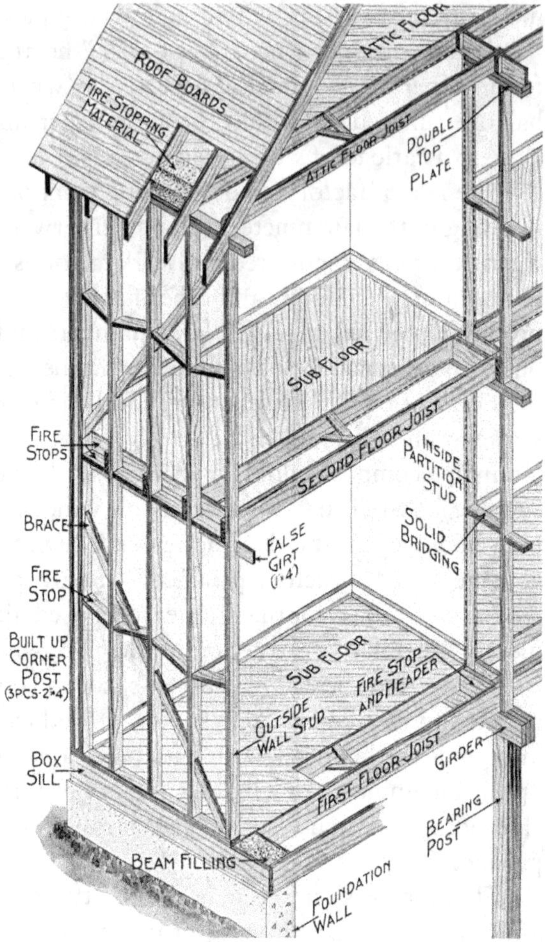

Figure 4.7. Balloon framing, a common form of light wood framing that makes use of dimensional lumber fastened together with nails.

Source: Weyerhaeuser Forest Products, *High Cost of Cheap Construction: A Book for Home-Builders on the Importance of Right Construction in House Building* (St. Paul, MN: Weyerhaeuser Forest Products, 1922), 18.

put up," replacing the laborious mortise-and-tenon connections used in heavy timber structures.[85]

Despite technological advances, however, the cutting and assembly of wood framing still required judgment and care. Innovative companies such as Sears and Aladdin delivered precut house kits, predominantly to small-town customers, which removed the work of selecting and trimming materials.[86] Yet, as Buster Keaton's character showed in the silent comedy *One Week* (1920)—a story of self-building gone hilariously wrong—these kits did not guarantee a problem-free experience. Kate Wilder, a builder who competed with kit houses in the 1920s, warned potential customers that the "so-called ready-cut house" was a building method "in which much time is lost in sorting the various parts."[87] Despite the challenges of housebuilding—precut and not—there was plenty of room for the future owner of a modern, urban house to contribute to its construction. As Richard Harris explains, owners could hire contractors for the most skill-intensive work, such as structural framing or electrical work, depending on their own skills and interests, while doing other parts of the job themselves. Reduced cost was, of course, a great benefit of this, as were the satisfaction and the learning experienced while building.[88]

The labor of housebuilding changed with the adoption of new technology, but these changes did not simply deskill the process. They eliminated difficult, unskilled work, as well.[89] Excavation required less manpower, for example, when workers had access to compressed air picks and automatic loaders, while the skilled operators of big machines such as steam shovels and trenching machines were empowered by technological advance. The labor of horses was beginning to be replaced by trucks that could carry materials more quickly over larger areas. A truck could be outfitted with a hydraulic dumping bed, reducing the labor of shoveling sand and gravel.[90] These did not provide effortless service, however. The operators of open-cab trucks still endured winter cold. They had to apply chains to their tires before proceeding over muddy or snow-covered, unpaved roads, then remove the chains again before returning to the paved surfaces to avoid damaging the tires. A mixture of alcohol and glycerin and a rag for wiping could help with a fogged-over window.[91] Still, "gasoline, compressed air and electricity [were] superseding hand power in many instances," as one industry commentator noted, adding, "gasoline furnishes cheap power and saves the time of expensive labor."[92]

The technology-led reduction of unskilled tasks extended to interior work. As the American Floor Surfacing Machine Company illustrated in a striking advertisement, the payroll for one mechanical sander operator was smaller than that for six hand sanders. In the ad, the machine operator is dressed in a crisp black outfit and tie, juxtaposed with six manual sanders on their hands and knees, in wrinkled work clothes and suspenders. The man in black represents the worker whose prestige has risen from his engagement with new technology and suggests a more impressive representation of the building industry to its various audiences, including clients and prospective workers. While it is not clear whether they wore black clothes on the job, one of the more up-to-date flooring subcontractors in Detroit did advertise that its crew would use the "latest dustless machines."[93]

Conclusion

Urban decentralization was the work of many hands, and Detroit's ubiquitous bungalows and two-flats reflected a range of efforts to modernize building products and process. Policy makers, material suppliers, and building contractors all saw opportunities to do more and better work in the boom of the 1920s. The most immediate shapers of the city's modern houses were workers: skilled tradespeople and laborers who dug utility trenches and laid foundations, assembled and sheathed wood frames, and applied siding and shingles. Others laid flooring, ran wiring, and painted. Their efforts gave them and the rest of the city's workers access to a new, higher standard of material comfort and prestige. As both producers and consumers, housebuilding workers helped to make urban development Detroit's second great industry, next to automobiles. Their efforts were amplified not only by new building products and machines, but also by the rising clout of real estate agents, who showed lots and speculative houses to prospective buyers, adopting a dual identity as both straitlaced professionals and confident predictors of the future.

5

DETROIT'S OTHER INDUSTRY

*Real Estate and the Culture
of Elusive Security*

> Prosperity and real estate activity go hand in hand. . . . [T]here is not a shadow of doubt but that the two greatest elements of business life and activity in Detroit today are automobiles and real estate.
>
> —H. T. Clough, Detroit Real Estate Board

Plan-book designers and builders gave modern houses their form, but these dwellings' dollar value and cultural meaning were subject to the dynamics of a real estate market. Real estate agents, through their advertisements and sales advice, exerted significant influence in shaping these values and meanings. They engaged with workers seeking houses and with the investors and builders adding to the available stock of houses for rent and purchase. Along with local business leaders and the federal government, they helped to construct the period's social contract in which hard work was rewarded with access to modern housing. To workers who were skeptical about the products they offered, agents responded with a barrage of warnings and promises. Staying in an antiquated neighborhood risked lost social prestige, they explained, while moving to a better neighborhood promised rising status. Failing to invest in homeownership risked ageing without economic security, while real estate investments could deliver large and fast increases in wealth. The value of Detroit's real estate grew by nearly ten times across the 1910s and 1920s.[1] Real estate agents facilitated this boom, working to drive customers to the city's expanding periphery. In the process, they made promises of working-class social advancement and economic security that were set on the unsteady foundations of racial segregation and excessive speculation.

Rise of the Realtor

In the late nineteenth and early twentieth centuries, American real estate agents increasingly institutionalized their practices through local real estate boards, positioning property as a sound investment and themselves as trusted advisers. Agents formed the Detroit Real Estate Board (DREB) in 1886 and joined the local board to the National Association of Real Estate Boards in 1908.[2] The national board established standards for ethical practice and advertised that fact, distinguishing its members from other agents by taking on the title "realtors," one that only members in good standing could claim. The DREB lobbied for favorable tax policies, urged members to make wartime Red Cross donations, and kept its members informed about plans for road and streetcar expansion that might bring new value to outlying property.[3]

Though realtors remained in the minority among real estate agents through the 1910s and 1920s, they succeeded in raising the bar for agents' practices more broadly. The DREB successfully lobbied for the Michigan License Law, enacted in August 1919, "to promote clean real estate transactions," making Michigan one of just three states to adopt real estate regulations and licensing requirements by that time. The terms of the law applied to all agents in Michigan, requiring registration fees and some oversight and discouraging informal brokerage practice.[4] Realtors assured their clients that they could be counted on to honestly represent properties' value and to adhere to a uniform schedule of fees and commissions.

When the Los Angeles realtor Harry Culver addressed the DREB in 1927, from the height of a mid-1920s housing boom, he could claim that realtors had made significant gains in public trust. He illustrated the point with a casually sexist anecdote about an attorney who had recently called a local real estate board to find out whether a certain broker was, indeed, a certified realtor. "I have a client who is a widow," the attorney had said, "negotiating a deal with this broker, and . . . I find it impossible to be here the day that the deal is closed." Learning that the broker was indeed a realtor, the attorney was relieved, concluding, "I shall now be able to advise her that she can proceed with all safety. She is doing business with a realtor."[5] In the 1920s, leveraging their rising professional clout and riding high on the Motor City's extraordinary economic growth, Detroit's real estate brokers advised their clients to invest aggressively and to reap the rewards of an economic boom with no end in sight.

Faith in Growth

Selling Detroit real estate was selling the city's future prospects, and the real estate agents of the 1910s and 1920s consistently forecast strong growth—and, thus, rising value—for well-chosen properties. "The past," one agent explained in the 1920s, "is but a mirror of the future," and the city's past performance had been extraordinary.[6] In 1912, with Detroit's population around half a million, William Hannan, a prominent real estate agent, began to undersign his advertisements with the confident projection: "Detroit a Million in 1925." Though Hannan died in 1917, his associates lived to see his once audacious forecast beaten. The city reached one million residents shortly after 1920—years ahead of Hannan's prediction. Detroit agents would not repeat Hannan's mistaken modesty. The city's amazing growth in the 1910s fueled a real estate culture of magical thinking in the 1920s. A 1922 DREB article boasted "Detroit—Two Million in 1930," a claim supported by the "conservative predictions of statisticians" and repeated in agents' advertisements (Figure 5.1).[7] In 1928, Hannan's successor firm, the Hannan Real Estate Exchange, claimed, "No one can question the contin-

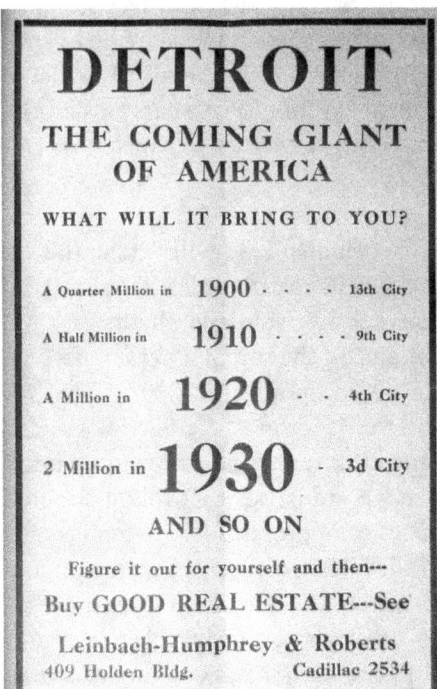

Figure 5.1. In the 1920s, many real estate agents advertised the value of their products by predicting that Detroit would continue to grow exponentially, as it had in previous decades. In fact, the city's population reached only about 1.6 million by 1930.

Source: Real Estate Files, Burton Historical Collection, Detroit Public Library.

ued rapid growth of Detroit. . . . [C]onservative estimates made by the public service corporation name 1945 as the date of the third million."[8]

Predictions of two million and three million residents would go unrealized by the municipality of Detroit, which, constrained by a ring of fast-growing independent suburbs, reached its peak decennial population in 1950 at 1.85 million. But amid the extraordinary growth of the 1910s and 1920s, when Detroit's proportional growth outpaced that of the nation's other large cities, and its automobiles were transforming urban life nationwide, no claim seemed to be too great. One booster was so inspired by the city's recent growth that he predicted, in 1928, that Detroit would surpass even New York City, claiming, "Fifty years from now men will be saying 'New York is what Detroit was 25 years ago!'"[9]

When the growth of the automobile market appeared to be plateauing in the late 1920s, Detroit agents began to tie their future projections to a new industry: aviation. Under a section titled "Prosperity without Limit," the Hannan Exchange's sales manual *The Hannan Bible* advised salesmen, "Since the airplane is only an automobile with wings, it was inevitable that the aircraft industry center in Detroit [and] make real estate history repeat itself in this Wonder City."[10] The development of private aircraft promised a surge in industrial growth, and, moreover, just as the automobile had, aircraft might open vast new territories to urban development. Frank Lloyd Wright, for example, included views of helicopter-like personal aircraft in his 1935 exhibition of Broadacre City, a utopian vision of urban decentralization.[11] Five years earlier, the Hannan Exchange was already predicting a further expansion of Detroit based in aerial commuting:

> Very soon we will all see the day when airplanes will extend the residential districts of every city out 50 to 100 miles . . . , and, just as a bird comes down with exact precision and alights on a limb, we will come down and alight on the top of a skyscraper, and get off and take the elevator down to our office.[12]

Real estate observers did not hang all future hope on aviation, however. They pointed to other prospective industries that might support growth without end. Paul Rohr, an author of promotional pamphlets for Detroit real estate firms, suggested that "Detroit's next greatest industry" would be electric refrigeration, which was in its infancy in the mid-1920s. In his view, it "promise[d] to attain a size comparable to the auto industry." Rohr imagined a future in which Detroit's economy would be bolstered by the desire for iceless refrigeration machines in "every high class apartment" and "every modern home for families of moderate means."[13] He and other observers also looked forward to the opening of the St. Lawrence Seaway, which would bring Detroit "an average of 650 miles nearer to Europe" via direct oceangoing ships and, perhaps, make Detroit a competitive port for the shipping of midwestern grain.[14] While waiting for these promising future industries, Rohr urged steadfast faith in the automobile industry, as well, for if "2,000,000 machines are completely scrapped each year," then "these must be replaced," suggesting that market "saturation is a long way off at this rate."[15]

Succession Theory in Practice

Real estate agents' growth projections bolstered the property market, and their sales practices helped to shape it, both physically and socially. They conceptualized the city's growth as occurring in successive rings of outward expansion and encouraged clients to see those rings as a dynamic social ladder that a canny buyer could climb. Detroit's relatively flat and featureless surrounds meant that the city could expand with relative ease, as Harry Carman, a professor of history at Columbia University, observed in the 1920s. He foretold that the city's industrial might and unimpeded terrain positioned Detroit to become the "greatest city on the Western Hemisphere" in subsequent years.[16] Indeed, Hannan had predicted sprawling outward growth for Detroit even before the Model T was developed, projecting around 1906 that "Detroit is destined to become one of the largest cities on earth, and will not stop until the limits of Wayne County have become the limits of the city."[17]

Succession implied that a "natural" stratification would develop in the city's outward growth. "Drop a rock in a pond," Hannan observed around 1906, "and the succession of waves . . . will follow each other and spread to the outermost limits of the water." It was, he argued, "just so in REAL ESTATE." As Detroit grew, "Every year has added one more circle about the city's heart, in which, if a man invested a little money he would be certain to realize a handsome profit, and in many cases, independent wealth."[18] The social significance of urban growth rings was theorized by the Chicago School sociologist Ernest Burgess in 1925, in his concentric zone theory of urban social structure (Figure 5.2).[19] Like Hannan, Burgess used biological metaphors to make the complex process of urban growth legible. He argued that city growth tends to proceed in succession, with new arrivals continuously pouring into the

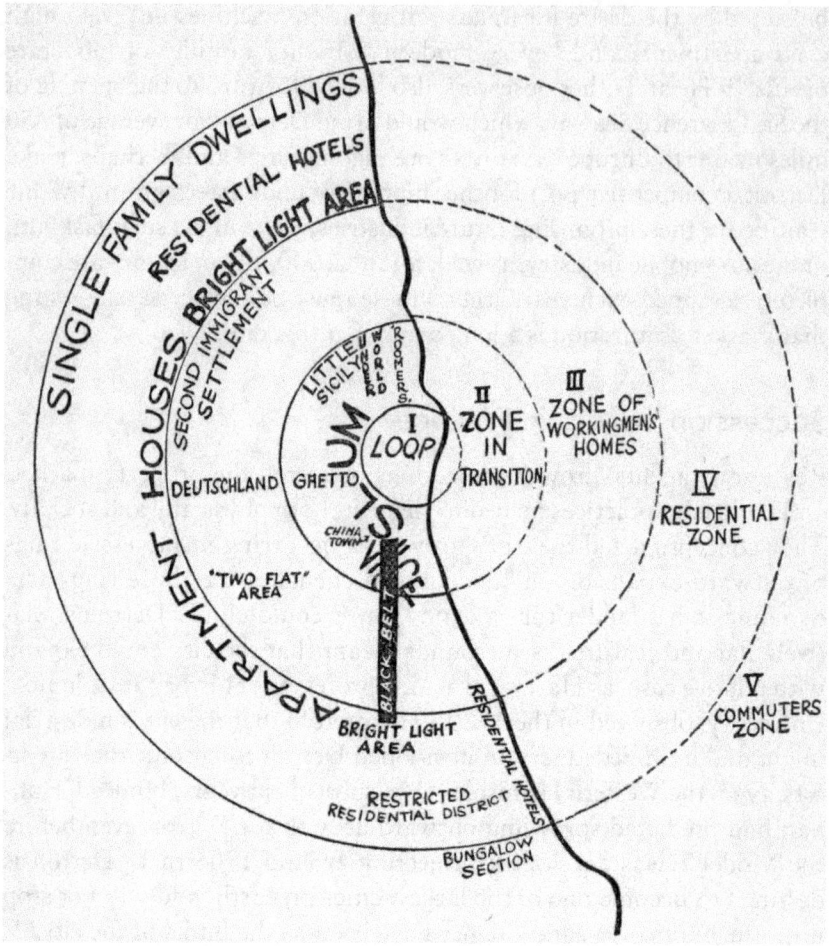

Figure 5.2. Ernest Burgess's concentric zone model of urban social structure, based on Chicago.

Source: "The Growth of the City: An Introduction to a Research Project," in Robert E. Park, Ernest W. Burgess, and Roderick D. McKenzie, *The City* (Chicago: University of Chicago Press, 1925), 55.

slums, the "Zone in Transition," encircling the business district. From there, many would eventually filter outward into the better "Zone of Workingmen's Homes," and perhaps even into the more exclusive middle-class zones beyond. As residents succeed through such a system, though, it continues to change dynamically around them. As the overall urban population grows, in a "moving equilibrium of social order," each concentric zone grows outward and tends "to extend its area by the invasion of the next outer zone."[20] In its simplicity Burgess's model obscures some of the complexities of urban geography—missing the presence of peripheral workers' housing among affluent suburbs, for example—but it legibly described a real estate dynamic that agents and their clients had long been aware of and exploiting.

Urban succession was a speculative game that real estate agents took part in through their buying and selling. To win, buyers had to invest in lots beyond the built-up sections of the city, with faith that growth would reach them and boost their property's value.[21] The realtor Roy Swanson dramatized succession with a commercial poem, acknowledging and seeking to overcome the skepticism of prospective buyers:

TOO FAR OUT

'Twas back in nineteen hundred ten
Detroit we know was smaller then,
And Real Estate men told you why
Their Real Estate was good to buy.
They told you how to make some dough,
But you, old man, seemed filled with doubt,
You only said, "It's too far out." . . .

Detroit will grow as ne'er before
And values here will upward soar.
And Ground you think far out today
Tomorrow big returns will pay[22]

In addition to increased wealth, buyers could take advantage of the rising social prestige associated with an outlying subdivision, either for themselves as owner-occupiers or, if planning to rent or resell the property, for their own customers. Burgess's zone three, for example, was defined by what its residents had left behind: the "Zone of Workingmen's Homes" was inhabited by "the workers in industries who have escaped from the area of deterioration" nearer the center.[23] In this system, working-class parents might position their children to enter a higher social class by buying or renting in the city's new outer subdivisions. The Hannan Exchange advised its salesmen that "parents with daughters of eighteen, nineteen and twenty years of age are splendid prospects for a lot and new home in a better community where the inevitable mating may be on a higher social level."[24]

The federal government reinforced succession theory in its efforts to promote mortgaged homeownership after World War I. In 1923, Hoover's Commerce Department published the pamphlet *How to Own*

Your Home and distributed it widely to provide advice and encouragement to potential buyers. The text acknowledged the high stakes that home buying represented to those of modest means. It warned that navigating the geography of urban change poorly by, for example, buying in a declining neighborhood or purchasing beyond one's means might "cause discouragement and a loss of all one's savings."[25] But the manual provided some reassuring tools. *How to Own Your Home* included a chart that buyers could use to determine the size of mortgage that their income could comfortably bear, taking into account taxes, insurance, upkeep, and other expenses that the inexperienced homebuyer might fail to anticipate.

The Commerce Department's pamphlet encouraged decentralized modern housing by discouraging the practices of the nineteenth-century ethnic enclave. It implicitly suggested that homebuyers leave their old neighborhoods for new, superior ones identified by class or occupational group—advice that many early twentieth-century Detroiters followed, as Olivier Zunz has shown.[26] "While a family may think that it would like to live close to relatives and friends," the document explains, "this factor should not be given too much weight. Nevertheless, the general type of people living in the neighborhood is important, especially if there are children in the family, who should be brought up in the right kind of surroundings."[27]

While a well-sited house promised upward mobility, real estate agents warned that the opposite was true, as well: the continued outward expansion of slums near the city center threatened social depreciation. Agents presented a new house in a "better community" as an opportunity to escape this fate and to protect the threatened physical and moral security of the family. Samuel A. Merchant's 1916 advertisement for Elmwood Park, for example, promised the father of the family "a place where his wife and children will be happy, healthy, contented, safe—so he can work all day long with a song in his heart instead of a fear and a worry." For "The Mother," the company promised

> an ideal place for her dear ones to grow up in, where the little ones are not deprived of playgrounds or clean, bright surroundings—where autos will not kill them, where alley-gangs will not corrupt them.

Children growing up in a secure environment, "a good home in a good neighborhood with good boys and girls and good influences," would learn the "whole curriculum of things that make life a success." The

Figure 5.3. Advertisement for B. E. Taylor's Kenmore development, located well outside of the "congested area."
Source: Real Estate Files, Burton Historical Collection, Detroit Public Library.

advertised houses themselves were within the reach of an unskilled worker at $2,200, which would buy the privacy and sanitary technologies that industrialists, reformers, and advertisers urged: "six rooms, bath, full cellar, brick foundation, hot air heat, electric light, etc."[28]

Burgess understood the paradoxical destructiveness of rapid growth through succession. During a real estate boom, he argued, the balanced "metabolism" of succession was upset. Under such rapidly changing conditions of "social disorganization," he noted, urban growth tends to "speed up expansion, to speed up industry, to speed up the 'junking' process in the area of deterioration [near the city center]."[29]

The Detroit developer B. E. Taylor vividly illustrated the dynamics of junking by succession. In an advertisement, his company depicted an upwardly mobile middle-class family stepping up and away from the expanding "congested area" of old Detroit toward Taylor's more prestigious developments at the northwestern edge of urban growth (Figure 5.3). Yet this advertisement would not have been a welcome sight to residents of Taylor's innermost developments, Southlawn and Westlawn. There, the growing "congested area" was beginning to loom close and perhaps to threaten these residents' security—in terms of social status or house value—with depreciation. Under succession, it was wise to avoid becoming rooted in one community and, instead, to continue to climb the steps of upward mobility toward the urban periphery. Once prized areas could decline rapidly, as the Hannan Exchange explained in 1928:

> North Woodward, which a little while back was considered "the only place" to live, is, with the exception of a few good streets, fast giving way to this new order of things. Even as far north as Highland Park the pressure is felt. Who *wants* to live in a city where these conditions prevail . . . if there is something available which gives us all the charm of old Detroit and just fifteen minutes further away[?][30]

As *The Hannan Bible* teaches, "Good property is where you *make* it. It has to be *created*"—that is, from a green field.[31] To the client who complained "I can buy property cheaper three miles further in," not understanding the concept of succession, the Hannan salesman was instructed to reply, "Sure! But look at it! Look at the neighborhood and surrounding tendencies. Are the restrictions such as will safeguard your investment? Or do you just not care who or what your neighbors may be?"[32]

Security in Homeownership

Agents and developers championed working-class homeownership as a source of economic security as one aged. In an advertisement for "High Class Workingmen's Subdivisions," for example, F. S. Prikryl and Company presented a drawing of a semi-bungalow with a low, shining sun behind it, perhaps a subtle suggestion of time running out. Less subtly, the ad included an unfurled banner below the house with the word SECURITY written across it.[33] Playing on the fear of aging in an economy that favored the young, Detroit's real estate sellers emphasized that homeowners could live rent-free in retirement if they had paid off their house loans. As Robert and Helen Lynd discovered among glassworkers in Muncie, Indiana, in the 1920s, industrial labor was becoming a young person's game, where the value of youth and speed were replacing the traditional craft-based values of seniority and experience. Under the new paradigm, it was not uncommon for workers to be forced into retirement in their late forties as their physical capacity for intensive production began to decline. Aging was thus a source of anxiety. As one glassworker's wife explained, "The only thing a man can do is to keep as young as he can and save as much as he can."[34] Hannan taught his Detroit realtors to leverage this anxiety when selling real estate, encouraging clients to picture themselves in "old age" and to explain:

> We have from 21 to 40 to accumulate a home. If we have not accumulated a home by that time the chances are we never will, and must be compelled to go into old age homeless, dependent upon a landlord for shelter for ourselves and little ones.[35]

Taylor leveraged the fear of aging in his advertisements for the working-class Brightmoor neighborhood, using a cartoon in three scenes. In the first, a confident young man questions his friend's decision to buy a house, saying, "There is plenty of time to buy a home later. What is the rush? I believe in letting each day take care of itself." In the second image, the man's confidence is lost and he has aged considerably. He explains to his wife that they need to move into a cheaper rental. "You know," he says, "it is getting hard to pay rent as I get older. My salary is not as large as it was when I was a young man." In the third scene, the aging man is evicted from his house by an unsympathetic sheriff. "Oh! Where will I go?" the man asks. "I am too old to work and I can't pay rent. . . . I wish I had bought a home in my younger days." The sheriff replies, "Sorry, my dear sir, but it is too late now."[36]

Compounding these fears was the thought of leaving one's family, through death, without adequate financial means to sustain the way of life they had known. Life insurance was popular among unskilled Ford workers surveyed in 1929, who paid an annual premium of $60 for it, but the average coverage provided only a $2,076 death benefit, just over 120 percent of their average annual earnings.[37] This would help, but it would not provide lasting security. Paul Rohr's real estate booklet *Am I My Dollar's Keeper?* urged that "the average man's earning capacity today begins to decline at the age of 45" and that, upon his death,

> *Out of every 100 widows—*
> *18 are left with some means*
> *47 must supplement the little left by going to work*
> *35 are in real want.*

But readers of the booklet could still protect their families, as Rohr explained that "a well-chosen real estate investment would be the most solid insurance, not easily dissipated and not declining in value."[38] The choosing of such an investment required subtle calibration, particularly on the question of how close a worker's family should live to the industrial facilities that shared the urban periphery with the new subdivisions.

Selling the Great West Side

Investors, observing the growing congestion of Detroit's inner-city rail junctions, had constructed an outer belt rail line in 1905 that cut through Detroit's rural periphery and encircled the city.[39] Industrialists quickly began to develop modern factories along this line. The Ford Motor Company created its Highland Park plant on the north side of the belt line and then built its successor, the massive River Rouge plant, on the line's west side. Real estate developers worked to provide modern houses amid the west side's new factories, creating a closely interwoven pattern of work and housing in this area that the booster Walt Clyde referred to as the "world's greatest industrial center" in 1925.[40]

New roads and infrastructure were crucial to the success of Detroit's west side. Understanding this, the large-scale developer Robert Oakman purchased a twelve-mile right of way for a new public roadway and streetcar line in the mid-1910s. He called the new artery Ford Highway, "named in honor of Henry Ford . . . whose unparalleled industries . . . not only made this highway desirable, but absolutely necessary."[41] The Ford Highway (today Oakman Boulevard) arced through Detroit's western periphery, paralleling the rail belt line and connecting Ford's Highland Park and River Rouge plants by streetcar and automobile road, opening the miles of farmland between these plants to new development. Oakman, of course, purchased land adjacent to his highway and was able to profitably sell residential lots from his portfolio of holdings.

Representations of the west side's new houses held competing domestic ideals in a tension. Real estate agents and boosters sold the west side as a site of growth, change, and modernization. At the same time, in a nod to the nineteenth century "cult of domesticity," they described the area's dwellings in terms of security, permanence, and proximity to nature.[42] A worker seeking to live near the Ford Highway, the *Detroit News* argued, would find subdivisions "where he may live in reasonably close proximity to his work and still enjoy the blessings and pleasures of a quiet, modest little home" (Figure 5.4).[43] Agents' illustrations of Detroit's west side feature rail lines and smokestacks—signifying work and wages—alongside clusters of gabled houses set among trees (Figure 5.5). You could, these trees suggest, have the best of both worlds on the west side. In practice, tolerance of the noise and smoke of industry had

Figure 5.4. Detail view of a southwestern Detroit real estate advertisement by Walt Clyde, implying that the district could provide both a stable, pastoral domestic life and access to the economic benefits of a dynamic industrial city.

Source: Walt Clyde, "Great South and West Area of Yesterday—Today—Tomorrow," *Greater Detroit Magazine*, reprint, 1925, Real Estate Files, Burton Historical Collection, Detroit Public Library.

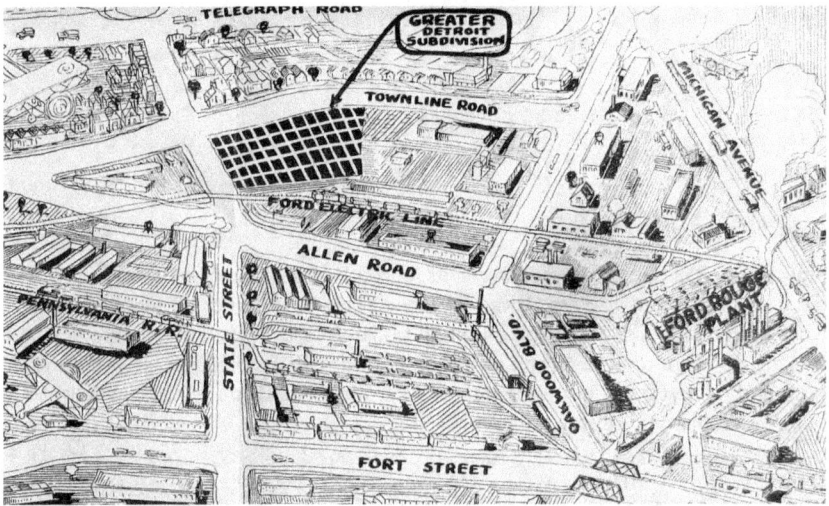

Figure 5.5. An advertisement presenting the Greater Detroit Subdivision's proximity to Ford's Rouge Plant as an amenity, providing easy access to "the very hub of the world's greatest industry." It does not acknowledge how that industry might affect the neighborhood's environmental conditions or its long-term sustainability.

Source: O'Connor's Greater Detroit Subdivision Advertisement, Real Estate Files, Burton Historical Collection, Detroit Public Library.

to be balanced with the benefits of a short commute.[44] On the west side, spaces idealized for their security and permanence—the house, playground, and cemetery—were thus juxtaposed with spaces of dynamic growth and change, including the most productive automaking facilities in the world.

The neighborhood known today as Springwells (area 1 in Figure 5.6) reflects the density and close proximity of work to housing that exemplified western Detroit.[45] Situated between a major rail juncture and the

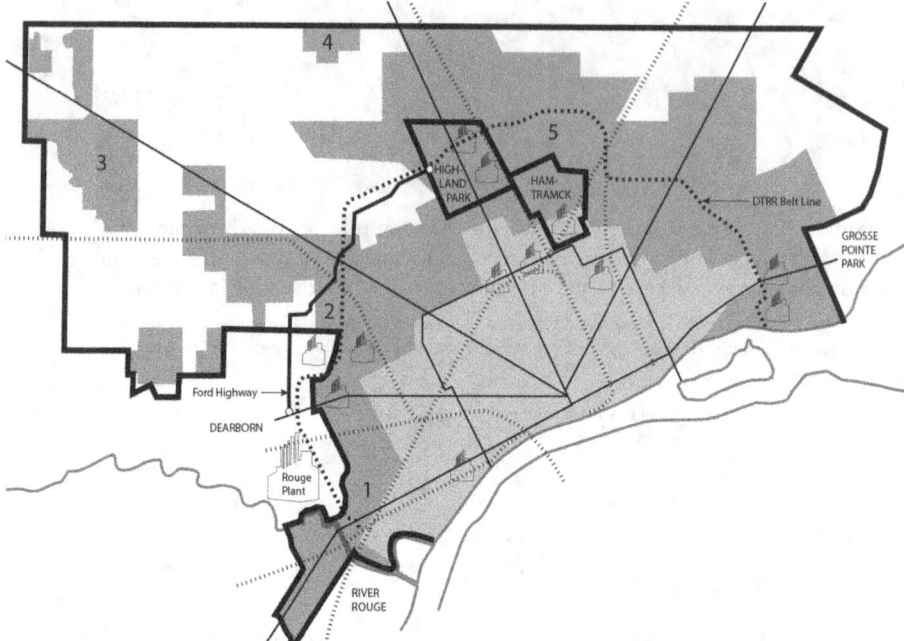

Figure 5.6. Railroads, automobile plants, and urban development. Areas discussed in the chapter are (1) the Springwells neighborhood; (2) the James W. Fales Subdivision; (3) Brightmoor; (4) Eight Mile-Wyoming; and (5) Hamtramck and the Polish northeast. Urban development from 1910 to 1930 is shown in dark gray, and railroads are indicated with dashed lines. The Detroit Terminal Railroad belt line and Ford Highway are noted.

Source: Illustration by the author, with reference to Constantinos A. Doxiadis, *Emergence and Growth of an Urban Region: The Developing Urban Detroit Area* (Detroit: Detroit Edison, 1966), 69; Sanborn Map Company, *Insurance Maps of Detroit, Michigan*, vols. 5–8, 1910, University of Michigan, Ann Arbor; Olivier Zunz, *The Changing Face of Inequality: Urbanization, Industrial Development, and Immigrants in Detroit, 1880–1920* (Chicago: University of Chicago Press, 1982), map 12.2.

expansive Woodmere Cemetery, the area was incorporated into the city as part of a large annexation in 1906.[46] Most of its houses were built during a period of intensive construction between 1913 and 1918.[47] Jobs were close at hand, with Ford's Rouge Plant just on the other side of the cemetery, Michigan Central's Railroad Shops at the neighborhood's northern edge, and Delray's salt works just to the south. The New York Central rail line bisected Springwells, adding many smaller shops to the mix including a refinery, a meatpacking plant, and several manufacturing shops and coal yards.[48]

Through the middle-class eyes of a 1920s geographer, the exterior appearance of the houses in Springwells left something to be desired. He described the neighborhood as consisting of "one and two story detached frame houses, unpainted or weatherbeaten, plain and unornamental, but serving their purpose adequately well."[49] No single description could capture the social diversity of the area. The value of houses in Springwells varied substantially based on where in the neighborhood they were located, as a 1940 survey of house values in the area illustrated. The most prized houses and lots were located on the northern edge, farthest from the area's industrial plants and along the greenspace of the cemetery. The blocks near the rail line bisecting Springwells, and near the Hungarian and Armenian district of Delray to the south, had lower values.[50] Racial and ethnic discrimination were reflected in house prices. A 1926 real estate ad for a Springwells residence played on this by claiming that it was located in an "American Neighborhood." This persistent distinction between "Americans" and "new immigrants" illustrates the limits of the melting pot project. Even as many immigrants assimilated toward American identities, ethnic distinctions remained meaningful in social life, and real estate agents touted the ethnic affiliations of their products.[51] Increasingly, they also leveraged anti-Black racism in their pursuit of sales.

"Restrictions Are an Asset"

Real estate agents helped to drive the outward march of urban succession and the depreciation that followed it. At the same time, they emphasized that properties with restrictive covenants in their deeds were protected against depreciation. Covenants not only could block the encroachment of commercial or industrial uses in a residential district—in the absence of zoning prior to 1940—but were also used as a tool of segregation on the basis of race, religion, and class.[52] As Ann Durkin Keating and Jon Teaford have pointed out, deed restrictions were part of the curated package of amenities that property developers and their agents sold to customers alongside features such as a desirable location and access to utilities.[53]

North of Springwells, Lambrecht, Kelly and Company developed the Fales Subdivision, offering residential lots "in the heart of the new industrial development" (see Figure 5.6, area 2).[54] For an investor who would rent the property or a worker seeking homeownership, the location added value: the Paige Detroit Motor Car and Detroit Seamless Steel Tube plants were located within a mile's walk, and the Ford Highway streetcar could connect the site to Ford's large Highland Park and River Rouge plants. The developer promised that lots would have "the necessary improvements for immediate occupancy," and since the land had been annexed by the city of Detroit in 1916, municipal water service and street paving were indeed forthcoming.[55] Advertisements for the subdivision not only touted its deed restrictions but also sought to instruct those who were new to this concept. They explained that "restrictions are an asset," a means of protecting residents from risks to their social prestige and property values. The advertisement was explicit: the minimum cost of construction at Fales was set at $2,500; saloons and pool rooms were prohibited; and the development's "property shall at no time be used or occupied by a colored person."[56]

During the 1920s, real estate professionals justified and even took pride in their efforts to restrict Black, Jewish, and other minority groups' access to new developments, framing their practices as good stewardship of property values. As the historians David Freund and Elaine Lewinnek have pointed out, the National Association of Real Estate Boards' *Code of Ethics* for 1924 was explicitly segregationist. In its "relations to customers and the public," the organization warned:

> A Realtor should never be instrumental in introducing into a neighborhood a character of property or occupancy, members of any race or nationality, or any individuals whose presence will clearly be detrimental to property values in that neighborhood.[57]

A realtor who promoted racial change or introduced "detrimental" building types—perhaps a tenement or pool hall—faced sanction. Realtors or local real estate boards who failed to live up to their "grave social responsibility and . . . patriotic duty" to following the code of ethics would face "disciplinary action."[58] With the support of government, whose laws backed restrictive covenants until 1948, real estate agents and developers worked to define the modern social contract as a privilege belonging to white Christians.

Among this privileged group, there were those who sought homeownership but were daunted by the cost or complexity of acquiring a modern house. Among the excluded, the formal real estate market could be a hostile place. For both, the strategy of incrementally improving a spartan house at the urban periphery offered a solution.

Satellites: Brightmoor and Eight Mile-Wyoming

Beyond Detroit's outer belt line, B. E. Taylor purchased land in 1921 to create a large development of highly affordable houses and lots. There, as noted in Chapter 4, one of the only restrictions was that residents be white. He called it Brightmoor (see Figure 5.6, area 3). The development was sold as a different kind of value proposition from the west side neighborhood of Springwells discussed earlier: Brightmoor lacked utilities and proximity to work, but did offer a path to homeownership at an exceptionally low cost.

Despite the distance, getting from Brightmoor to industrial jobs was essential for Taylor's prospective buyers, so he arranged for a bus service between the development and the city's employment centers. Because of the bus, Taylor's advertisements could make the claim that Ford's "Rouge [Plant] and Brightmoor [Are] Next Door Neighbors," despite the five or so miles between them. The company reinforced the point with a diagram illustrating the connection, displayed in the front window of its realty office.[59] To overcome Brightmoor's isolation, Taylor built a community center with a small library for residents in 1922, a hub of community sociability and a place where hired social workers could help residents assimilate to their new context. As Americanization programs had done for newly arrived immigrants in the 1910s, the Brightmoor community center in the following decade focused on the assimilation of white American migrants, many from rural Appalachia. Its recreational programs and gardening and cooking classes sought to introduce this group to the ways and standards of an urban and industrial life.[60]

Brightmoor houses ranged from the four-room model illustrated in Chapter 4 to a six-room model. Each of the bedrooms was outfitted with one window, even where wall space could accommodate more. These houses were heated by stoves and lacked basements and indoor bathrooms, falling short of the modern ideal of the five-room-plus-bath house available in other Detroit subdivisions.[61] This was no oversight. Taylor was practiced at building modern houses—at Crescent Heights, for example, he advertised that "the Great American Family demands the comforts of the bath, hot and cold running water, sewage disposal, electric lights, well-kept streets, etc."—but he bet there was also a market among new arrivals with little cash who would prioritize immediate homeownership over waiting and saving to buy a better house.[62] Too far out to access Detroit's utilities and services, Brightmoor's residents lived on largely unlit and unpaved streets, unpatrolled by police, and received water from trucks furnished by Taylor. Under these conditions it is unsurprising that area residents "vote[d] themselves into Detroit" by annexation in 1925 to receive utility services.[63] Prior to that, as Carolyn Loeb has written, investigators found that inadequate sewage disposal was causing widespread illness among Brightmoor's children. Some residents opted not to purchase one of Taylor's houses and instead bought a lot, where the absence of building regulations allowed them to live in "tents, tar paper shacks and some garage homes" as a provisional strategy while they saved to build a more substantial dwelling.[64]

As humble as Brightmoor houses were, Taylor sold them with buyers' aspirations in mind. He brought out-of-state prospects to Detroit and provided a meal and a room at a downtown hotel before showing them the fields northwest of the city where Brightmoor was emerging.[65] A house purchase in that distant subdivision was thus presented as an accessible way to gain a foothold in an impressive, growing city.

For those who had caught on to the merits of speculation, the developer made the "combination offer," which included a Taylor-built house on its own lot plus one additional "[racially] restricted" Brightmoor lot as an investment property. The total cost of the combination was $2,834, financed by Taylor's company and "payable $35 per month, with small payment down." Instead of renting a modern bungalow in the city for a similar cost, this strategy involved sacrificing some domestic comforts in exchange for the future windfall that the second lot, as it rose in value, might eventually provide. When the house was paid off, Taylor predicted, the buyer's family would achieve significant wealth: the original house and the second lot would likely be worth as much as $8,000 in ten years, allowing the Brightmoor household, who had delayed gratification, to sell and purchase a much finer house in a location of their choosing.[66] In ten years, buyers might transform themselves from cash-poor migrants into the upwardly mobile owners of a modern house. Once the sale was made, Taylor encouraged his mortgagees to make extra payments if they could, one year offering two hundred turkeys and two hundred chickens to the first comers who made extra payments around Thanksgiving and Christmas. Aware of the competition for comfort and prosperity that motivated his clients, the community builder noted that "turkeys are scarce this year. . . . [G]et one from B.E. Taylor."[67]

Excluded from Brightmoor and much of the city's formal real estate and credit markets, Black Detroiters sought homeownership at the city's northern edge—Eight Mile and Wyoming—in a satellite development of their own (see Figure 5.6, area 4). As Thomas Sugrue explains, residents in this district built incrementally, combining scavenged building materials and new, the latter bought with cash as family necessity and income allowed.[68] The wood-frame shacks, garages, and other provisional shelters that resulted from this process were often not intended to be permanent houses. Instead, they were part of a process in which residents' future income and savings might allow for more substantial construction, and greater comfort, in the face of the racial inequality that so limited African Americans' access to property.

The material conditions at Eight Mile-Wyoming were informal—tar paper could be found in place of wood siding and outdoor water and toilet facilities often had to suffice—but residents were relatively rich in land, with many forty-foot-wide lot frontages. In western Detroit, by contrast, workers' subdivisions provided greater proximity to jobs and access to city utilities, but their narrow lot frontage of twenty-five to thirty-five feet and stricter regulations allowed for less spatial flexibility. At Eight Mile-Wyoming, large front yards and adjacent empty lots could serve as gardens to grow flowers or food. The neighborhood's frame structures were variously aligned at the front, middle, and back of their respective lots, according to their builders' decisions rather than a uniform setback requirement (Figures 5.7–5.8). The area's flexibility is further illustrated by the presence of many churches within small residential-type buildings in the area, where residents established African Methodist and Baptist congregations.

The outward development of Detroit's formal real estate market approached the Eight Mile-Wyoming satellite in subsequent decades, and the neighborhood came under increased scrutiny and pressure. The difference between its ad hoc construction and the formality of the subdivisions around it was starkly illustrated in the citywide property assessment conducted by the Works Progress Administration (WPA) in 1940. The WPA perceived that most of the housing in north Detroit was in good repair but categorized Eight Mile-Wyoming as a distinct outlier, with houses "needing major repairs [to floors, roof, plaster, walls, or foundation] or . . . having no private bath."[69] Infamously, in 1941, the culture of segregation that had pushed Black Detroiters to this marginal space to begin with was reinforced with a half-mile-long, six-foot-high, one-foot-thick concrete wall. It was built to meet the segregationist requirements of the Federal Housing Authority, which required separation between Eight Mile-Wyoming and a new white residential subdivision that would be built next to it. By the 1950s, government surveyors considered Eight Mile-Wyoming unsalvageable, scoring the area as being of the "[most severe] intensity of blight," a rare candidate for slum clearance and redevelopment on Detroit's urban periphery.[70]

Figure 5.7. Backyards in the Eight Mile-Wyoming neighborhood, illustrating the varied setbacks of the houses and the small outbuildings that residents constructed on their lots. Note the concrete wall, built by a developer in 1941 to separate Eight Mile-Wyoming's Black residents from a new, whites-only subdivision they planned to build on the other side of the wall.

Source: *Detroit News* photograph, Archives of Labor and Urban Affairs, Walter P. Reuther Library, Wayne State University, Detroit.

Figure 5.8. A house in the Eight Mile-Wyoming neighborhood, depicting its spacious context and residents' informal gardening practices. Note the modernizing presence of electricity and the children gathered in the house's shade.

Source: John Vachon, "House in Negro Section, Detroit, Michigan," LC-USF34-063747-D, U.S. Farm Security Administration/Office of War Information Collection, Prints and Photographs Division, Library of Congress, Washington, DC.

Selling Polish Detroit

While real estate agents sold some neighborhoods on their "American" identity, they addressed a different market by touting the working-class Polish identity of other subdivisions, such as in Hamtramck and northeastern Detroit. Nearby Ford and Dodge Brothers plants served as major employment centers for those Polish-majority areas. As the factories came online in the 1910s, Hamtramck grew from a village of 2,559 to a dense enclave with a population of 48,615 by 1920. This represented "the greatest community growth for that period in the United States," according to local authorities.[71] While Hamtramck incorporated as an independent city in 1922, its cultural and economic life were interdependent with the city of Detroit's, and Detroit grew northward to surround it.[72]

As developers shaped the Polish northeast with a gridiron of residential blocks and thousands of plus-or-minus-thirty-foot-wide lots, real estate agents advertised these properties to workers in the local Polish-language newspaper *Dziennik Polski* (*Polish Daily News*). Their ads presented many of the same themes that appeared in the city's English-language real estate ads (Figure 5.9). Hannan, for example, posted a Polish-language advertisement in 1916 for the west side's Sonk Subdivision, where deeds were "properly limited" and "the air is clean and fresh."[73] E. D. Preston—another realtor of Anglo Saxon origin, judging by his surname—advised in a *Dziennik Polski* ad that, "before prices rise[,] the safest and most reliable way for you to make money is to buy a lot." He promoted the Fleming Subdivision near the center of Hamtramck by touting its advantages. Its properties featured site improvements (cement sidewalks and municipal water "already accessible on some streets"), proximity to factories and two streetcar lines, and crucially, an offer of credit: lots were available at "$5 [down] and $5 a month," with a promise that payments could be suspended in case of illness or unemployment.[74] A third advertisement urged Polish readers to consider the benefits of a good real estate investment. "Make yourself and your family happy," it suggested, adding, "Money makes us happy and brings profit."[75]

Polish-language ads spoke to the difficulty of accumulating wealth through wage labor, suggesting that real estate was the worker's rare opportunity to bring in investment income. "Aren't you weary," one advertiser asked, "of . . . working from morning till late evening to earn a living and pay the rent[?]" Why do so, the ad continued, when lots were available for purchase on credit for just $5 per month and were

KUP DOM DZISIAJ!

Nie Płac Rentu.

Po 5-ciu latach nie będziesz miał nic więcej, jak tylko pokwitowania za płacenie mieszkania, które nie będą miały żadnej wartości.

Figure 5.9. "Buy a House Today!" An apparent interethnic partnership emerged in Hamtramck between the well-known American-born Homer Warren (active in Detroit industry and real estate) and the less prominent Lesiński-Leszczyński Company (Polish by surname). The partnership advertised in the Polish-language press that it had finished constructing six houses "to be moved into on the spot," with credit offered such that $150–$200 down and $25 per month, plus interest, would secure the deal. The ad emphasized that the houses "are all built of first rate materials and make, with oak wood floors and Georgia Pine finish." Photographs illustrate the houses' front-gabled façades, clean and new and crossed by a gleaming strip of sidewalk.
Source: Warren and Lesiński-Leszczyński, advertisement, *Dziennik Polski*, July 11, 1914.

predicted to grow so rapidly in value that buyers could "build up [their] capital ten times in a couple of years"?[76] Another seller explicitly directed an appeal "TO WORKING PEOPLE!" It urged them to take "the only real chance in your life": the chance to have a house to show for all of their labor. "Stop putting forth your efforts," the ad continued, "and contending with your fate. Stop grasping and yearning for your own home. The chance to possess a house has come. Take it."[77] Finally, a third agent targeted the appeal toward the brashness of young buyers. Addressing "POLISH YOUTHS!" he advised, "Instead of depositing money in banks at ridiculously small interest," they could "buy realties to make a fortune." Despite the economic uncertainty of 1914, this seller promised that fortune would favor the bold—those with "strong will, energy, flexibility, self-confidence and power"—and that his lots in the Polish district would quickly double or triple in value.[78]

Agents sought to tailor their appeals to the concerns of newly arrived Polish immigrants. Calling on readers' rural understanding of the value of livestock, one noted that by "keeping hens" on their property in the Edgewood Park Subdivision, buyers could "always have fresh eggs."[79] In the early days of the war in Europe—an event that Detroit's Poles were surely following with intense interest—Preston framed the war not as a threat to his readers but as an opportunity to prosper in Detroit's labor market. He wrote:

War in Europe
   Means more business, jobs and prosperity in America.
   In Austria, Serbia, Germany, Russia, England, France and Italy men are drafted to armies from fields, factories and offices. ... [T]hese men will not produce anything[, and] the industries in all these countries will be stopped during the war.
   SO THEY WILL HAVE TO BUY EVERYTHING FROM US IN AMERICA.

Moreover, he argued, demand for labor in Detroit would only be strengthened as some immigrants returned from the city to Europe to join the fight.[80]

The Hamtramck developer Jan B. Sosnowski used the salutation "Dear Compatriots" in one of his advertisements, presenting himself as a trusted fellow Pole. In addition to property, he sold ship cards for travel to Europe, offering a free car ride to the train station as a sweetener.[81] Houses and lots were his main products, and Sosnowski framed Hamtramck property as a way for buyers to invest wisely while retaining their Polish identity. "Do not let yourselves, Fellow Countrymen, be driven into other surroundings, to other countrymen," in districts "far from big factories, schools and churches." His office, as one advertisement pointed out, was located just opposite the Sweetest Heart of Mary Catholic Church, a beloved institution in Polish Detroit. If all of this was not enough, he also had a "big automobile" and was ready to take clients out for driving tours to see his properties.[82]

Ford workers purchased most of the twenty-five houses Sosnowski had built in Hamtramck by 1914. Drawing on the company's authority in housing matters, he added that his houses and contracts "had first been examined by Ford Company inspectors ... [and found to be] most suitable for a worker." Sosnowski assured prospects that doing business with him was "good and safe for you" and explained in another ad that all of his houses were "built to stand long, and they are based on stone foundations not on piles." This was an assurance that B. E. Taylor could not make to his buyers in Brightmoor.[83]

Real estate agents encouraged Polish-language readers to use their day off, Sunday, to look at subdivisions and provided automobile tours to make the experience more leisurely. This practice appears to have been common. One agent urged his prospects to get only in a car with a green flag on it, apparently concerned that someone else might intercept them and show them a different subdivision.[84] In 1914, an automobile ride was a luxury that most workers had seldom, if ever, experienced. It helped to downplay the distance of new subdivisions from the city core and allowed prospects to enjoy a sense of their rising consumer clout in the thrill of mechanical acceleration.

Conclusion

Agents' projections of Detroit's boundless future growth proved elusive, even as workers placed their bets as buyers and renters in the city's new subdivisions. The outward growth of Detroit itself ceased in 1926 as surrounding suburban villages resisted annexation.[85] Large automakers enjoyed havens from the city's governance and taxation as Highland Park, Hamtramck, and Dearborn gained independence from Detroit in 1918, 1922, and 1927, respectively, each centered on a major plant. Further, while the succession-based model of valuation unfolded, providing upward mobility and security to workers at the outermost edge of development, it left an expanding zone of crowding and depreciation in its wake, where pockets of abandoned real estate emerged as early as the 1920s. This suggests that Detroit's property abandonment, strongly associated with the city's population decline over the past fifty years, is in fact a manifestation of a century-old process of decentralization.

In 1928, the geographer Jerome Thomas described an increasingly vacant district of small, aging industrial and residential buildings west of downtown Detroit as "gaunt and abandoned." There, too far west from the commercial center to attract new investment and filled with deteriorated residential structures that "no one will have the energy to improve or replace," was a languishing district in the midst of the fast-growing city. Detroit's developers were focused on peripheral greenfield sites, and its real estate agents were actively downgrading the value of the older sections of the city. "These ramshackle frame structures," Thomas added, "mere shells of residences, today stand as mute testimony to the fact that even worse conditions than slum congestion can result from decadence. . . . I see no future for this area" (Figure 5.10).[86]

Figure 5.10. "Ramshackled Frame Houses on West Side." The house to the left appears to be abandoned, with its door and lower windows papered over with advertisements.

Source: Jerome Thomas, "The City of Detroit: A Study in Urban Geography" (Ph.D. diss., University of Michigan, Ann Arbor, 1928), fig. 89.

His words prefigure the loss of purpose that would come to so many of Detroit's houses, and to Ford's Highland Park plant itself, as residents and the auto industry continued their relentless march away from the city center.

Detroit's housing boom made the city's early twentieth-century industrialization possible, providing new comforts and social advancement to a fast-growing cohort of modern workers. Real estate agents assured these workers that the industrial economy would continue to grow, that peripheral subdivisions would provide social prestige and access to nature, and that homeownership could offer economic security as one aged. Building and selling new subdivisions, the real estate industry reinforced social divisions—between Detroiters at the city's periphery and its center, between white and Black, between Polish and American cultural identities—encouraging households to seek individual advantage in the exclusion of others. Agents, with the aid of employers and the federal government, helped to normalize the risks of chasing a rising standard of living, even as workers' employment prospects rose and fell with economic and seasonal cycles. As a social worker among the city's Polish immigrants observed, however, two weeks of unemployment was often all that stood between domestic comfort and a family crisis, in which rent or loan payments, and grocery bills, would go unpaid.[87] Accepting these risks and developing a diversity of household strategies for dealing with them, Detroit workers sought better lives in modern houses.

6

BETTER LIVES

Making Do in Modern Houses

> Detroit is largely composed, today, of seemingly endless square miles of low-density failure.
> —Jane Jacobs, *The Death and Life of Great American Cities*

The Motor City's development model has long been a foil for urban theorists. To Jane Jacobs, its neighborhoods lacked the density and fine-grained diversity of a place like Greenwich Village. To the modernist architect José Luis Sert, writing twenty years earlier, an aerial view of Detroit illustrated a city reduced to "a monotonous and unending series of real estate developments."[1] Though they disagreed strongly on the value of centralized planning, both critics describe Detroit's gridiron of lots and blocks as "endless." From their distanced view, though, neither urbanist could see how important the city's houses were to those who lived in them. The recorded memories of its residents, by contrast, suggest that for all its flaws, Detroit's wood-framed, for-profit urbanism was an experientially rich and socially meaningful environment. For working-class Detroiters, the city's new houses represented a hard-earned stake in the project of modernization, a way to gain social advancement through a life of disciplined labor. These houses helped to establish the ideal that in modern America, work should be respected and well rewarded. The fuller meaning of this urbanism, in its success and its failures, is too complex and variegated to be understood from a distance.

This chapter takes a closer look. It explores photographs, oral histories, and an International Labor Office survey of Ford workers' budgets while also considering life in contemporaneous Muncie, Indiana. There, the sociologists Helen and Robert Lynd studied the 1920s working-class experience in unparalleled detail, shedding light on national cultural trends. These artifacts provide a measure of access to workers' daily lives, their spending and saving, and their rest and play. They suggest the kinds of aspirations workers held and the choices they made amid an extraordinary urban transformation. It was through their daily practices, ultimately, that workers became coauthors in the emerging social contract, giving a lifetime of work in pursuit of modern houses. Workers "made do," as Michel de Certeau puts it, within the constraining order of the industrial city and its housing market and in this way found agency in a modernization process over which they had limited control.[2] In common and spectacular acts, making their houses meaningful, wage earners produced a highly textured urban condition. They constructed distinct ethnic identities, in the house and in the streets, and navigated neighborhood relationships. They also outfitted, updated, and maintained their houses in ways that made each bungalow or duplex significantly different from the one next to it, even where outside appearances might be similar. Detroit workers created a city composed not of one modernity, one definition of a better life, but of many. This diversity was often constructed at an intimate scale—a scale that fiction, through informed, imaginative leaps, can bring to the fore.

Harriman's Houses

In 1903, Detroit was still a midsize manufacturing center, and the Ford Motor Company was in its infancy. Yet workers were already beginning to grapple with the opportunities and challenges of modernization. In this context, the Michigan author Karl Harriman wrote *The Homebuilders*, a short story collection focused on the incremental transformation of Polish immigrants' houses in Detroit.[3] Working in the "realist" tradition, Harriman reveled, to a romanticizing degree, in the details of space, material, and experience in workers' houses.[4] At the same time, he illustrates how meanings inhere in domestic objects, from the new stove to the old chair, in a period of transition. These stories are not, of course, a transparent lens with which to read working-class Detroit at the turn of the century. Harriman's characters' simple, colloquial language and chaste, thrifty lives reflect his paternalism as much as any on-the-ground cultural insight. At the same time, his empathic imagination puts the built environment in motion, animating it with the kinds of exhilaration and fear that immigrants likely experienced as they navigated urban modernization.

The title story, "The Homebuilders," follows two young protago-

Figure 6.1. Jefferson Avenue, where the city's elite constructed fine houses beginning in the nineteenth century and where Harriman's Henry Brosczki dreamed he might live.

Source: *Detroit News* photograph, Archives of Labor and Urban Affairs, Walter P. Reuther Library, Wayne State University, Detroit.

nists—the tobacco stripper Julia Fernowicz and the sand hauler Henry Brosczki—who meet at a "Polonia Hall" dance and begin courting. Discussing marriage, they embrace the cultural ideal of homeownership with which they have been raised, and the pair began spending their savings at a delirious pace to acquire the material requisites for marriage in their community. They put a down payment on a lot and buy a used cottage, which they have relocated to the lot. It is, for Henry, the realization of a dream, even though the cottage is a far cry from the grand brick house on Jefferson Avenue that he had dreamed of owning (Figure 6.1).[5] Their lot is filled, in its own way, with the promise of great things to come: the block has been wired recently for electricity, which promises future indoor lighting. As the couple walks in their new yard one evening before the wedding, planning a future flowerbed and chicken coop, the house is "gleam[ing] in the electric light" of the street lamps.[6]

There are plenty of ways to improve the new cottage, and Henry takes the opportunity of his wedding gift to Julia to make a big one.

Following two days of wedding celebration with food, drink, and dancing, the newlyweds return, exhausted, and enter their new house together for the first time. Various gifts wait for them there, but Julia moves immediately toward the greatest of them: the kitchen stove that is Henry's gift. The house is not yet wired for electricity, so she lights a match. Examining the stove with "rapturous delight," she says, "It's a beauty."[7] The outfitting of a house, as Harriman suggests, could be about more than material improvement. It could be entwined with the building of household relationships, as well.

The new stove, like many furnishings, fixtures, and spaces, takes on deeper meaning in the intimate context of a house, transcending its mere commercial value. It has the capacity to be what Mary Douglas calls "a memory machine," opening access to the past and anticipation of the future in an imaginative space punctuated by daily, seasonal, and life cycles.[8] Gaston Bachelard, for example, describes the wardrobe as a space "filled with memories," evoking the comfort of having "good things held in reserve."[9] When feeling protected in a favorite corner of their house, one may experience a remembered or projected sense of enclosure as much as an actual one. For Harriman's Julia, perhaps, the new stove is entwined with past experiences of domestic intimacy or winter cold and with anticipation for the couple's private future—for shared meals and, with good fortune, abundant fuel for heat.

In the face of rapid change, the domestic space of the immigrant worker's cottage could also be animated by pain and loss, as Harriman explores in "The Wages of His Toil." In this story, Ladislaw Adamowsky, an aging hauler at a stove works, takes dinner wordlessly with his two sons at the kitchen table, where a fourth chair, in its emptiness, reflects the recent death of Ladislaw's wife.[10] The man's health declines rapidly in the story, and as he becomes weaker, his paternal authority gives way to the rising influence of his sons and daughter-in-law. The latter, having worked as a kitchen maid, seeks to introduce "American" domestic tastes into his house. The children refurnish the house in the image of their own desires, all around Ladislaw, who looks on as "a chair would vanish overnight; a shelf would disappear," until "after a month the changes had been so many that . . . the memory in him died." The older man responds by moving into the backyard shed with his milk cow.[11] Yet while the fictional Ladislaw withdraws in the face of cultural change, many of Detroit's newly arrived workers saw opportunity in it—opportunity to build new houses and to construct a diversity of modern identities.

Making Houses: Practices and Purchases

Detroit's streets were a stage for conscious and unconscious performance, as illustrated by the neighborhood processions of the city's ethnically Polish community. In 1913, the *Detroit News* documented one such procession, believed to be the funeral cortege for St. Albertus's pastor, Father Mueller. It began, according to the paper, with "the deep tolling of the bells in the steeple." As the sound rang out, a regalia-clad group raised their religious banners and began to make their way through the residential neighborhood adjacent to the church as local children looked on from the sidewalk.[12] Such practices continued as the Polish American community grew in subsequent decades. In 1939, commemorating the Polish Constitution, a west side parade made its way to St. Hedwig Church for a celebratory mass as neighbors watched from their porches (Figure 6.2). One onlooking household flew an American flag, perhaps reflecting their hybrid identity.

More often, the life of Detroit's working-class neighborhoods was spontaneous. In 1915, in the fast-growing enclave of Hamtramck, a

Figure 6.2. A 1939 parade commemorating the Polish Constitution makes its way along Junction Avenue, on the west side. The event ended with a celebratory mass at St. Hedwig Church.

Source: *Detroit News* photograph, Archives of Labor and Urban Affairs, Walter P. Reuther Library, Wayne State University, Detroit.

social worker observed "37 children on roller skates, hanging on the tail end of a team [of horses] that was galloping down the concrete street."[13] Alarmed, and finding no apparent humor in the situation, he made a note in his report. There and elsewhere, children's activities animated the corridor of the residential street, and neighbors negotiated the extents of their responsibility to mind one another's children at play. One Detroit resident recalled a watchful system of "eyes on the street" in his oral history—something that Jacobs might have appreciated.[14] There, neighbors spent social evenings on the porches of their newly built bungalows and duplexes, and "if there were somebody from outside the neighborhood, they were spotted. They were watched."[15] Another resident recalled the "extended family relationship" they experienced with neighbors. This was a liability for children: "If you did something bad, you got a spanking from [the neighbor who saw you]. When you got home, you got a second spanking."[16]

The closely monitored, developmental play of small children was facilitated by the length and smoothness of the modern sidewalks. Frank Diplock and Bob Kermode, for example, played with a pedal car on the east side's Gladwin Avenue in 1924. Bob, the older of the two boys, gave Frank a ride. In an apparently staged photograph, someone, perhaps a parent, captured the younger boy behind the wheel, despite his being too small to operate it. The scene echoed the increasing access to real automobiles in this relatively affluent neighborhood, where skilled tradesmen such as a steamfitter and a carpenter lived alongside a white-collar clerk, and many residents had added alley-facing auto garages to their properties by the end of the 1920s.[17] Even among Ford's unskilled workers, forty-seven in one hundred surveyed had new or used cars parked outside their houses by the end of the 1920s, a consumer durable that, the survey found, was "becoming more and more a part of the family equipment for recreation."[18]

The front façade of the house, then as now, provided more than shelter. It could stand for the larger house and its meaning symbolically and was therefore often used as an honorific background for family photographs, which served to tie memories of relationships and events to the house and neighborhood for posterity. Front-yard photographs posed their subjects amid other indexes of household care: trimmed lawns, decorative trees, and cultivated plants (Figure 6.3). In their sociological analysis of 1920s Muncie, the Lynds associated this façade care with the more prosperous and image-conscious section of the working class, which tended to have "a tidy front yard; whether [their] home is of the two-floor variety, a bungalow, or a cottage, there are often

Figure 6.3. Groups pose for photographs on Detroit's west and east sides, in their early-twentieth century neighborhoods.

Source: WestSiders, *Remembering Detroit's Old Westside, 1920–1950,* 101 (*top*); Detroit Historical Society (*bottom*).

geraniums in the front windows, neat with their tan, tasseled shades and coarse lace curtains."[19]

In one neighborhood on Detroit's west side, which current and former residents refer to as "the Westside," Black Detroiters gained access to modern houses in the early twentieth century. Those who grew up in the neighborhood in that period recall how important their houses' appearance was to their parents. "This was their property," said one resident in his oral history. "They wanted this property. They wanted to keep their homes up, paint them, have lawns, all of that sort of thing." In a city where most new neighborhoods were hostile to Black residents, having a modern house was "a big deal," and maintenance practices celebrated it.[20] "Mama paid me a penny a dandelion," another Westsider recalls, "which we had to get out with a dandelion weeder because cutting them does not do anything but promulgate more dandelions." She performed this task, and "the sons would do the mowing."[21] Perhaps her father, as others had, took pleasure in watering the lawn to keep it green or in gardening to produce fresh vegetables. Another interviewee recalled the dread that home beautification brought him as a young man, recalling, "As soon as the snow melted, I had to turn up the dirt all around the fence. My mother loved flowers. She was known as 'The Flower Girl.' So I had to go all round the fence and turn up the soil around there. I hated this."[22]

The front door of the house is emphasized in bourgeois discourse as a symbolic threshold that separates "home," as refuge, from the demands of work and from the moral impurity of the city beyond.[23] The Detroit-based poet Edgar Guest spoke to this with sentimental verse in 1916. For him, the front door is where, at the end of the workday, one pauses to acclimatize oneself to the rarefied space of the house. At the door he sees a significant challenge and a choice: to leave or not leave the burdens of the day at the doorstep:

The day is done, and here I leave
The petty things that vex and grieve;
What clings to me of hate and sin
To them I will not carry in.[24]

But what have workers said about the meaning of the front door? What relationship did they seek to foster between the house and the world outside through their modern domestic practices?

It appears that passing through the door with a smile, ready to cheerfully engage with the rest of the household, was harder for those who did physically demanding work than Guest might have imagined. Muncie workers, in their interviews for the Lynds' *Middletown*, expressed the challenge of balancing hard labor and family life. Wishing she could do more with her children, one woman noted: "I'm too tired to do it even when I have the time. . . . I just can't get up any energy." Her spouse was similarly taxed by his labor, being "so tired when he comes home from work that he just lies down and rests and never plays with the children."[25] Yet for many, it was hope for children's social advancement and their better lives in the future that gave meaning to work. One Detroit worker's son remembers, for example, that when his father spoke of his job, he made it clear the work he was doing was not something he wanted to see his children end up doing. It was "hard and dirty and we could see that by how [my father] looked when he came home. And he talked about the fact that he didn't wish to see us in that kind of situation."[26] Explaining why she woke at 5:30 A.M. each day for work, a Muncie woman described the family's bungalow, but also the future ease and choice the children raised there might enjoy. "The two boys want to go to college," she noted, "and I want them to. I graduated from high school myself but I feel if I can't give my boys a little more all my work will have been useless."[27] In these views, the house is less a refuge from the world than a staging point from which the household's members might better position themselves in that world.

In the early twentieth century, as now, women faced gender-based wage discrimination, but their incomes were crucial to many working-class household economies. The labor-force participation rate of married women grew rapidly nationwide in the 1920s, and nearly 30 percent of wage-earning women were married by decade's end. A second earner's wages made a big difference in a household's ability to save and spend. The woman who aspired for her children to go to college was proud of the nearly paid-off brown-and-white bungalow, electric washing machine and iron, and vacuum sweeper that her wages had helped to make possible. She described the family's Studebaker to her interviewees in detail and added, "I have felt better since I worked than ever before in my life."[28] The particular fortune of her family, though, should not obscure the importance of compromise in the early twentieth-century working-class pursuit of material advancement.

One compromise that workers' households made was to defer home-ownership, instead renting a modern house because of the difficulty of saving for a down payment. Others compromised in the other direction, deferring modern comforts to achieve ownership more quickly—buying a small house without a bathroom in Detroit's Brightmoor development, for example. Households' compromises were not abstract things. They helped to shape the sensory experience of daily life. Among Ford workers' families interviewed in 1929, "some . . . kept their rooms very warm during the winter months on account of the small children, while others practiced economy in fuel and light even to the extent of being uncomfortable." In the same group, two of the one hundred workers interviewed walked thirty to sixty minutes to get to their jobs, rising earlier and returning home later to save on streetcar fare or automobile expenses. Home haircuts, at least for children, were a common economizing practice.[29]

The kitchen could be a major site of strategic compromise. One Muncie woman, for example, explained that she had achieved significant savings in groceries over the previous year, "partly because we trade at a cheaper place and partly because we're economizing."[30] One could accept canned milk instead of fresh, for example, and eat more beans and

Figure 6.4. Paired ads encouraging married women to be "judicious" consumers on behalf of their families, noting that an Adora phonograph could be enjoyed now and paid for over the course of a year.

Source: *Marriage Record and Hints on Housekeeping: An Indispensable Household Guide* (Detroit: B. B. Schermerhorn, 1920), 64–65.

potatoes instead of meat. In Detroit, full-time industrial workers might also seek to earn extra money in their off-hours, compromising their leisure time. The Ford Motor Company introduced the five-day workweek in 1926, removing Saturday shifts, but its employees traded some of their leisure for side income, such as "carpentry work, painting, repairing automobiles, repairing shoes, or working in a store."[31]

The tension between a desire to economize and a desire for new comforts was not lost on product sellers and advertisers. They urged consumers to see themselves as managers, both of their finances and of their households' emotional well-being. Thoughtful purchases could create an "atmosphere" conducive to the household's happiness. If the full cost of a phonograph, for example, was too great in the short term, payments could be made "gradually, as convenient" (Figure 6.4).[32] Consumer credit was on the rise nationwide in the 1920s, and "nowhere," one observer noted at the time, "is the system of installment purchase more enthusiastically lauded and practiced than in Detroit."[33] Among one hundred surveyed Ford families, twelve had invested in consumer durables in the previous year, including stoves, washing machines, radios, and pianos, and all but one had done so on an installment plan.[34] Other product sellers appealed strictly to economy, forgoing any emotional appeal or discussion of credit. The department store People's Outfitting, for example, advertised its clearance sale in the Polish-language *Dziennik Polski* with an angle for buyers who knew how to do their own repair work: "Our warehouse is still full of damaged furniture which we sell at cheap prices."[35] In sum, the pursuit of better lives was a balance of income, risk tolerance, and desire, but the rising standard of living is clear in the household budgets of surveyed workers. They showed regular spending on visits to doctors and dentists; new, ready-made hats and clothes; daily newspapers and occasional restaurant lunches; and an average of thirty-three motion picture show tickets per household in a year, used mostly by the children.[36]

Inside the working-class house, spatial limits required compromises and flexibility. While many five- and six-room bungalows included a dining room, for example, that was accessed from the living room through a cased opening, B. E. Taylor's four-room Brightmoor houses did not. Adapting to this—as a promotional photograph from a *Building Age* article shows—the living room could be arranged to support dining, as well (Figure 6.5). Perpetuating a nineteenth-century strategy, buyers of inexpensive Brightmoor houses consolidated their activities into a multiuse front room, containing the house's single heat source—the stove.[37] In another spatial compromise, the bedroom beyond the doorway (at the left in the photograph) functioned as a "sitting room" by day, and its pull-out couch was transformed into a bed at night. The curtain at this room's threshold was likely used to keep heat from escaping the living room space into what could have been a cold bedroom at night. Despite the house's modesty, though, its dining table was arranged in an honorific position, near the light of the front window and the warmth of the stove, and finished with a tablecloth and decorative centerpiece.

In a sitting room-turned-bedroom, or in the street-turned-parade route discussed earlier, spatial limitations could be overcome by the tactical reimagining of available space. With its furniture moved, the modern living room could become a place for holiday events and other occasional celebrations. As the phonograph proliferated in the 1910s and 1920s, such parties were often animated by recorded music.[38] As Lizabeth Cohen points out, music could be a means to tailor an event to the shared conventions of a coethnic group of family or friends—

Figure 6.5. Inside this Brightmoor house, the living room doubles as a dining room, and the front bedroom (*beyond at left*) also does double duty: it serves as a "sitting room" and is equipped with a sleeper sofa.

Source: H. C. L. Jackson, "Building a Bungalow City in 18 Months," *Building Age*, August 1924, 86–87.

Polish, Italian, or Mexican records, for example, might fill the transformed living room with shared language and cultural affiliation on the occasion of a gathering. The record industry also offered regionally specific music to Black and white audiences who had migrated from the American South.[39] Music could transcend ethnic and regional niches, as well. James Gregory notes that American popular music was "southernized" by the proliferation of musical forms such as jazz, blues, and country that coincided with the outmigration of many southerners.[40] In this context, it is easy to imagine the appeal of an Adora phonograph, whose "clear, liquid tones" could bring new life to an upcoming celebration and be paid for in installments over time.

Dining rooms were included in all three of the Sibley Lumber stock plans examined in Chapter 4. Yet whether eaten in a dedicated dining room or in the living room or kitchen, a household's meal together could be what the anthropologist Mary Douglas calls "a conclave," a private setting for the negotiation of close relationships.[41] It could provide opportunities to coordinate the household's rules and schedules. Yet picturing the table conclave through the lens of a bourgeois ideal, on a weekday morning at breakfast or in the evening after the close of business, would obscure the complexity of many working-class schedules. When the Ford Motor Company reduced its work shifts from nine to eight hours, in 1914, it did so in part to more efficiently use the twenty-four-hour cycle. This meant that three eight-hour shifts could be run each day. It also meant that many workers would be employed on evening shifts, or overnight, putting them on a schedule different from that of the rest of their household.⁴² Second- and third-shift families would have to schedule their conclaves around the demands of modern industry. Even day-shift work could pose schedule challenges. In Muncie, as the Lynds describe, social status was often indexed in a household's waking hours and visible from the street:

> About six o'clock of a winter morning one notes two kinds of homes: the dark ones where people still sleep, and the ones with a light in the kitchen where the adults of the household may be seen moving about, starting the business of the day.

The former tended to be from the business class, who might arrive at work at 8:30 A.M., and the latter tended to be workers, who often started at 7:00 A.M. Waking in the dark in winter, a working-class parent would be more likely to eat "hastily in the kitchen in the gray dawn" and be at work before the children needed to be at school.⁴³

In private bedrooms, the children of Detroit's modern houses might sleep through the waking ritual of a working parent—a comfort harder to achieve in the small cottages of an earlier generation. They might also be segregated by gender, a significant priority in the emerging early twentieth-century culture of privacy.⁴⁴ Navigating the period's ideals of comfort and privacy, working households made do. Two or three bedrooms did not go far in a family of two adults and eight children, for example. Felix Seldon, who grew up in such a household in the Westside neighborhood, recalled the need for "lots of bed covers" in winter, in the unheated attic of his parents' bungalow, on the bed that he shared with two brothers.⁴⁵

Ford Motor Company sociological investigators were keen to photograph workers' bedrooms, documenting what higher wages and paternalistic interventions had done to improve living standards.⁴⁶ In keeping with company practice, discussed in Chapter 1, residents themselves were often excluded from these photographs. Nevertheless, and despite the photographers' biases, these photos suggest something of the real use and meaning of these spaces to those who inhabited them. Daylit windows and bright white linens might tell the intended story of reform, but other subtle choices enter the scene (Figure 6.6). Catholic iconography gives special meaning to this bedroom in two hung pictures, edges slightly curling: one a heavenly scene depicting God in three persons—Father, Son, and Holy Spirit—and the other a Madonna and child. Below these is a third, perhaps secular image: a seated woman with two kneeling children and an infant around her. Cycles of regular prayer

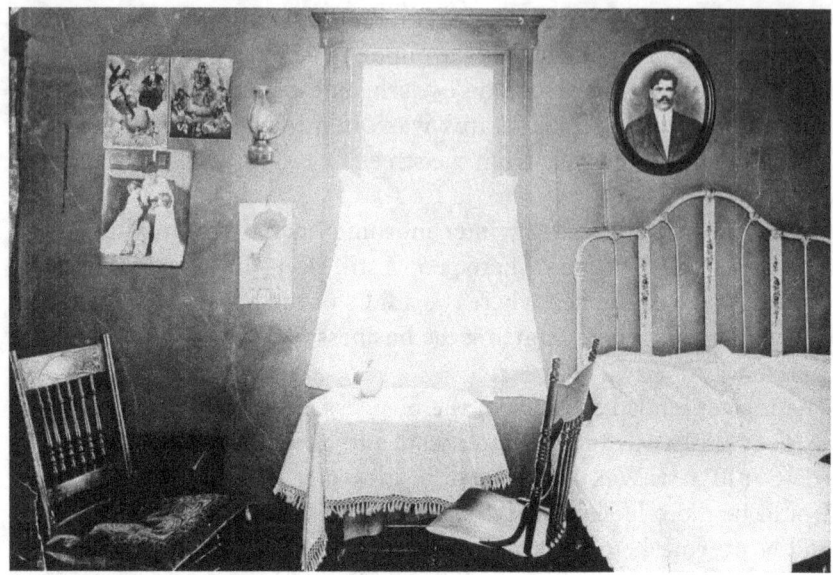

Figure 6.6. "Bedroom of an Improved Home, 1914." Photograph by the Ford Motor Company Sociological Department.
Source: Image from the Collections of The Henry Ford, Dearborn, MI.

appear to have been practiced in the quiet and the privacy of this room, as a rosary is hung on a nail to the left of the religious pictures. Other cycles are reflected in the room's tabletop clock and wall calendar, turned to November: modern cycles of work, appointments, and planned events, and perhaps each morning the need to wake before the rest of the household to light the stove or feed the furnace.[47]

The bedroom was also a place where birth and death took place and in those roles could gain an honorific significance in household memory. One Detroiter recalled the front bedroom of his childhood house as the room where he was born—a spatial memory that was important enough to his family, and passed on to him, that he recalled it eighty years later. "Most of the family was born there in the home," he added.[48] A death in the bedroom, as Edgar Guest's poetry suggests, could cause the space and the larger house to become "dearer" in the emotional lives of its residents, even "sanctified."[49]

Home Economics

Early twentieth-century home economics discourse framed the kitchen as a predominantly technical environment, a message that young women encountered in the city's modern school system. Detroit's public schools more than doubled their enrollment in the 1920s, to 250,000 students, and rapidly expanded facilities and staff. These schools increasingly emphasized the "platoon" method of instruction, where cohorts of students would alternate between periods of traditional academic study and periods of enrichment and vocational study, in art and physical education and in manual training and home economics.[50] Home economics courses, with the backing of countless advertisements, framed the kitchen as a woman's sphere of responsibility, and one that could be managed more easily with modern tools and techniques. Kitchen work could be made more efficient in much the same way factory work was, through time studies of the physical movements required for kitchen tasks.[51] In 1922, Detroit's Merrill-Palmer Motherhood and Home Training School advised public and private schools on home economics pedagogy with the publication *Outline for the Teaching of Home Making*.[52]

Outline framed the modern kitchen as a design problem that women had the agency to solve in how they selected, updated, and used the space and its equipment. Emphasizing this, one suggested assignment challenged students to lay out a hypothetical kitchen's appliances and furniture with ease of use in mind:

Select a floor plan for a house and locate in the kitchen the following equipment:

1. Sink
2. Stove
3. Table
4. Storage—Supplies, Utensils, China, Cutlery, Linen
5. Refrigerator
6. Chair

In locating equipment consider:

1. Light on working surfaces, day and night
2. Distance to be travelled between working spaces
3. Perform following duties and trace route:
    a. Clear dining table and wash dishes
    b. Prepare mashed potatoes and serve

The *Outline* called for iteration on this design exercise, requiring students to "try various arrangements and compare [their] desirability by tracing [the] working path." As a final step, it asked the student to engage with their own mother for a critique of their chosen design, asking her, "Can the kitchen equipment be arranged so that it will be more convenient?"[53] In this way, the suggested homemaking course would prompt an intergenerational dialogue within the household about the ideal kitchen and its practices. At the same time, it would shed light on the distance between a textbook ideal and each household's particular economic limitations or preferences.

Kitchens, even in houses that appear similar from the street, were differently equipped, depending on their residents' budgets and choices. Sinks, for example, were fed by a hot water heater in 65 percent of surveyed Ford workers' households by the end of the 1920s, a significant but by no means universal dispersion of the technology.[54] Among workers' kitchens that were considered "improved" by Ford Motor Company investigators in 1914, a range of conditions are evident. One inspected kitchen featured stylish wallpaper and a countertop work surface and stove that were conveniently near the sink—helpful when preparing mashed potatoes.[55] In a second, "improved" kitchen, however, the sink was off by itself and awkwardly positioned next to the back door (Figure 6.7). Nevertheless, signs of care and indexes of the household's daily practices are clear in the second kitchen. A decorative curtain is hung below the sink to hide pipes and any stored items, and a mat is placed at the back door for residents and guests to wipe their shoes before entering. In both kitchens, dishes are carefully displayed in glass-fronted cabinets, and both households likely did a bit of tidying up for the photographer.

Home economics discourse emphasized the cleanliness of the modern house and body and was supported by advertisements for cleaning products of all kinds.[56] Seventy-two of one hundred surveyed Ford workers' households had gained an indoor bathroom by 1929. This made bathing easier than by the old method, as recalled by Guest: a wooden tub in the kitchen filled with stove-warmed water.[57] Still, it would be misleading to read these modern baths as labor-free spaces. A 1920 corset ad from inside a Detroit household's copy of *Marriage Record and Hints on Housekeeping* illustrates some of the many demands the modern domestic ideal placed on women. In it, a woman is undressed to her corset as she gives a child a bath. The corset exerts, according to the company, "a gentle urge toward perfection in figure," even as the child playfully threatens to throw a wet sponge at her. A decorative heat diffuser suggests an atmosphere of warm and comfortable central heating—a feature of forty-four in one hundred surveyed

Figure 6.7. A worker's kitchen, photographed by the Ford Motor Company's Sociological Department and used in the publication *Factory Facts at Ford* (1915) to illustrate the improvements that had been achieved in employees' housing conditions.

Source: Image from the Collections of The Henry Ford, Dearborn, MI.

workers' houses.[58] In the advertisement, there is no crying or struggle in the bathing process, and the woman's unpaid labor seems to disappear. In the real world of early twentieth-century Detroit, the modern house was a site of significant and meaningful work, as illustrated in the stories of African American families who migrated to Detroit and managed to gain modern houses.

Better Lives in Black Detroit

The dream of a modern house had particular meaning for Black Detroiters, given the discrimination they faced. East of downtown, the Black Bottom neighborhood became an increasingly crowded African American ghetto amid rapid migration and residential discrimination, as discussed in Chapter 2. Racially restrictive covenants and neighborhood violence showed newly arrived African Americans that they were largely unwelcome outside of Black Bottom.[59] Despite the hardships of segregation, however, Black Bottom's residents constructed meaningful domestic lives (Figure 6.8). The adoption of spatial hierarchies, from the profane to the sacred, was one reflection of this. One resident of this district, for example, enforced strict rules on music in her house. As her grandson recalled, "The blues and jazz [were] controversial" in the

Figure 6.8. A couple and an infant pose on their porch in the Black Bottom neighborhood. Little is known about them, but the image offers a reminder that domestic pride and care were not absent from the neighborhood east of downtown where most Black Detroiters lived. The photograph was taken by Harvey C. Jackson around the 1930s, part of a series of photographs of his family, friends, and neighborhood.

Source: Harvey C. Jackson Collection, Burton Historical Collection, Detroit Public Library.

1920s, and "a lot of people didn't want jazz in their house because jazz came from whorehouses." His grandmother refused to have these styles of music played in her parlor, though she allowed them in the kitchen or on the back porch. "I don't want that devil music in here," she had said.[60]

Others, despite the racially restrictive covenants that governed most new subdivisions, gained a foothold in the neighborhood residents called the Westside around 1915. There, Black Detroiters began to establish their own culture of modern houses and social advancement.[61] The sociologist Forrester Washington described this mixed-class group of workers and professionals as "the most promising element in the Negro community . . . ; the bone and sinew of the race," believing, unfairly, that they were uniquely "hard-working and thrifty."[62] In the Westside neighborhood, Black workers found both opportunity and the persistence of segregation. One son recalled the pride and ambition that his father, who worked for the Ford Motor Company, expressed at the decision to buy a house on 30th Street, after renting half of a two-flat in the area for some time: "He told my mother, 'I am going to buy that house,'" and the family did.⁶³ Despite their achievements, however, Black residents' mobility was limited by the lines of race that defined this neighborhood's edges.

The streets bounding the Westside in the 1920s were Epworth, Warren, Tireman, and Grand. As one resident recalled, Tireman divided Blacks from American-born whites, and Warren divided Blacks from Polish Americans. Tense racial and ethnic lines were not limited to the African American experience. In early twentieth-century Detroit, a Jewish Detroiter recalled, "It was just understood that if you were Jewish, you didn't move into a WASP area, which [the Woodward corridor] was at that time."⁶⁴ Where a Jewish district met a Polish American district, he remembered, "If you walked past the border line, you were likely to get beaten up. If they came over, some of the guys on our side would reciprocate."⁶⁵ Such lines were not impermeable, however. One African American resident recalled leaving the Westside neighborhood and crossing into an adjacent Polish American district on occasional shopping trips. By contrast, "The only Blacks that crossed that [Tireman] line [into the American-born white district] were workers in the homes over there."⁶⁶

In 1920, one-fifth of the U.S. workforce was female, and among Black women, more than 40 percent worked for wages in the early twentieth century, including many who labored in the houses of middle-class whites.⁶⁷ Westside women often worked, as their interviewed children recalled: one was a social worker, for example, while others did "day work," cleaning and ironing in other peoples' houses.⁶⁸ Much additional labor was performed, by Westside adults and children alike, in cleaning and maintaining their own houses. "My Mother would not have tolerated your not making your bed before you left out of the house," one Westsider remembers, "because something might happen to you and someone might have to bring you back"—and therefore see the condition of the house's interior.⁶⁹ Children polished wood furniture and floors, washed clothes and cleaned dishes, and practiced at the piano in the neighborhood, some rewarded for their efforts with access to the radio during Sunday evening programs. The work these African American residents put into beautifying their houses and protecting and disciplining their children and neighborhood can be read as a form of resistance in the context of racial segregation, as further discussed in Chapter 7.⁷⁰

Conclusion

In their recollections, Detroiters describe an early twentieth-century city that was anything but "endless" and undifferentiated. Instead, its grid of blocks, lots, and new houses was patterned with practices of identity formation large and small. Racial and ethnic lines charged the experience of urban geography with meaning, as did everyday efforts at neighborly cooperation. Between one house and another, workers' domestic practices, possessions, and values set their households apart, even where the outward architectural forms of their houses were similar. Each bedroom and kitchen represented a negotiation between ideals and real constraints in pursuit of self-defined better lives. Modern houses were hard-earned, manifesting each household's labor, risk-taking, and pride. They brought new spatial experiences and technologies—new comforts and aspirations—within reach of working-class households as never before.

At the same time, Detroit's modern houses divided. To a significant extent, they split the economic interests and identities of one household from the next, and one neighborhood from the next. A commentator in the *New Republic* captured this in 1927, describing Detroit as "a city of strangers" and, as such, the "essence of America," where the pursuit of better lives was centered on independent houses and in neighborhoods often defined by lines of ethnicity and race.[71] Helping to construct racial segregation in housing, even with violence, white workers distanced themselves from their Black colleagues, seeking advantage in a competition for social advancement as if it was a zero-sum game. In turn, Black Detroiters struggled for a fair share in the modern social contract, even at great personal risk.

PART III

STRUGGLE

7

GLASS AND STONES

Materials of Race and Neighborhood Violence

> Despite the brutal reality of racial apartheid, of domination, one's homeplace was the one site where one could freely confront the issue of humanization, where one could resist.
> —bell hooks, "Homeplace (A Site of Resistance)"

African Americans faced bitter segregation in white-dominated early twentieth-century cities, yet the Black family's house, as bell hooks writes, could be a restorative place amid a hostile context. The outer walls of the house could frame a sense of protection and dignity for the people and practices within. In Detroit, however, in the summer of 1925, white mobs threatened these walls. They sought to break through the protective enclosures of Black families' houses in a series of racist attacks. Many of them were focused in western Detroit, a district that the *Detroit Free Press* referred to as the "Storm Area" during the crisis.[1] On several evenings, angry white crowds filled the district's streets, lawns, and porches. They intended to terrify those few African American households who had dared to move into what had previously been all-white neighborhoods. The *Free Press*'s storm metaphor suggested that the violence was a menacing natural occurrence, but this was certainly not the case. Residents constructed this violence in the name of white supremacy, and the form that it took was influenced by the district's modern houses themselves. As Dianne Harris argues, houses are "so pervasive and seemingly ordinary as to become critically unobserved," but in fact they have long been leveraged in the social construction of race.[2] In this sense, Detroit's new subdivisions were more than shelter for a growing workforce in the early twentieth century. They were material representations of whiteness itself, reflect-

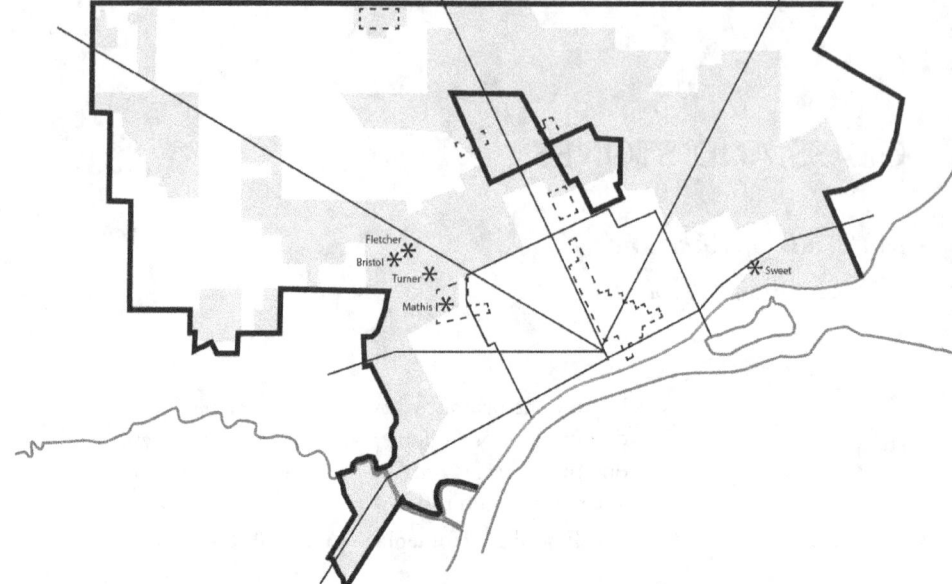

Figure 7.1. Map of Detroit's neighborhood racial violence, 1925. Concentrations of Black residents are depicted with a dashed line, and the five major mob riots of the summer of 1925 are indicated with stars and labeled by their victims' last names. The light-gray area indicates where housing was developed between 1910 and 1930.

Source: Illustration by the author, with reference to Jerome Thomas, "The City of Detroit: A Study in Urban Geography" (Ph.D. diss., University of Michigan, Ann Arbor, 1928), fig. 6; Richard W. Thomas, *Life for Us Is What We Make It: Building Black Community in Detroit, 1915–1945* (Bloomington: Indiana University Press, 1992).

ing the upward mobility that whiteness permitted. The city's industrial economy relied on the labor of both Black and white workers, but only the latter were entitled to the benefits of the modern social contract. Whiteness in this context was a privileged identity, and an anxious one. Confronted with neighborhood integration in the 1920s, white Detroiters feared the loss of their racial privileges and responded with a brutal sense of entitlement.

Detroit's neighborhood violence of 1925 included the well-known mob attack at Dr. Ossian and Gladys Sweet's east side house (Figure 7.1). The Sweets, affluent African Americans, had moved into an all-white neighborhood, and the rioters outside of their house sought to force them to leave. A white rioter was shot, and the besieged Black family was acquitted of murder in what Reynolds Farley has called the "nation's foremost civil rights trial of the 1920s."[3] This chapter revisits the summer of 1925 to consider another riot—this one perpetrated against a Black working-class household. It puts particular focus on the "architecture" of that violence: the ways that the attack, and the household's response, were performed through the physical space of a modern house and neighborhood. As the "storm" unfolded, perpetrators used the physical environment as a tool for committing violence, and the victims resisted in and through those same spaces, each making claims about modern housing and race, about who was entitled to participate fully in the city's modern social contract

Prehistory: Chicago's Red Summer

Detroit's neighborhood violence was part of a nationwide rise in white supremacist activity that followed World War I. As Black and white southerners moved northward, and populations shifted from rural to urban contexts, increased interracial competition for jobs and housing sparked deadly riots across the country in the Red Summer of 1919.[4] Thirty-eight people were killed in a week of rioting in Chicago—twenty-three Black and fifteen white—and more than five hundred were seriously wounded.[5] Thousands of U.S. soldiers ultimately quelled Chicago's violence.

Housing was central to the Chicago conflict. The movement of African American residents into formerly white enclaves, such as Hyde Park, was a major source of tension.[6] In response, white residents formed neighborhood associations, organized public protests, and undertook a campaign of threats, mob intimidation, and bombings. Whites, fearing neighborhood racial integration, set off at least twenty-six bombs, targeting the houses of newly arrived African Americans and the offices of the realtors who dared to serve them. These attacks, carried out in secret, created fear and extensive property damage and caused the death of a six-year-old girl.[7] The tragedies of 1919 were on the minds of Detroit officials six years later, when that city's residents took to the streets. Urging calm, but also revealing great uncertainty, Mayor John Smith released a statement advising that "the condition which faces Detroit is one which faced Washington, East Saint Louis, Chicago and other large cities" and adding, "The result in those cities was one which Detroit must avoid if possible."[8]

The "Value" of a Neighborhood

Detroit had already experienced instances of racial violence in 1917 and 1920, and Mayor Smith realized that rapid Black and white in-migration from the South, and continued segregated development, had made the city that much more explosive by 1925.⁹ The intervening years had only hardened white supremacist sentiment in the city, as the modern real estate industry promulgated a profoundly racist idea: that the presence of Black residents was a signal of neighborhood decline.¹⁰ As discussed in Chapter 5, developers and realtors introduced racially restrictive covenants as a property amenity, as insurance against feared racial integration, and they were legally enforceable through the 1920s and beyond, until the Supreme Court struck them down in the *Shelley v. Kraemer* decision in 1948. The backing of government and real estate agents gave perceived legitimacy to the idea that integration should be feared.

White workers' racist fears were exacerbated by their precarious social and economic position. For "new immigrants" from southern and eastern Europe, for example, whiteness and its privileges had only recently and provisionally been achieved in the early twentieth century. Detroit culture was still dominated by an Anglo Protestant elite, and mainstream newspaper articles persisted in distinguishing "Polaks" from whites.¹¹ In this context, anxieties about social and racial status could be fodder for real estate speculation. An investigator for the Associated Charities, Forrester Washington, interviewed Black and white real estate agents in 1920. He found that the majority of white agents believed the arrival of Black residents—or "invasion," as one put it—reduced the market value of nearby property from 25 percent to an absurd 100 percent. This idea, Washington noted, created the opportunity for unscrupulous real estate investors to "commercialize on race prejudice and fill the neighborhood with colored people who are made to pay higher down payments and higher rents than had previously been charged in the neighborhood."¹² As N. D. B. Connolly has written, the American real estate industry had much to gain in producing and reproducing housing segregation, as it "limited the mobility of consumers, thereby confining demand, manufacturing scarcity, and driving up prices on both sides of the color line."¹³

White renters, fearing a loss of social prestige, might leave a neighborhood undergoing integration, allowing the houses' owners to charge a higher rate to incoming Black renters. White homeowners, fearing the same and worried about a precipitous loss in their house's market value, might sell quickly, even at a loss.¹⁴ Once racial integration began, individual owners might rush to move and spark a panic sell-off in which many white neighbors would leave the area at increasing financial loss, selling, as one sociologist of the period observed, "because of hysteria and without regard to market value."¹⁵ Working-class homeowners leveraged beyond their means with multiple mortgages might be financially ruined by such depreciation.¹⁶

In 1925, however, in the city's newly built white neighborhoods, residents refused both integration and the prospect of leaving. Instead, they choose to violently "defend" the racial exclusivity of their neighborhoods. These residents formed "neighborhood improvement associations," which provided a forum for neighbors to act as a coracial group against perceived threats rather than as competitive individuals in a real estate market.[17] As one mid-century scholar of Detroit's neighborhood associations writes, these groups often worked to defend property values by "keep[ing] the neighborhood constantly stirred up against the inmigration of Negros," raising funds to take breakers of restrictive covenants to court and waging intimidation campaigns against those who crossed the color line.[18]

The Material Construction of Race

The physical condition of the city's neighborhoods reinforced what the sociologist Harold Black called the "circular logic" of the race-based depreciation concept.[19] By confining much of the fast-growing Black population to an aging district east of the city's downtown, Black Bottom, Detroit's white residents and realtors fulfilled their own belief that African Americans did not maintain their houses well. This stereotype did not account for the crowding and exploitative rents that Blacks faced in this district due to their forced crowding. It did not consider the advanced age of the structures available there or the expansion of factories and garages that also contributed to the degradation of housing in Black Bottom.[20] Neither did it acknowledge that Black Bottom and the adjacent Paradise Valley commercial district—despite their housing problems—were a diverse space of African American life and culture, where members of the city's Black elite lived and worked alongside those struggling with poverty and inadequate housing.[21]

The depreciation concept was supported not only through whites' outward perceptions but also through their self-perceptions. It emphasized the good care that many white families felt they took of their houses, without acknowledging how employers, reformers, housebuilders, lenders, and realtors all went out of their way to help them, providing access to new, often well-equipped bungalows and duplexes and the means to furnish them well. The Waterworks Park Improvement Association, for example, could call on the pride of white residents and a threatening other in rallying fearful neighbors to a "self-defense" meeting against racial integration in 1925. "Do you want to maintain the existing good health conditions and environment for your little children?" it asked.[22]

Figure 7.2. "Decadent Frame Cottage Now Part of the Negro Section."

Source: Jerome Thomas, "The City of Detroit: A Study in Urban Geography," (Ph.D. diss., University of Michigan, Ann Arbor, 1928), fig. 86a.

Blackness was constructed through the material conditions of ghetto housing in many cities. A federal report on "Negro Housing" released in 1932 found it was commonly believed that "deteriorated areas . . . are alone [African Americans'] by right of race," and members of this imagined Black monoculture were generally "happier in their own neighborhoods."[23] Even in academic culture, the explicit belief in a race-based hierarchy of human difference persisted into the 1930s, supported by scientific discourses such as eugenics.[24] Reflecting this belief, a University of Michigan geographer of the 1920s described Detroit's near-east side, including Black Bottom. He perceived unmodern material conditions and behavior and attributed them to "Negro" culture, without considering the effects of poverty and segregation (Figure 7.2). The extent and detail of his paternalistic, stereotypical descriptions bear quoting at length:

> The Negro problem in Detroit is of minor importance as long as those residents realize that they are to be restricted to a type area [*sic*] of their own. As long as they stay in this area it becomes typically Negro. The congestion and carefreeness of the population is evidenced by the ramshackle character of their buildings, by the multiplicity of their store types, by the picturesque gaudiness of their decorations and street attire, the teeming colorfulness of their street life, the lounging and lolling groups of all ages, sexes, and colors who bring to Detroit a landscape far different from that which existed in the same region, on the same streets, and veritably in the same buildings only a few short years ago.[25]

Like-minded Detroiters could not see Blacks' attempts to leave this crowded district as a relatable desire for the comforts of modern housing. Instead, they perceived African Americans' residential movements as a threatening desire to intermix socially with white people.

White Womanhood

The modern worker's house was designed in part to guard against unsanctioned sexual relationships. Toward this end, its private bedroom and bathroom walls, among other things, staged paternalistic control of women's social contacts. Reflecting this impulse, Ford Motor Company's Sociological Department agents spoke of the importance of separating walls, since without them, in a boardinghouse, for example, there was nothing to stop intercourse between "landladies" and their male boarders.[26] In 1925, the prospect of racial integration called up a related discourse on the male protection of white women, or "white womanhood," from feared interracial marriage with Black men. Living side by side in similar houses, white residents feared, Black and white neighbors might begin to meet as social equals. The greatest threat of intermarriage—as the sociologist Gunnar Myrdal noted in the 1940s—was that it would provide a "supreme indication" of social equality between two married people, undermining the interracially married white spouse's claims of racial superiority and, by extension, all whites' claims of superiority.[27]

Whites invoked a special sensitivity with regard to the bedroom in their rejection of neighborhood racial integration. A white man from Detroit's west side, for example, wrote in the 1940s that he believed in "the God-given equality of men," but he also believed in his and his white neighbors' God-given "right to choose the people we sleep with."[28] To "protect" white peoples' bedrooms, by extension, was to protect against interracial marriage. As a Ku Klux Klan (KKK) author of the 1920s explained, "The chastity of women [is] a sacred trust, and sanctity of the home . . . an inviolable obligation."[29] Another Klansman of the period conjured the fear of white sexual propriety violated—while attacking Catholicism—by imagining the encounter of Black parish priests with white Catholic women. The author asked, "What will be the effect upon our civilization and social status" if parishes became racially mixed? Dramatizing this threat, the author conjured the image of "negro priests sit[ting] in the confessional where white women must answer the most intimate and suggestive sex questions."[30] In truth, the author had little to fear: the historian John McGreevey has shown that Catholic parishes, including a cited example from the east side of Detroit, typically shared the KKK's desire to keep their churches racially segregated.[31]

The Klan in Detroit

The KKK grew rapidly in American cities in the 1920s—a major resurgence for an institution that had been in decline.[32] The urbanization of cities such as Detroit created a cultural space where Klan ideology thrived. In the 1920s, Detroit was charged with what the historian David Levine calls the "polyglot intensity" of its distinct and competitive identity groups, including many Catholics from southern and eastern Europe. By attacking papal authority and parochial schools, KKK thought leaders played on white Protestants' anxieties as they shared the shop floor and the city with "new immigrants."[33] The KKK articulated a doctrine of white supremacy and called for stronger legal defense of the residential color line.[34] For white workers who believed their economic and social gains were at stake, Klan discourse was affirming. It acknowledged their fears and created a forum to act in solidarity against perceived threats. The national leader of the KKK invited pros-

pects in this period to join the organization in "the sacred duty of protecting womanhood" and to become part of an organization that was "the soul of chivalry and virtue's impenetrable shield."[35]

The KKK also made tailored appeals to women and children in Detroit and elsewhere. The national leader of the organization's women's groups urged her audience to appreciate the protection that men were providing, keeping alcohol, gambling, and sexual impropriety away from their houses:

> The red in our national banner speaks in no uncertain way of manly blood that has been and will be shed for woman's protection. The white of our flag's folds cries out for unstained purity and virtue in manhood and womanhood, and bears silent testimony that the men of the nation would rise as one to protect the honor and chastity of our home-builders—our women.[36]

Recruiting intensively in Detroit, the Klan rolls in the city grew from three thousand in 1923 to twenty-two thousand eighteen months later, reaching a high of thirty-two thousand.[37]

Recruiters used spatial strategies in the design of their mass-initiation rallies. While drawing on Detroit's large pool of prospective members, the KKK held large gatherings in the fields outside the city, avoiding government and police interference and maintaining a sense of secrecy.[38] The city's automobiles made this possible by allowing thousands—carpooling, surely—to quickly converge on an obscure rural site, pass a makeshift checkpoint, and enter the ceremonial field (Figure 7.3). There, the altar and its pyrotechnics created a pseudo-religious sense of drama, invoking the solidarity of those gathered. In November 1923, 2,500 new members were initiated in a field west of Detroit, on Seven Mile Road, where an acetylene tank was arranged to feed fuel to a monumental cross made of pipe. When the organizers lit the device, "it blazed forth," as a KKK journalist reported, "and as its white light

Figure 7.3. Ku Klux Klan Labor Day event, 1925. The event was held near Pontiac, Michigan, thirty miles north of the Motor City. *Pipp's Weekly* noted that the crowd was "made up very largely of Klan members from Detroit." Emphasizing the fearsome strength of the organization, *Pipp's* added that the photograph "reveals only a part of the machines, only those within range of the camera from one point."

Source: "A Gathering of the Ku Klux Klan—And Its Political Significance," *Pipp's Weekly*, September 26, 1925, 12.

Figure 7.4. "Do you Want Klan Rule?"

Source: *Pipp's Weekly*, October 17, 1925.

penetrated the semidarkness a mighty cheer arose that seemed to fairly shake the earth."[39] Thereafter, "a hush fell over the crowd" as the assembled leaders began to speak the "oath of Americanism . . . in deep and solemn tones." The mass of assembled candidates repeated the words in unison.[40] At the height of the Detroit Klan's power, just before its favored mayoral candidate, Charles Bowles, was narrowly defeated in November 1924, the organization drew a broadly estimated crowd of twenty-five thousand to fifty thousand people to a Saturday evening rally in Dearborn Township, west of Detroit.[41]

The city's business elite did not welcome the rise of the Klan or the uncertainty created by racial violence, despite their role in constructing Detroit's segregated geography. Their Americanization classes and housing reform discourse had offered full citizenship and social prestige to white workers in modern houses while denying these things to African Americans. Fearing the phenomenal growth of the KKK, however, and the possibility that Bowles would come to power, the business magazine *Pipp's Weekly* focused a 1925 issue on the threat the Klan represented. It argued that Detroit's houses—far from being a cause of unrest—were actually a bulwark against political extremism and that Detroit, through its phenomenal growth, had attained a reputation for tolerance and neighborliness. It was known "as a progressive city, a home-loving, home-supporting city, because it has had citizens who have prided themselves in their homes, their families, and the general betterment of the community." This reputation—and, presumably, future business prospects—were at stake in the election. The magazine asked: "Do you want your city to be known the world over as a Klan city?" (Figure 7.4).[42] The article did not acknowledge that white supremacy was endemic to the city's "home-loving" neighborhoods. Detroit's cohort of potentially violent racists was much larger and more diverse than the KKK itself, even as the semisecret organization provided a conspicuous symbol of a much broader problem.

Detroit Neighborhoods in Crisis

Prior to the infamous attack at the Sweet residence, several other Black households had been assaulted in the summer of 1925.[43] The earliest and least studied attack of that summer, at the Mathis residence, can shed new light on neighborhood racial violence. Fleta Mathis, who survived the attack, recorded her memories of the incident in the community-based publication *Remembering Detroit's Old Westside* (1997), detailing the material and spatial practices that gave meaning to neighborhood violence and its resistance.[44]

The newly developed Westside African American neighborhood discussed in Chapter 6 expanded during the 1920s. It was the pride of the city's Black elite and reformers, a place where professionals and prosperous workers lived, negotiating a culture of domestic pride. Reform-minded Black women created the Entre Nous club in the area, for example, to promote a culture of Black domestic respectability with cleanup campaigns and housekeeping awards and by pressuring residents whose houses did not meet standards.[45] At the same time, the social identities and behavior of the expanding Westside's residents were diverse. Fleta and Aldine Mathis, recent migrants from Georgia, did not keep the socially preferred nuclear family household. Rather, they shared their lower duplex flat with another man and woman, their small baby, and that man's brother. Aldine worked in a furniture store, and the two other men worked in automobile factories. This made it easier to pay the rent and provided supportive friendships within the household. Fleta, looking back, called it Aldine's and her own "first venture at housekeeping."[46]

The Mathises had participated in the Westside neighborhood's expansion by moving into their duplex flat. It was located on Northfield

Figure 7.5. The Northfield Street duplex where Fleta and Aldine Mathis moved with three others in 1925, breaking a west side color line. In the 1920s, neighboring houses were located on each side of the duplex, but they apparently had been demolished by the time this undated photograph was taken.

Source: WestSiders, *Remembering Detroit's Old Westside, 1920–1950: A Pictorial History of the WestSiders* (Detroit: WestSiders, 1997), 103.

Street and required crossing into an all-white area adjacent to the Black-dominated Westside. Their arrival caused alarm among white neighbors, and the white family in the flat above them quickly moved out (Figure 7.5).[47] Within days, a group of white neighbors assembled to plan a response to the Mathises' presence. The group's efforts were supported by the KKK—Fleta recalls that the group sent threatening letters to her new home—and some neighbors may well have been members.[48] Detroit's Mayor John Smith, who at the time was running for reelection against the Klan-endorsed Bowles, claimed that the organization's members had gone "from house to house . . . where resentment is strongest against members of the Negro race[,] and have whispered their criminal propaganda."[49] Klan members and sympathizers surely did live in the vicinity of the Mathises' new residence. Their favored candidate, Bowles, enjoyed strong support on Detroit's west side and did best in neighborhoods east of Grand River, just a mile from the Mathises' flat.[50] The mayor, as *Pipp's Weekly* had, preferred to blame neighborhood unrest on the KKK rather than acknowledge Detroit's broader problem of white supremacist sentiment.

Fear of racial integration motivated white residents to create "defense" coalitions, uniting neighbors who otherwise were political adversaries. American-born Protestants were likely to support Bowles's anti-vice and anti-parochial schools positions at the polls, while Smith's winning coalition of immigrant Catholics and Jews joined with African Americans in opposing Bowles at the ballot box. Yet a southern-born white Protestant worker and a European-born Catholic worker were more alike than different in an important way: both, having achieved precarious social advancement in modern neighborhoods, likely believed that their gains depended on segregation from African Americans.[51] The "close proximity to oppression" that conditionally white immigrants still felt, as David Roediger argues, helped to motivate their opposition to residential integration even as they partnered with Black workers in the electoral realm.[52] Reflecting on the attack at the Sweets' residence, one author in the 1920s found irony in the fact that the neighborhood's residents, most of whom had "Polish, Swedish and German sounding names," felt so entitled to racial superiority that they joined the fight against integration.[53] "The bitterest man," he added, "was an Assyrian."[54] In the 1930 census district surrounding the Mathises' duplex, there were three times as many European immigrants and their children as there were whites of American parentage.[55] The composition of the mob that attacked the Mathises is unknown, but these demographics suggest that it was a diverse white assemblage with a shared interest in housing segregation.

Violence and the Material Negotiation of Race

Efforts to remove the Mathises were initially discrete. Overt violence, even in the name of "defense," would surely undermine the perceived security of the neighborhood in the eyes of residents and the broader real estate market, even if the perpetrators succeeded in restoring segregation. Given this, the defenders' first attempts to intimidate the Mathises took the form of inconspicuous provocations: the KKK sent threatening letters, and a group knocked on the front door. The house call was made during the day, Fleta believes, because the group wanted to avoid directly confronting the men—who presumably would be away at work—but, "to their surprise," one of the men was home.[56] The visitors nonetheless communicated their demand. They did not require immediate action but assured Fleta and her housemate that if they did not move out by the end of the month, "there would be trouble."[57] Provoked by the threat, Fleta's autoworker housemate, who was large in stature, *"told them off."* Having delivered their threat, the white neighbors retreated immediately.[58] The Mathises received other warnings in subsequent days, and Fleta's husband, Aldine, reported them to the police.[59]

The Mathis household paid the next month's rent in defiance of the neighborhood "defenders," a move that provoked new intimidation tactics that overtly and strategically breached domestic conventions. Dropping the pretense of respect for the Mathises' duplex that the mailed and personally delivered threats reflected, the defenders began to vandalize the duplex when no one was home. Fleta does not describe the vandalism in her account, but whether it consisted of broken windows, surfaces marked with paint, or thrown eggs, the tactic was a powerful one. Vandalism punished the Mathis household with costly repairs, paid in cash and in time spent cleaning or filing police reports, and it did a great deal of cultural work: conspicuous damage to the two-flat set it apart from the field of closely spaced bungalows and duplexes surrounding it, a move that might humiliate the house's residents. One vandalized house among many well-tended neighboring houses visually reinforced the Mathis household's otherness from the neighborhood while at the same time highlighting a seeming unity among the many unmolested "white houses" surrounding them.[60]

When vandalism failed to remove the Mathis household, the group assailing them once more changed tactics and mounted an overwhelming show of force. A white mob estimated at five thousand people—several times larger than the mob that would later attack the Sweet residence—surrounded the Mathises' duplex in the evening of April 9. A friend happened to be visiting that evening, traveling on foot, and warned that "many folks were gathering" on the streets nearby.[61] The process of mob building is not entirely clear, but it is likely that a group of core instigators—perhaps including those responsible for the earlier letters, house calls, and vandalism—called local residents from their houses and set in motion an intensifying spectacle that drew others outside. An evening attack was likely planned to ensure that the victims, and the maximum number of perpetrators, would be home from dayshift work.

Converging on the duplex and surrounding it, the mob performed a fearsome inversion of the very domestic ideals they were gathered to "defend." The house—embodying secure family independence and social acceptance within the neighborhood—was transformed by the surrounding mob into an isolated, vulnerable place from which the Mathises and their housemates could not escape. The many windows of the modern duplex—a pleasure in daily life similarly inverted—became a terrible liability, shattering one after another as the mob threw stones and bottles. The *Detroit Free Press* reported that the crowd "managed to smash every window in the Mathis dwelling and had threatened to set fire to the house," all before the police arrived in force.[62] It is a testament to the household's fear and desperation that Aldine and his visiting friend took up firearms as the violence began.[63] In the American South, the lynch mob remained a serious threat in the 1920s, as Reynolds Farley notes, and the Mathises had no way of knowing how far the mob would go.[64] Apparent warning shots were fired early in the assault, with no injuries, though the newspaper could not confirm whether they were fired from the crowd or from within the Mathises' flat.

In June and July, similar mob attacks were carried out nearby. North of Tireman Avenue, a crowd of four thousand descended on the house of the African American waiter John Fletcher and his family and boarders, and another mob of five thousand attacked the Black physician Alexander Turner's house.[65] In each of these attacks, the instigators appear to have coordinated their efforts with groups outside of the immediate neighborhood. Recorded details suggest that the crowds were bolstered by participants who arrived by automobile to take part in the violence. The author Marcet Haldeman-Julius interviewed Ossian Sweet during his trial and described the gathering crowd around the Sweets' house this way:

> Already the schoolyard was full! So was the space around the grocery store! People were in the alley, on the porches of the two-flat houses opposite! Cars were coming and parking—two deep.[66]

In the Motor City, mob violence was reflected in masses of automobiles. As the crowd gathered near the Sweet residence, a police lieutenant reported, traffic was thick with approaching cars that did not belong in the neighborhood, forcing police to divert vehicles off Garland Avenue.[67] As the mob surrounding the Mathises' duplex formed, police similarly worked to direct traffic to gain control of the situation.[68] While Turner's house was under attack, that same summer, traffic was "hopelessly stalled" on Detroit's major northwestern artery, Grand River Avenue.[69]

The reported size of Detroit's neighborhood mobs is startling. In the context of the Mathis house for example, a crowd of five thousand would be comparable to the entire population of every house and flat in sixteen blocks.[70] Standing in perfect rows, three feet on center, this number of participants could completely fill Northfield Avenue for the entire length of the Mathises' block, with hundreds left over and spilling into the adjacent roads.[71] In actuality, the mobs of the summer of 1925 dispersed over larger areas, filling nearby porches, streets, alleys, and schoolyards. While a core of assailants surrounded the target house—throwing stones and shouting threats—many other participants remained some distance from the riot's center. The *Detroit Free Press* described these more passive participants in the Mathis incident as an

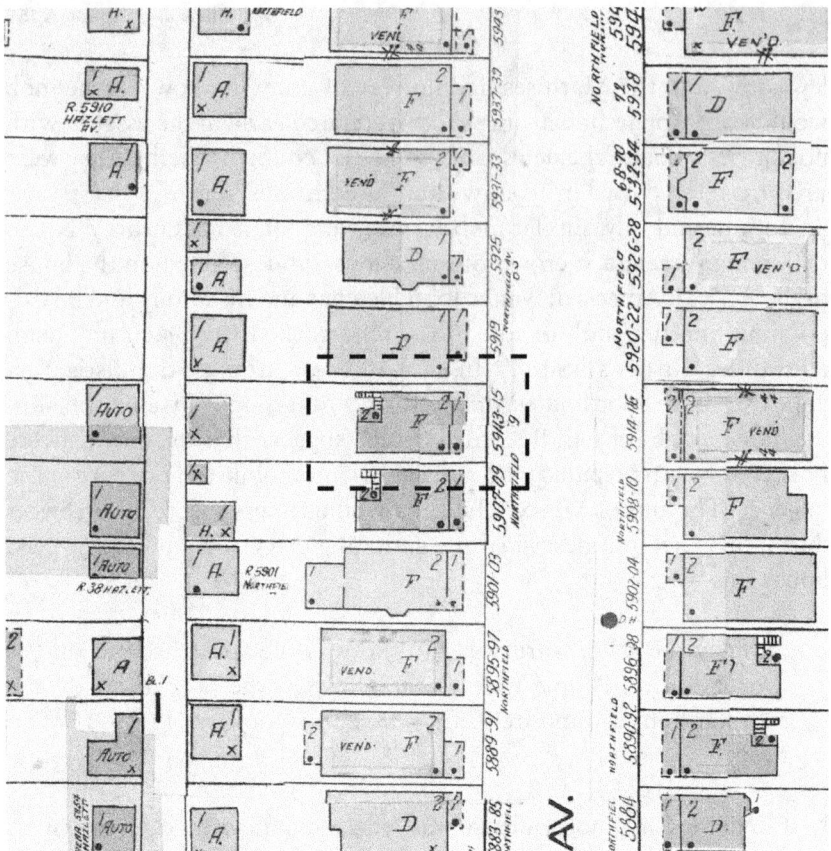

Figure 7.6. Map of Northfield Avenue illustrating the close spacing of the houses, which gave the narrow spaces between them a sense of privacy. The assailants of Fleta, Suzie, and Belle lurked in one of these spaces before throwing their bricks. The Mathises' duplex at 5915 Northfield Avenue is identified with a dashed outline.

Source: Sanborn Map Company, *Insurance Maps of Detroit, Michigan*, vol. 6, sheet 11, 1910–January 1951, Library of Congress, Washington, DC, http://hdl.loc.gov/loc.gmd/g4114dm.g03985195106.

"orderly" crowd, "in a naturally curious mood," papering over their complicity in the violence.[72]

In the days following the attack, the Mathises and their housemates began to rebuild. Despite being renters, and despite the fact that their flat's windows had been broken by others, they took it upon themselves to have the windows reglazed. In this way they restored, in an act of resistance, the dignity of their house.[73] The cost of these repairs was surely daunting, but Fleta recalls that the household's Baptist church donated funds in support of their cause. The fight for the Northfield duplex's meaning was not over, however, and the house's conventions of privacy and security would be breached one more time.

Days after the mob attack, Fleta and her female housemate Suzie lay together in one of the house's bedrooms, with Suzie's infant daughter, Belle. In keeping with the standard duplex type, this bedroom was tucked behind the street-facing living room and stairwell and its windows opened onto the narrow space between houses (Figure 7.6). Shielded from the street view, these bedrooms reflected the ideal of the modern household's privacy.[74] When assailants entered the narrow yard between the Mathises' flat and the house next door, they surely understood the charged meaning of their presence. Fleta recalls that the infant began to cry and that suddenly—perhaps having heard her—the lurkers outside threw two bricks through the bedroom window. The bricks and shards of glass landed on the bed where Fleta, Suzie, and Belle lay. The mother and infant rushed to the safety of a windowless corner of the dining room, and Fleta picked up a gun. She fired twice through the bedroom window, and the bullets struck the house next door, with no injuries. Fleta was arrested briefly but not prosecuted.[75] Incredibly, the Mathises continued to persevere in the house. They were not removed until their landlord sold the duplex to a new owner, who was opposed to their presence and promptly discontinued their rental contract.[76]

Conclusion

In the 1920s, Detroit's rapid growth was accompanied by a spike in white supremacist organizing. Through so-called neighborhood improvement associations and the KKK, white workers claimed many of the city's modern neighborhoods as their own by right of race. Their views were emboldened by the support of employers, government, and property developers who helped to normalize and defend housing segregation. Real estate agents' on-the-ground efforts put segregation into practice, producing profit from white workers' fear of integration and from Black workers' desperate need for housing. In this context, white supremacists called on gendered notions of the well-kept modern house and of domestic privacy in their construction of whiteness and their imagination of a threatening other: Blackness, associated with the city's crowded, antiquated core.

When the Mathises moved to Northfield Avenue, their white neighbors were alarmed and felt entitled to respond with threats, vandalism, and violence to restore their sense of superiority. At once attempting to terrify the Mathises and to reinforce white solidarity, these neighbors inverted the very domestic ideals they held dear, such as the care and maintenance of the house and the privacy of the bedroom, in a series of violent attacks. At least for a time, in another turn of material meaning, the Mathises reasserted their dignity in an act of domestic care, repairing windows that the mob had broken. What white workers did not appear to see, while "defending" their neighborhoods against the perceived threats of integration, was that a very real threat to their domestic security loomed just on the horizon. Despite the assurances of boosters and the city's real estate industry, Detroit's extraordinary economic growth could not go on indefinitely. Black and white workers alike were vulnerable to a downturn, to say nothing of a crash.

8

SOCIAL CONTRACT IN CRISIS

Welfare, Eviction, and Activism in the Depression

> Their Home! Their Home! They had lost it! Grief, despair, rage overwhelmed him . . . [at] the sight of strange people living in his house, hanging their curtains in his windows, staring at him with hostile eyes!
>
> Only think what he had suffered for that house—what miseries they had all suffered for it—the price they had paid for it!
>
> —Jurgis Rudkus, in Upton Sinclair, *The Jungle*

Upton Sinclair's protagonists, the Rudkus family, lost their cottage near the Chicago stockyards when brutal misfortune left them unable to make their payments on a land contract. Their loss of shelter was an acute concern, but the deeper injury the family felt was the loss of years of difficult work and years of payments on the land contract, only to be left empty-handed. This fictional scene illustrated a real vulnerability in urban working-class life at the start of the twentieth century—one that grew as workers rented and bought larger and better-equipped houses in the 1910s and 1920s, becoming more dependent on industrial employment and rising house values. Powerful employers and government agencies had idealized these modern houses, and workers had embraced them, forming an implicit social contract in which hard work would be rewarded with domestic security and upward mobility.

Mass unemployment tested this contract in the early 1930s, as the threat of widespread eviction and foreclosure provoked working-class activism and a major political realignment. Sinclair joined in this struggle. In 1937 he published another novel reflecting on the anxieties of the worker's house: *The Flivver King*. Named for Henry Ford and the Model T, popularly known as the "flivver," the book was published by the emerging United Automobile Workers (UAW) union, which printed

200,000 copies for its members. With the recent success of its "sit-down" strikes against General Motors in Flint, the UAW was turning its sights on the Ford Motor Company, and the novel illustrated what was at stake in the fight for greater working-class political power. It follows the rise of Abner Shutt as he works his way up to become a subforeman at the Ford Motor Company and as his family leverages credit to buy a modern six-room house.

The Shutts abide by the new social contract and reap rewards. At home, after a day's work, Abner happily tends a garden of onions and turnips. He watches his children grow in security and thinks: "Mr. Ford was right, as usual; it was a good thing to own your own home."[1] Yet in Sinclair's story, and in real American cities, the gains of the 1910s and 1920s came under threat in the global Depression, when mass layoffs raised the threat of an eviction and foreclosure crisis in the early 1930s. Many exhausted their savings, defaulting on debts accrued in the boom years of the 1920s. The modern social contract was in crisis, but not destroyed. Instead, its terms became the subject of intensive struggle.

City government and employers developed welfare programs, seeking to relieve growing fear and anger. Workers, emboldened by communist political organizers, pressed their own demands. Without income, as Sinclair illustrated, the modern house could be a fearsome place. The Shutts became so cash poor in the Depression that even though they owned their house, they lacked the capital to make tax payments on it. They abandoned the ideal of privacy, renting out all but two rooms of their house to boarders and taking in their evicted adult children. We might imagine that some of the Shutts' boarders were workers who had been evicted from their own houses for nonpayment of rent. The Shutt family learned to live in tight quarters and began pawning their possessions, at great loss.[2] "What were they supposed to do with that home," Abner wondered. "Sit in it and freeze to death, or starve, or both? They couldn't sell [the house] for anything."[3]

The economic crisis pressed a question that had been deferred in the prosperity of the 1920s: who was responsible for securing the modern social contract now that its debts were being called? Frank Murphy, a liberal Democrat elected mayor of Detroit in 1930, promised city aid. With the support of labor, European immigrants, and the National Association for the Advancement of Colored People, he framed support for the unemployed not as charity but as a right of Detroit citizens and a responsibility of government.[4] He, and the city's workers, looked to employers to take a greater role in resolving the crisis, with little success.

Though industrial corporations provided some aid, they largely avoided responsibility for their laid-off employees' domestic security. Though these negotiations took place in the context of a crisis, it was one that was not entirely unexpected. Even as Detroit's real estate boosters had predicted endless growth in the 1920s, critical observers had begun to warn of trouble ahead.

Ramsay Muir, a British author and liberal politician, had criticized Detroit's industrial culture in his sardonically titled *America the Golden* of 1927. He framed the Motor City, with its extremes of rapid economic growth and anti-union corporate power, as the exemplar of a new American doctrine of progress: "Detroitism." It was not only "the home of mass-production, of very high wages and colossal profits," but also a site of "lavish spending and reckless installment-buying," heading for trouble.[5] The automobile industry appeared to be slowing, and history had shown that Detroit's employers preferred to "waste men rather than materials," by hiring and firing workers as consumer demand rose and fell, to avoid producing any surplus.[6] "Cocksure," just as Muir had described them, the city's business leaders deflected the criticism. They seized on his term and redefined it, removing any hint of class conflict. Writing in the business newspaper *Pipp's Weekly*, they claimed that the "Detroitism" of international renown was a doctrine of upward mobility and security for workers "to the end that the average man, woman, and child may be better fed, better housed, better educated, better protected in health and morals, with more of the comforts and pleasures of life, and have enough left for old age."[7] The innocence of *Pipp's* Detroitism, however, and of the 1920s social contract that it reflected could not survive mass unemployment.

By October 1930, about eighty thousand Detroit workers had registered as unemployed through city relief agencies, while those who managed to retain employment faced deep cuts in pay and work days.[8] A supervisor in the Crankshaft Department at Ford's Rouge Plant recalled that most employees' wages were cut back from $7 to $4 per hour during the Depression. "We worked three days a week one week, and the next week we'd work two days a week. We did that for some time," he explained, "trying to spread the work out."[9] With construction at a standstill, unemployment in the building trades was widespread. Job loss and reduced wages created the risk that workers would cease to meet their rent obligations and default on debts, from installment-purchased furniture and phonographs to mortgages and land contracts. In Detroit and nationwide, the Depression drove what the economist Miles Colean, writing in the 1940s, called "the greatest wave of urban home foreclosures in our history."[10] Critics lambasted the consumer culture of the preceding decades, arguing that its celebration of "homeownership" had obscured the fact that most "owners" were in fact "debtors"—they were owners of mortgages, not of houses.[11]

Detroit's real estate market collapsed in the Depression, and major banks, heavily invested in real estate and mortgages, failed. The average house dropped to 60 percent of its original value, putting many owners "under water" on their loans.[12] In 1933, when the federal government created the Home Owners Loan Corporation (HOLC) to stabilize the market, Michigan was the second largest recipient of rescue loans for homeowners facing foreclosure—aid extended to the owners of 31 percent of all mortgaged, nonfarm, owner-occupied dwellings in the state.[13] Older workers with debts carried an especially difficult burden in the crisis. They, facing foreclosure, experienced a cruel reversal of the ideal of security in homeownership. Research on Detroit homeowners in default found that half of the applicants for HOLC rescue loans were fifty or older, as older workers were more likely to face unemployment. "Firms requiring high-speed work, and especially those with pension plans," the researcher noted, "have quite well-recognized policies of employing only younger men." Since older workers were unlikely to find well-paid work again when the factories reopened, many would ultimately lose their houses, and principal investments, despite HOLC help, unless they had working-age children to contribute to their family economies.[14]

Mayor Murphy understood that the threat of eviction and foreclosure, and the cold and hunger that many Detroiters were experiencing, threatened the city's social stability. He worked aggressively, in the absence of support from the federal government, to sustain the domestic security of the unemployed through local initiatives. Murphy's Unemployment Committee tailored its programs to provide relief for unemployed workers with houses and families. These workers, whose social status had risen sharply in the 1910s and 1920s, were more than individual citizens in need. They were central to the Motor City's identity and to America's identity as a land of working-class prosperity. As eviction notices arrived, with installment-plan furniture repossessed and pantries and coal stores emptied, Detroit's fundamental premise was thrown into question. Alarmed, the committee extended legal aid to families to forestall eviction. It worked with landlords and mortgage holders and, by the end of 1930, claimed to have postponed eight hundred evictions and hundreds of foreclosures. The nationwide housing crisis might have been considerably worse, but many landlords forgave unpaid rent in the Depression, either out of charity or pragmatic acceptance that rent-paying tenants could not be found.[15]

Detroit's unemployed workers registered themselves with city government to request relief. In turn, the city sent caseworkers to interpret the worthiness and needs of each household and began to take up responsibilities and social authority once held by wage-paying employers. Giving preference to workers with families, the city extended grocery vouchers, rent and utility assistance, free hospitalization, and job placement.[16] For those who had accepted the intrusive visits of Ford investigators years earlier, receiving city investigators would have been a familiar indignity. Yet in both 1914 and 1930, the economic benefits of compliance for most outweighed the humiliation of having one's private life scrutinized, and they opened their doors.

In addition to legal aid and welfare assistance, the city coordinated an employment program to direct what meager jobs were available toward the workers with the largest families. The Unemployment Committee's jobs bureau asked all city employers to coordinate their hiring through city government, which would direct jobs to workers—both men and women, white collar and blue—based on their number of dependents. As the *Detroit News* explained, "Men with seven or more dependents are being given first call. There are about 3,500 in this group. Men with six dependents will be called next, and so on."[17]

With so many prospective workers and so few jobs at hand, the committee created work for some unemployed workers by providing apples and bags of sand to sell. The city worked to ensure that even such modest efforts were targeted at those it considered most worthy. Learning that unauthorized apples and sand were being sold outside the auspices of its program, the committee urged buyers to demand that sellers show their city-provided credentials. "Our men are chosen because they are in hard straits and have large families," explained the secretary of creative employment.[18] Any sand would make one's sidewalk less slippery in winter, but only a city-sponsored seller was ensured to be "a worthy man who is out of work," who would "put every cent they earn back into circulation . . . , buy[ing] food, clothing and other necessities for their families."[19] City-led relief efforts proved expensive. In 1930–1931, Detroit's per capita relief spending was twice the national average, surpassed only by Boston among major American cities.[20] Defending his policies, Murphy argued that "welfare work has minimized radicalism," adding, "Detroit would have been on fire without relief."[21]

Critics of welfare treated single workers with particular scorn in their efforts to undermine Murphy's program. The business newspaper

Detroit Saturday Night argued that many in the unmarried cohort were "bums" from out of town, taking advantage of local resources, and not long-term Detroit workers. Many, it charged, were not legitimately unemployed, just unwilling to work.[22] Despite this opposition, Murphy urged that the city fund lodging houses for those who were unemployed and not married, given the preference that married workers were receiving in rehiring and relief spending.[23] He framed single unemployed workers as a party to the same besieged social contract as their married peers. They were "self-respecting, sensitive men, willing to do some kind of work but unable to find it . . . ; [an] entirely new type of man."[24] This new sensitivity, for single and married workers alike, had been built over fifteen years of rising working-class standards of living, followed by the crash. The city ultimately did pay private lodging houses to room the unemployed. General Motors and Studebaker contributed, as well, donating the use of idle factory buildings, where the displaced slept on army cots.[25]

Even as workers accepted welfare to survive, the city's Depression-era culture continued to celebrate the pride of independence. If one had to ask for help, it should be done only with great pain. In 1930, the *Detroit News* featured just such a figure in Joe Vandervoort. An autoworker, married father of one and a homeowner, he had been unemployed for a year when the paper discovered him. Months behind on house payments, the Dutch immigrant's family was ineligible for city welfare because their house was located just north of Detroit. Vandervoort stood conspicuously along Washington Boulevard in the fall of 1930, in Detroit's central business district, holding a placard that read, "Who will help me get a job? I do not want charity" (Figure 8.1).[26] The *News* feature celebrated Vandervoort's pride and independence. It dramatized his psychological pain at asking for help, noting that he could not bring himself to display the placard until his third trip down to the boulevard. He finally did so "with tear-filled eyes . . . with his heart, as he explained in his own words, 'shriveling up inside him.'"[27]

Other workers, finding no room or refusing the paternalism of the municipal lodging houses, faced homelessness. Thousands took shelter in outdoor encampments in Depression-era Detroit, though a turn of bitterly cold weather might drive some back into the shelters.[28] Several hundred created a conspicuous settlement in the city center's Grand Circus Park, while others settled in outer districts.[29] In the winter of 1932, the *Detroit Free Press* described a "community of tin and tarpaper shacks" at a dump site on Detroit's west side, where the Springwells neighborhood met the Michigan Central rail yards.[30] Such "Hoover-

Figure 8.1. An unemployed autoworker pleads for work, but not charity, in 1930.
Source: *Detroit News* photograph, Archives of Labor and Urban Affairs, Walter P. Reuther Library, Wayne State University, Detroit.

villes," named for the president at the time of the economic collapse, emerged in many U.S. cities in this period. In southwestern Detroit, the residents of these settlements collected scrap metal and rags, which they could sell for ten or fifteen cents per day. Even in this provisional setting, workers reproduced the segregated conditions of the formal city they had left behind, establishing "Negroes' shacks in one cluster and the whites' in another."[31] The encampment was short-lived. In winter, zero-degree temperatures drove away most, and the fifty residents who remained in this unsanctioned space received no sympathy from law enforcement, who, following reports that residents had stolen coal, "routed" the group from the site four days before Christmas, putting their shelters to the torch.[32]

Work in the Garden

To protect pride in work and generate some food for the unemployed, Murphy's administration created a subsistence gardening program. Those it found worthy and willing to work under supervision would be given the means to grow their own produce—seeds, tools, and land.

Patterned after the city's gardening program in the 1893 economic crisis, Murphy's "Thrift Gardens" of the early 1930s aimed to preserve the "work habits" of the unemployed.[33] Gardens required labor of their beneficiaries, making them more ideologically palatable to opponents of direct welfare. They were also relatively inexpensive to administer. Powerful private-sector institutions embraced gardening, including the Detroit Real Estate Board, whose members lent land for cultivation, and the Detroit Board of Commerce, whose representative helped to plan a fundraiser for the project. The Ford Motor Company developed its own parallel gardens program on company-owned land.[34] The "privilege" of cultivating a garden, Murphy argued, could restore workers' threatened identities and provide a hedge against unrest, reducing "the psychological effect of idleness," which he saw as "dangerous to the safety and morale of our country."[35]

Unemployed workers could participate in the program by growing food on their own residential lots, on nearby vacant lots, or in one of twenty-seven city-managed garden sites (Figure 8.2). The city gardens were regulated and supervised according to an exacting set of rules and prescriptions that replicated the demands of formal employment. One had to apply and have one's need assessed to be given a forty-by-one-hundred-foot space at one of the city's gardens. Applicants signed a pledge to consume and not resell their produce. They agreed "to plant their gardens according to prescribed diagrams, to keep them in good condition, free from weeds; to keep a record of the amount harvested and to respect the rights of neighboring gardeners."[36] The program served more than 1,600 home gardens and 2,700 city garden plots in 1931 and was extended for another year, "with unemployment conditions seemingly no better [at year's end] than they were in the spring."[37]

Field overseers walked the Thrift Gardens from "7 A.M. until 7 or 8 P.M.," providing advice and instructions to gardeners. The program's "Model Layout" prescribed thirty-two rows of staple foods such as corn, beans, and carrots, and allowed eight rows for the "gardener to plant what he chooses" (Figure 8.3).[38] These rules, as one overseer in the southwestern neighborhood of Delray found, were difficult to enforce. Oversight created tension, as gardeners with diverse tastes and cultural affiliations confronted the generic, thrift-oriented model. One overseer, approached by the *Detroit News* while in the in the midst of a debate with gardeners, explained:

> Our gardeners come from different parts of the globe. The majority were raised on farms and have definite ideas about garden-

Figure 8.2. Children and adults gather at a Thrift Garden well, ca. 1931.
Source: Detroit Historical Museum.

ing which they brought from the old country. . . . We had to make some deviations from the blue prints of the model garden supplied to us by agricultural experts to suit racial tastes. Yes, we are raising chili beans and kapusta [cabbage] and petrezselyem [parsley]. And we will raise enough paprika to satisfy all the needs of the Hungarians in Delray.[39]

In this way, unemployed workers found agency and meaning in the gardens. In Delray, the *News* reported, many even "smiled good naturedly, looked with love upon their garden plots and were optimistic about the future."[40] Some of those interviewed by the *News*, however, faced bleak economic prospects. One fifty-eight-year-old man, two years unemployed, had "a wife and four children to support," and another, sixty-five and recently laid off from the Department of Public Works, would face age discrimination in any future attempt to enter the workforce. Despite their diligent labor—in the industries of the 1920s and the Thrift Garden of the early 1930s—they would likely struggle to resume rent or mortgage payments when the crisis receded. Gardens

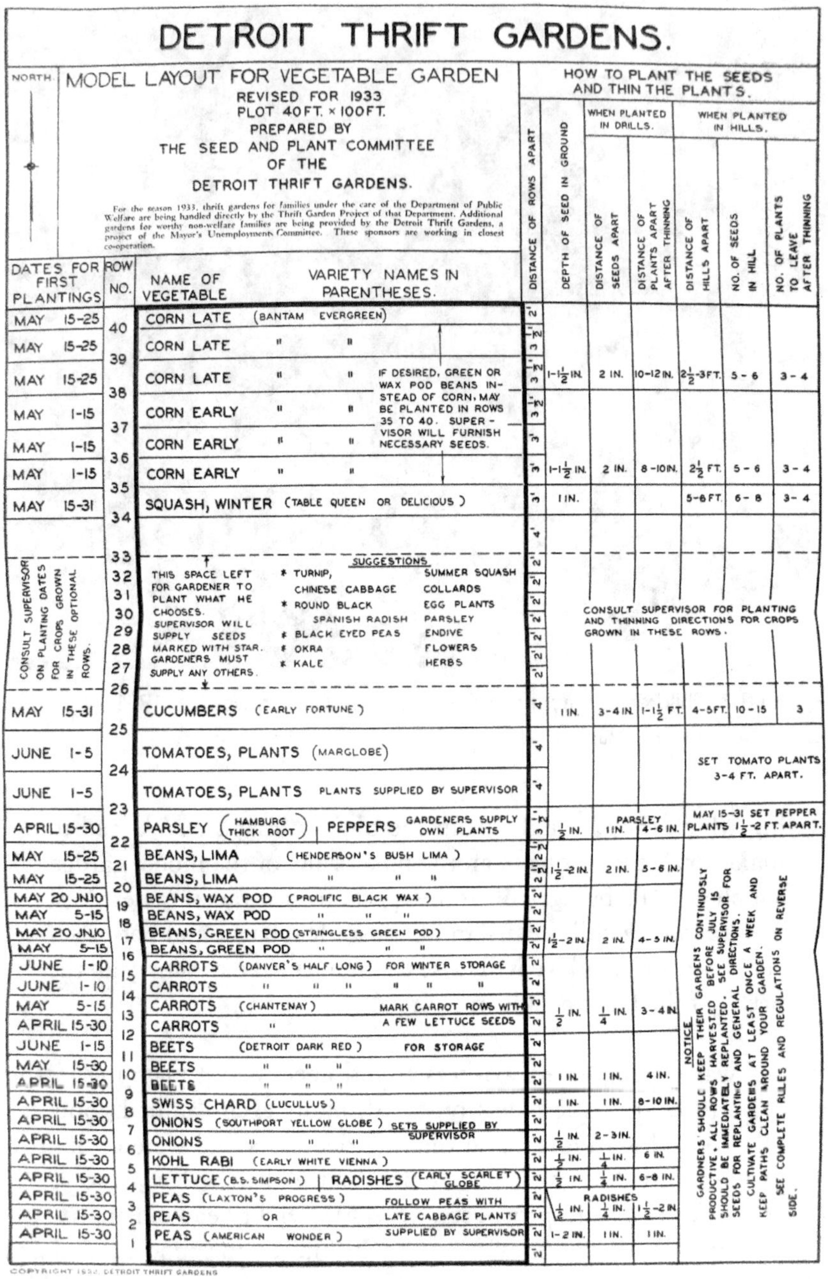

DETROIT THRIFT GARDENS.

NORTH.

MODEL LAYOUT FOR VEGETABLE GARDEN

REVISED FOR 1933
PLOT 40 FT. × 100 FT.
PREPARED BY
THE SEED AND PLANT COMMITTEE
OF THE
DETROIT THRIFT GARDENS.

For the season 1933, thrift gardens for families under the care of the Department of Public Welfare are being handled directly by the Thrift Garden Project of that Department. Additional gardens for worthy non-welfare families are being provided by the Detroit Thrift Gardens, a project of the Mayor's Unemployment Committee. These sponsors are working in closest co-operation.

HOW TO PLANT THE SEEDS AND THIN THE PLANTS.

DATES FOR FIRST PLANTINGS	ROW NO.	NAME OF VEGETABLE (VARIETY NAMES IN PARENTHESES.)	DISTANCE OF ROWS APART	DEPTH OF SEED IN GROUND	WHEN PLANTED IN DRILLS: DISTANCE OF SEEDS APART	WHEN PLANTED IN DRILLS: DISTANCE OF PLANTS APART AFTER THINNING	WHEN PLANTED IN HILLS: DISTANCE OF HILLS APART	WHEN PLANTED IN HILLS: NO. OF SEEDS IN HILL	WHEN PLANTED IN HILLS: NO. OF PLANTS TO LEAVE AFTER THINNING
MAY 15-25	40	CORN LATE (BANTAM EVERGREEN)	2'						
MAY 15-25	39	CORN LATE " "	3½'						
MAY 15-25	38	CORN LATE " "	3½'	1-1½ IN.	2 IN.	10-12 IN.	2½-3 FT.	5 - 6	3 - 4
MAY 1-15	37	CORN EARLY " "	3½'						
MAY 1-15	36	CORN EARLY " "	3'						
MAY 1-15	35	CORN EARLY " "	3'	1-1½ IN.	2 IN.	8 -10 IN.	2½ FT.	5 - 6	3 - 4
MAY 15-31	34	SQUASH, WINTER (TABLE QUEEN OR DELICIOUS)	3'	1 IN.			5-6 FT.	6 - 8	3 - 4
			4'						
CONSULT SUPERVISOR ON PLANTING DATES FOR CROPS GROWN IN THESE OPTIONAL ROWS.	33–26	SUGGESTIONS (see below)	2' (each row)	CONSULT SUPERVISOR FOR PLANTING AND THINNING DIRECTIONS FOR CROPS GROWN IN THESE ROWS.					
MAY 15-31	25	CUCUMBERS (EARLY FORTUNE)	4'	1 IN.	3-4 IN.	1-1½ FT.	4-5 FT.	10 - 15	3
JUNE 1-5	24	TOMATOES, PLANTS (MARGLOBE)	4'				SET TOMATO PLANTS 3-4 FT. APART.		
JUNE 1-5	23	TOMATOES, PLANTS — PLANTS SUPPLIED BY SUPERVISOR	4'						
APRIL 15-30	22	PARSLEY (HAMBURG THICK ROOT) | PEPPERS — GARDENERS SUPPLY OWN PLANTS	3½'	½ IN.	PARSLEY 1 IN.	4-6 IN.	MAY 15-31 SET PEPPER PLANTS 1½-2 FT. APART.		
MAY 15-25	21	BEANS, LIMA (HENDERSON'S BUSH LIMA)	2½'						
MAY 15-25	20	BEANS, LIMA " " "	2½'	1½-2 IN.	2 IN.	5 - 6 IN.			
MAY 20 JN.10	19	BEANS, WAX POD (PROLIFIC BLACK WAX)	2'						
MAY 5-15	18	BEANS, WAX POD " " "	2'						
MAY 20 JN.10	17	BEANS, GREEN POD (STRINGLESS GREEN POD)	2'	1½-2 IN.	2 IN.	4- 5 IN.			
MAY 5-15	16	BEANS, GREEN POD " " "	2'						
JUNE 1-10	15	CARROTS (DANVER'S HALF LONG) FOR WINTER STORAGE	2'						
JUNE 1-10	14	CARROTS " " " " " "	2'						
MAY 5-15	13	CARROTS (CHANTENAY) — MARK CARROT ROWS WITH	2'	½ IN.	¼ IN.	3 - 4 IN.			
APRIL 15-30	12	CARROTS " — A FEW LETTUCE SEEDS	2'						
JUNE 1-15	11	BEETS (DETROIT DARK RED) FOR STORAGE	2'						
MAY 15-30	10	BEETS " " "	2'						
APRIL 15-30	9	BEETS " " "	2'	1 IN.	1 IN.	4 IN.			
APRIL 15-30	8	SWISS CHARD (LUCULLUS)	2'	1 IN.	1 IN.	8-10 IN.			
APRIL 15-30	7	ONIONS (SOUTHPORT YELLOW GLOBE) SETS SUPPLIED BY SUPERVISOR	2'						
APRIL 15-30	6	ONIONS " " "	2'	½ IN.	2 - 3 IN.				
APRIL 15-30	5	KOHL RABI (EARLY WHITE VIENNA)	2'	½ IN.	¼ IN.	6 IN.			
APRIL 15-30	4	LETTUCE (B.S. SIMPSON) | RADISHES (EARLY SCARLET GLOBE)	2'	½ IN.	¼ IN.	6-8 IN.			
APRIL 15-30	3	PEAS (LAXTON'S PROGRESS) — FOLLOW PEAS WITH	2'	RADISHES ½ IN.	¼ IN.	1½ -2 IN.			
APRIL 15-30	2	PEAS — OR LATE CABBAGE PLANTS	2'						
APRIL 15-30	1	PEAS (AMERICAN WONDER) — SUPPLIED BY SUPERVISOR	2'	1 - 2 IN.	1 IN.	1 IN.			
			2'						

THIS SPACE LEFT FOR GARDENER TO PLANT WHAT HE CHOOSES. SUPERVISOR WILL SUPPLY SEEDS MARKED WITH STAR. GARDENERS MUST SUPPLY ANY OTHERS.

SUGGESTIONS

* TURNIP,
CHINESE CABBAGE
* ROUND BLACK SPANISH RADISH
* BLACK EYED PEAS
* OKRA
* KALE
SUMMER SQUASH
COLLARDS
EGG PLANTS
PARSLEY
ENDIVE
FLOWERS
HERBS

IF DESIRED, GREEN OR WAX POD BEANS INSTEAD OF CORN, MAY BE PLANTED IN ROWS 35 TO 40. SUPERVISOR WILL FURNISH NECESSARY SEEDS.

NOTICE

GARDENERS SHOULD KEEP THEIR GARDENS CONTINUOSLY PRODUCTIVE. ALL ROWS HARVESTED BEFORE JULY 15 SHOULD BE IMMEDIATELY REPLANTED. SEE SUPERVISOR FOR SEEDS FOR REPLANTING AND GENERAL DIRECTIONS.

CULTIVATE GARDENS AT LEAST ONCE A WEEK AND KEEP PATHS CLEAN AROUND YOUR GARDEN.

SEE COMPLETE RULES AND REGULATIONS ON REVERSE SIDE.

Figure 8.3. Model layout for a vegetable garden in the Detroit Thrift Gardens program, 1933.

Source: Unemployed File, Burton Historical Collection, Detroit Public Library.

approximated work, paid in vegetables, and bought the city time, but any long-term economic resolution would require the assent of the federal government and that of the city's powerful corporations.

Risk and Responsibility

As Detroit's government worked to preserve a social contract in crisis, many called on the city's employers to take a greater responsibility. Within the Mayor's Unemployment Committee, for example, leftist and labor voices clashed with those of industry.[41] The former proposed regulating industrial work schedules: requiring factories to run five days a week and to spread out the work that they had, rather than concentrating it among a smaller staff. When a shop had an influx of work, Frank Martel of the Detroit Federation of Labor asked, "Why should men be working six or seven days a week, many of them between 10 and 12 hours a day, when we have in our city 100,000 unemployed?"[42] Work spreading was not unheard of and was practiced by large corporations, including Bethlehem Steel, General Electric, and General Motors, in the Depression, but John Lovett of the Michigan Manufacturers Association rejected any government mandate to do so. He argued that the Mayor's Unemployment Committee "has no business prescribing [working hours] to industry" and taunted his colleagues on the committee, saying, "Adopt your five-day week and see how far you will enforce it."[43] As Lovett suggested, the political power to force such a move was absent, and industry retained its autonomy with regard to work schedules.

The Ford Motor Company, the region's largest industrial employer, had cut its workforce precipitously, from 128,000 in 1929 to 37,000 by 1931.[44] An estimated 15 percent of Detroit's unemployed were former Ford workers, and Murphy and the Unemployment Committee argued that the company should take some responsibility for the cost of relief, which the city struggled to bear.[45] Detroit had little leverage, however, and received few tax dollars from the automaker, as it was based just outside the city's borders, in the adjoining suburbs of Dearborn and Highland Park. From this remove, Ford deflected the city of Detroit's arguments, criticizing its relief program as tainted by waste and fraud. As it had with gardening, the automaker created its own parallel relief program, providing meals to former employees living in Dearborn while continuing to evade responsibility for its large cohort of laid-off workers living in Detroit.[46] Though it had pushed its employees to buy modern houses in the 1910s, through the Five Dollar Day program, the company refused to defend those households' security in an economic crisis. Yet this was not the only challenge that Murphy's administration faced. It was also under fire from the left as the influence of Detroit communists rose.

With industrial capitalism in crisis and the Communist International calling for revolution from Moscow, the Communist Party of the U.S.A. developed Unemployed Councils in many American cities to rally the jobless. Its Detroit operatives framed local relief efforts as "wholly inadequate" and recruited many Detroiters to take their first working-class political action through council soup kitchens and political rallies.[47] Communist outreach among the jobless drew a diverse coalition that crossed dominant social divisions, bringing men and women and Blacks and whites together in a shared identity as unemployed workers.[48] Reflecting this, Sinclair's Abner Shutt, a proud "100 percent American" member of the Klan in the 1920s, was willing to march alongside Jews, Catholics, Blacks, and "Reds" to demand work, though he later felt ashamed of his participation.[49] Early in the crisis, in March 1930, the councils drew an unexpectedly large crowd of some fifty thousand to the city center to demonstrate.[50]

The Unemployed Council brought its demands to city government at an October 1930 meeting, as two thousand unemployed demonstrators gathered outside City Hall. They asked, as the *Detroit News* reported, that the material and domestic security of workers become a social responsibility and that "the families of unemployed persons be given $20 a week and $5 for each child or other dependent." They also demanded the "cessation of eviction proceedings; free light, gas and heat during the unemployment period; prohibition of the removal of furniture from workers['] homes for non-payment of installments; free meals, fares and clothes to school children, and free fares to unemployed; [and] that the city take over all vacant houses and vacant hotel rooms for housing the homeless."[51] These demands represented an entirely different politics from that of Murphy's welfare regime. Rather than bare subsistence aid, designed to protect workers' proud economic independence, and their ultimate responsibility for their houses, the communists' demands suggested the socializing of economic risks. Under the council's terms, the urgency to resume work would not fall on workers' households alone. It would be borne by the whole society, including government, lending institutions, property owners, employed taxpayers, and industry (Figure 8.4).

Murphy sought common ground in his exchange with the communists. He argued that their proposal for utility assistance had merit and emphasized that his government had effectively halted evictions. Defending his record, the mayor asserted, "There is no place on earth

Figure 8.4. Unemployed Council "Hunger March" demonstration, 1931. One visible placard states, "If you can't give us work give us wages. We refuse to starve," a demand that the risk of workers' unemployment should be borne by all.

Source: *Detroit News* photograph, Archives of Labor and Urban Affairs, Walter P. Reuther Library, Wayne State University, Detroit.

where greater measures have been taken for public relief than in Detroit, and that includes Moscow."[52] Categorically, though, he opposed the concept of income without work. Chiding the council's representatives, he added, "If I could get $20 a week from the City, free rent, food, light and carfare, I wouldn't work either."[53] Nearly a year later, presenting a more detailed proposal to the mayor with lower income requirements, the Unemployed Council's representative Philip Raymond raised the stakes, suggesting that social unrest was imminent. "We are trying to work within the present system of government," he said. "If we find no solution within it, the workers may be forced to solve their problems some other way."[54]

Raymond's threat came in the context of deteriorating conditions for the city's unemployed. In 1931, Murphy claimed that his administration had staved off widespread evictions, but this could not be maintained as the months dragged on.[55] That same year, facing rising budget deficits, the city reduced its spending on welfare and cut jobs in the Department of Public Works.[56] As the city cut rent subsidies, evictions

Figure 8.5. One of several evictions documented by the *Detroit News* in the period 1936–1938, this photograph being from the west side on DeSoto Street, 1936.

Source: *Detroit News* photograph, Archives of Labor and Urban Affairs, Walter P. Reuther Library, Wayne State University, Detroit.

spiked in the summer of 1931 to as many as 150 per day.[57] In 1932, a Mayor's Unemployment Committee report reviewed a sample of unemployed families and found that in one factory, 40 percent of 230 home-owning employees had lost their houses. Among a group of about one thousand renters, nearly one-third were behind on payments, and twenty-eight had been evicted. Ten percent of families with installment-purchased goods in their houses had seen them repossessed.[58]

With the economic crisis wearing on, households continued to face displacement—a fearsome spectacle of upward mobility reversed that was captured in 1936 in a *Detroit News* photograph. In it, evicted residents and their hard-earned possessions—a refrigerator, a crib, a chest of drawers—have been pushed to the curb, exposed to weather and to scrutiny (Figure 8.5). Not seeming to understand the gravity of their situation, two small children share what looks like a dining room chair, set in the middle of the sidewalk. The woman, working among the removed household objects, appears tired but stoic. Not everyone went so quietly. One family reportedly refused to yield their house to eviction, requiring a large police intervention to remove them. In two other, more

Figure 8.6. United Autoworkers members fought back against eviction in the late 1930s by returning workers' furniture to their houses after the authorities who had removed it left. This photograph was taken on the east side, on Lycaste Street, in January 1938.

Source: *Detroit News* photograph, Archives of Labor and Urban Affairs, Walter P. Reuther Library, Wayne State University, Detroit.

tragic cases, Detroit residents shot their landlords to defend against eviction. They were later acquitted.[59]

Groups from the Unemployed Council and, later, the UAW pushed back against evictions with acts of civil disobedience. They moved families' possessions, which the authorities had brought to the curb, back into their houses and covertly restored utility services cut for nonpayment (Figure 8.6).[60] Through these actions, workers and their allies asserted rights to the houses and the security they had worked so hard for in better times. Rather than facing the crisis as individual households, Detroit's Depression-era workers increasingly viewed their economic security as a matter of shared concern and took their demands to employers and government en masse.

Crossing the Line

The Ford Hunger March of 1932 was a turning point in workers' struggle for security in Detroit. In a daring move, the communist-led Unemployed Council and Auto Workers Union staged a march from Detroit, where their protest was permitted, into Ford's Dearborn, where it would undoubtedly be received with hostility. About three thousand unarmed workers and protesters participated, a group whose mixed composition illustrated the potential breadth of the working-class coalition. Maurice Sugar, a labor attorney who interviewed march participants, described the group as "men and women, white and Negro," not to mention the ideological mix of communist organizers and unemployed worker participants without Communist Party affiliation.[61] It was a group whose shared interests were stronger than the race and gender inequities that might divide them, and among the marchers' demands was a call to end racial discrimination in hiring. Gathered on the Detroit side, on a cold March 7, they walked up Miller Road, past Woodmere Cemetery and the frame houses of the Springwells neighborhood (Figure 8.7). Dearborn police and company agents awaited the marchers as if they were an invading army.[62] This dramatized the extent to which the municipal line between Detroit and Dearborn insulated the company from its laid-off employees. It surely tested the courage of the marchers.

As the marchers approached a roadblock defended by fifty Dearborn police and Ford agents, the Ford agents fired tear gas at them, escalating the encounter to violence.[63] Yet with overwhelming numbers, the march pressed past this checkpoint. Marchers threw stones, causing the fifty police and company agents to fall back to the plant. At the employment office's Gate Three, company officials and police made their stand, dispersing the marchers with tear gas, icy water hoses, and, finally, gunfire. They killed four of the protesters on the spot and wounded as many as sixty, and a fifth protester—a Black man—later died of his wounds, casualties that raised the stakes of Detroit's Depression-era social conflict to new heights.[64]

Hunger Marchers' houses were likely not far from their minds as they approached the militarized Detroit-Dearborn line. It was, after all, the deprivations of empty cupboards and coal bins and the fear or reality of eviction that drove many to activism. The work and wages that marchers demanded that day, to use a phrase Ford himself had coined years earlier, represented the "domestic destinies" of the assembled demonstrators.[65] The marchers sought the ability to organize labor within the plant and demanded direct material aid to address their lost domestic security. Marchers sought an end to "foreclosure on homes of former Ford workers." They called for "Ford to assume the responsibility for all mortgages, land contracts, and back taxes on homes until six months after regular employment" and to provide "five tons of coke or coal for

Figure 8.7. The Detroit-Dearborn line, photographed during a demonstration in 1933. This image illustrates the landscape where the Ford Hunger March of 1932 took place. From left to right, the image depicts the Rouge River, Miller Road (*beginning at the lower left and bending at the center*), a rail line, and Detroit's Springwells neighborhood (*right*).
Source: *Detroit News* photograph, Archives of Labor and Urban Affairs, Walter P. Reuther Library, Wayne State University, Detroit.

the winter" to each unemployed household, an ample supply given that an average household used 4.1 tons of coal per year.[66] The worker's house and its security, marchers reminded the company, were essential parts of the modern social contract to which industrial employers were a party.

If officials believed that killing protesters would stifle unrest, they were mistaken. A communist-led funeral parade for the protesters killed at Ford's Rouge Plant brought tens of thousands onto the streets of Detroit. Among the workers filling Woodward Avenue at Grand Circus Park, in the central business district, some carried a large banner that read, "Stop Ford-Murphy Police Terror" (Figure 8.8). This, at a time when the Detroit Communist Party's membership was about 1,500, could not be dismissed as a movement of far-left activists. It was clearly a broad and growing working-class social movement.[67] The city's

Figure 8.8. Funeral parade in downtown Detroit honoring those killed at the Ford Hunger March, 1932.

Source: *Detroit News* photograph, Archives of Labor and Urban Affairs, Walter P. Reuther Library, Wayne State University, Detroit.

workers had suffered exceptionally high unemployment and housing insecurity in the early 1930s but also found new political power in the crisis. Workers, especially the foreign-born, supported Franklin D. Roosevelt's presidential bid, not those of socialist or communist candidates, leading to his national victory. Black voters broke with the Republican Party in significant numbers, as well, and overall the Democratic Party received more than 59 percent of the Detroit vote in 1932. With a new administration in power, in 1933 the federal government expanded its response to the unemployment crisis and began to extend HOLC loans to restructure homeowners' unsustainable mortgage debts.[68] Workers made extraordinary gains in the years that followed. With new federal protections for collective bargaining, and leveraging sit-down strikes and other daring forms of worker resistance, they forced the auto industry to the bargaining table with the new United Automobile Workers union.

Conclusion

In the decades that preceded the crash, workers had labored in a growing industrial economy, and many gained access to the comforts of modern houses. The foreclosure crisis of the early 1930s exposed the fundamental economic insecurity that underlay these hard-earned gains. As industry shed jobs precipitously, workers' houses were transformed from sources of pride and security into anxious places, charged by the fear of eviction and the loss of hard-earned social prestige. Local relief programs, which often simulated work, could forestall the growing crisis for only so long.

Workers took collective action under the guidance of the city's communists but did not abandon capitalism. More so than a revolution, they sought the restoration of the implicit social contract of the 1920s and sought to have its terms insured. They pursued an electoral remedy and engaged in acts of civil disobedience: voting in a new president, Roosevelt, and defying eviction orders. The crisis and American workers' efforts to restore all that it threatened opened one of the most successful periods in the history of the global labor movement. Emboldened by new protections in the National Industrial Recovery Act of 1933 and organized by labor leaders, autoworkers would stage daring strikes in the mid-1930s. They began to win collectively bargained contracts.[69] They would continue to demand that the promise embodied in modern houses—hard work exchanged for security and upward mobility—be more than a celebrated ideal in American culture. It was an earned right that would be defended, in law and in the city's factories, streets, and houses.

CONCLUSION

> The city . . . does not tell its past, but contains it like the lines of a hand, written in the corners of the streets, the gratings of the windows, the banisters of the steps, the antennae of the lightning rods, the poles of the flags, every segment marked in turn with scratches, indentations, scrolls.
>
> —Italo Calvino, *Invisible Cities*

In Detroit today, century-old bungalows and duplexes still provide domestic comfort and pleasure. On the west side's Chopin Street, near the I-94 highway embankment, residents sit, dry their laundry, store their grills, and care for potted flowers on their porches. They decorate with holiday lights. One house features new porch supports and a new railing, built of still green treated wood, while the future of an abandoned corner store nearby is uncertain. Detroit's workers' houses, as Italo Calvino puts it, "contain a past," a story of an American city's modernization and workers' agency and experiences in that process. Workers negotiated a new social contract through these houses in the early twentieth century and helped to establish the cultural ideal that hard work should be respected and well rewarded.

Immigrant workers are crucial to the present-day U.S. economy, as they have been in the past, and yet they face discrimination and tight restrictions on their legal pathways to American citizenship. In this context, the story of Detroit's modernization provides a vivid reminder that many of today's "white Americans" are the descendants of immigrant workers. Their forebears often arrived with little cash and few possessions and with an uncertain commitment to the United States. They were received by a Progressive-era cohort of business leaders who were eager to invite them into American citizenship and to profit from their labor and future consumer purchases. Newly arrived workers tolerated employers' intrusive Americanization efforts, and many of them leveraged the new economic privileges available to white workers. They carried the memories of their difficult migration journeys with them as they pursued better lives, renting and buying modern houses on the growing urban periphery amid the city's newly emerging factories.

Detroit's houses contain their histories, as well as the stories of paths not taken, proposed models for the city that might have been. The city was modernized in the midst of a transatlantic debate about who, within an industrial society, should be responsible for housing. In the United States, with the backing of government, this responsibility was taken up by private, for-profit developers and real estate agents, who modernized their practices and produced an extraordinary amount of new housing in the 1920s. Yet European planners and architects, and like-minded Americans, illustrated an alternative: planned housing estates. Their proposals—built and unbuilt—concentrated higher-density housing in strategic locations while preserving more open space and protecting housing from harmful industrial adjacencies. Planners and architects included community amenities in their designs, putting schools, playgrounds, and laundries within easy reach of residents. These projects, moreover, reflected the idea that housing was a matter of broad social concern, managed by government or large employers, rather than the concern of individual households alone.

Who, today, should be responsible for providing high-quality, affordable housing in America? U.S. federal policy, since the early twentieth century, has oscillated between privatization and state intervention and more recently has moved back toward privatization. Amid the crisis of the global Depression, American policymakers began to augment the private market with interventions that would have been unthinkable under Herbert Hoover's watch. The New Deal federal government, empowered by workers' support, created the Home Owners Loan Corporation (HOLC) in 1933 to rescue the private market in Detroit as elsewhere. It bolstered private housebuilding with new Federal Housing Administration loan guarantees, but also resurrected the effort to build planned public housing in America.

Mid-century urban renewal policies extended U.S. public housing production to an ambitious new scale. Infamously, though, government support for public and private housing in this period extended the racial segregation established in earlier decades. These policies demolished Black-majority urban neighborhoods and replaced them with racially segregated public housing and new campuses for white-dominated institutions, such as hospitals and universities. Federal and local housing policies also promoted suburban growth at mid-century, and in this context, zoning regulation helped to segregate the expanding metropolis along race and class lines.[1] Policy makers did little to preserve the kinds of early twentieth-century housing that this book has focused on, despite the enormous amount of material and embodied labor that went into them. In the late 1930s, the HOLC labeled most of Detroit "definitely declining," or "hazardous" in its redlining maps of property risk, encouraging investment in a new layer of outward, suburban growth. The failures of U.S. government housing policy and postmodern criticism of mid-century urban renewal over the past half-century have helped to turn public opinion and U.S. policy back toward a market-based approach. Today, the most significant federal effort to ensure housing affordability is the distribution of Low-Income Housing Tax Credit (LIHTC) subsidies, which aim to increase the supply of affordable housing by subsidizing private-sector development.

While the failures of mid-twentieth-century public housing policy have been well recorded, the largely privatized housing system of today has proved inadequate, as shortages of affordable housing persist. The sharp economic swings of the past fifteen years have compounded America's housing problem. In the years following the Great Recession of 2008, more than 100,000 properties in Detroit, or about one-quarter of the city's properties, were subject to foreclosure for nonpayment of property taxes. The situation was made worse by erroneous assessments, which overstated house values in the city and placed an undue financial burden on Detroit's many low-income residents. Among the city's African American majority, the impacts have been profound: statewide, the Black homeownership rate fell from 51 percent to 40 percent between 2000 and 2016, a sharp decline in access to an important vehicle of wealth creation.[2]

As Detroit has recovered from the foreclosure crisis and its 2013 municipal bankruptcy, the city's economy has gained strength. Much development in this context has focused in the downtown and midtown districts, where housing is sought after by the city's growing professional middle class. This has raised rents and house prices generally, and construction of affordable units has not kept up with demand. A Hi-Lo warehousing vehicle operator, in present-day Detroit, can work more than full time at an entry-level wage and still be severely cost-burdened in a modest rental—an unsustainable burden. As inadequate as it is, the stock of regulated affordable housing may be set to decline further: LIHTC-funded projects are required to remain affordable for only fifteen years, and their costs will likely rise as units age out of this requirement and rise to market rate.[3]

Workers' early twentieth-century struggle for modern housing resonates today as workers continue to seek better lives within a challenging economic and social context. The hard-earned achievements of the labor movement, which grew out of the crisis of the 1930s, have been profoundly eroded in the past half-century. Across the United States, union membership has declined, and taxation has become less progressive. Income inequality has reached a level not seen since the 1920s.[4] Employers have long since withdrawn from any social responsibility for housing, a shift prefigured in the Ford Motor Company's abandonment of Fordson Village after World War I. Present-day corporations make no promise, implicit or explicit, that the wages they pay at the lower end of the scale are sufficient to cover rent or mortgage payments.[5] Even as workers' wages have risen, a recent spike in inflation has undermined these gains. The next economic crisis, whether personal or systemic, is always around the corner for those who pay more than they can comfortably afford for their house or apartment—waiting to erase their gains or even to thrust their possessions out to the curb.

The future of housing development will look different than it did one hundred years ago, when employers, government, and workers navigated an earlier phase of capitalist development that was marked by rapid growth. Looking outward from relatively compact urban centers, they saw opportunities to expand industrial productivity and wealth and to build a higher standard of living through new housing. Today, in the sprawling metropolises that these predecessors helped to create, there is no such simple development solution. There is no readily accessible periphery on which to build a better future. There is only the metropolis itself and the generations of housing developments of which it is composed, in their various states of repair. Often freighted with environmental contaminants and fortified by restrictive zoning ordinances, the contemporary city resists broad, generalizable modes of transformation. In Detroit, about eighty thousand housing units stand vacant, awaiting the complex work of rehabilitation or demolition—an extraordinary social challenge and opportunity.

Amid the fallout from the Great Recession, scholars have begun to reevaluate America's public housing history and to call for a return to socially ambitious government-led housing development. Brent Ryan has argued that in poor cities, such as Detroit, a profit-driven approach to housing development will never be adequate to improve conditions outside of a few privileged neighborhoods. Reinhold Martin, Leah Meisterlin, and Anna Kenoff have questioned the cultural ideal of private homeownership—the American dream. They point out that the seeming independence of the American household is in fact supported by vast public outlays, on everything from road maintenance to the mortgage interest tax deduction.[6] Why, they suggest, should we not have a public dream for housing development in this context? These projects are part of a larger conversation that must continue not only amid crisis, but in better times, as well, a debate about which social values should be reflected in the future of American housing.

The modern workers' houses of the early twentieth century were an American dream, but they were also more. They were part of a deal—a social contract. These dwellings reflected a negotiation among workers, employers, and government in which workers traded their hard, disciplined work for social and material advancement. Those workers found, within a mercurial economy, that better wages alone could not secure the terms of this contract. Only working-class political power could insure their gains. That remains as true today as it was in the 1930s. If workers increasingly demand solutions to the contemporary housing shortage in their places of employment, on the streets, and at the polls, their leverage may make the difference. These policy debates to come have much to gain by confronting the tragedy of modern housing development—the historical injustice of segregation that was hardened amid early twentieth-century growth. How might future housing policy begin to redress the multigenerational economic and social harm that segregation has caused African Americans?

The house is a highly political construct, but it is a locus of human experience, as well: a place where the social contract is *lived*. More than a question of unit counts and minimum standards, housing is a question about what residents want for their lives. The answers to this question will be multiple, and they will likely rest on the kinds of intimate details that meant so much to early twentieth-century workers. Seen in their historical context, Detroit's bungalows and duplexes reflect a great leap forward in workers' quality of life, one that might inspire ambitious affordable housing for the future. What transformative, future experiences of dwelling might match the impact of accessing a modern bathtub or private bedroom for the first time? What rich, identity-giving community rituals, large and small, might be staged amid future houses? Finally, and crucially, what is the prospect for working-class agency in future houses, through their selection, improvement, or transformation? The future of housing—the new dreams and experiences it makes possible—may give new meaning to work, as it did in the early twentieth century.

NOTES

INTRODUCTION

Epigraph: Factory Worker (Charlie Chaplin), *Modern Times*, dir. Charlie Chaplin (film, Charlie Chaplin Productions, 1936), 43 min.

1. Chaplin, *Modern Times*, 42 min.
2. Mason C. Doan, *American Housing Production, 1880–2000: A Concise History* (Lanham, MD: University Press of America, 1997), 1–14, 27–29.
3. See Irving Bernstein, *The Lean Years: A History of the American Worker, 1920–1933* (Chicago: Haymarket, 2010); Sydney Fine, *Sit Down* (Ann Arbor: University of Michigan Press, 1969).
4. Campbell Gibson, "Population of the 100 Largest Cities and Other Urban Places in the United States: 1790 to 1990," Working Paper No. POP-WP027, U.S. Bureau of the Census, June 1998, https://www.census.gov/library/working-papers/1998/demo/POP-twps0027.html.
5. Antonio Gramsci, "Americanism and Fordism," in *Selections from the Prison Notebooks of Antonio Gramsci*, edited by Quintin Hoare and Geoffrey Nowell Smith (New York: International Publishers, 1971); Ramsay Muir, *America the Golden: An Englishman's Notes and Comparisons* (London: Williams and Norgate, 1927).
6. Beth Tompkins Bates, *The Making of Black Detroit in the Age of Henry Ford* (Chapel Hill: University of North Carolina Press, 2012), 37, 61–64.
7. Wage data are from U.S. Bureau of Labor Statistics, *Wages and Hours of Labor in the Automobile Industry, 1922*, Bulletin No. 348, October 1923, 2–3. Cost of living data are from National Industrial Conference Board, *The Cost of Living among Wage-Earners, Detroit, Michigan, September 1921*, Special Report No. 19, October 1921, 14. See also Joyce Shaw Peterson, *American Automobile Workers, 1900–1933* (Albany: State University of New York Press, 1987), 71–93.
8. On married women's rising workforce participation in the early twentieth century, see Linda McDowell, *Gender, Identity and Place: Understanding Feminist Geographies* (Cambridge: Polity, 1999), 71–81.

9. See Joseph Bigott, *From Cottage to Bungalow: Houses and the Working Class in Metropolitan Chicago, 1869–1929* (Chicago: University of Chicago Press, 2001); Kim Hernandez, "The 'Bungalow Boom': The Working-Class Housing Industry and the Development and Promotion of Early Twentieth-Century Los Angeles," *Southern California Quarterly* 92, no. 4 (Winter 2010–2011): 351–392; Daniel Prosser, "Chicago and the Bungalow Boom of the 1920s," *Chicago History* 10, no. 2 (1981): 86–95.

10. Thomas C. Hubka, *Houses without Names: Architectural Nomenclature and the Classification of America's Common Houses* (Knoxville: University of Tennessee Press, 2013), 67. See also Shannon Mattern, "Closet Archive: A Stuffed History of the Closet, Where the 'Past Becomes Space,'" *Places Journal*, July 2017, https://placesjournal.org/article/closet-archive/?cn-reloaded=1.

11. David Allan Levine, *Internal Combustion: The Races in Detroit, 1915–1926* (Westport, CT: Greenwood, 1976), 42.

12. See Elaine Lewinnek, *The Working Man's Reward: Chicago's Early Suburbs and the Roots of American Sprawl* (New York: Oxford University Press, 2014); Olivier Zunz, *The Changing Face of Inequality: Urbanization, Industrial Development, and Immigrants in Detroit, 1880–1920* (Chicago: University of Chicago Press, 1982). Also, Lizabeth Cohen explores immigrant property ambitions and their possible origins in homeland experiences in "Embellishing a Life of Labor: An Interpretation of the Material Culture of American Working-Class Homes, 1885–1915," *Journal of American Culture* 3, no. 4 (Winter 1980): 762.

13. International Labor Office, *An International Enquiry into Costs of Living: A Comparative Study of Workers' Living Costs in Detroit (USA) and Fourteen European Cities*, 2d rev. ed. (Geneva: International Labor Office, 1931), 185. Data gathered in Richard Harris, "Working-Class Homeownership in the American Metropolis," *Journal of Urban History* 17, no. 1 (November 1990): 56, shows that in 1940 census data, in Detroit and elsewhere, homeownership was more common among skilled workers.

14. International Labor Office, *An International Enquiry into Costs of Living*.

15. Ibid., 17–19, 126, 185.

16. José Luis Sert, *Can Our Cities Survive? An ABC of Urban Problems, Their Analysis, Their Solutions* (Cambridge, MA: Harvard University Press, 1942). The demographic description of the Linwood neighborhood in the foreground, included in the caption for the photograph, is from Home Owner's Loan Corporation, "Description and Characteristics of Area [Detroit Area C29]," in *Mapping Inequality: Redlining in New Deal America, Residential Security Map of Detroit*, accessed April 7, 2022, https://dsl.richmond.edu/panorama/redlining/#loc=5/39.1/-94.58.

17. Jane Jacobs, *The Death and Life of Great American Cities* (New York: Random House, 1961), 204. For the persistent view that such houses were "oppressive" in their uniformity, see Brent Ryan, *Design after Decline: How America Rebuilds Shrinking Cities* (Philadelphia: University of Pennsylvania Press, 2012); Gwendolyn Wright, *Building the Dream: A Social History of Housing in America* (New York: Pantheon, 1981).

18. Gramsci, "Americanism and Fordism"; David Harvey, *Consciousness and the Urban Experience: Studies in the History and Theory of Capitalist Urbanization* (Baltimore: John Hopkins University Press, 1985), 46–47.

19. In *The Changing Face of Inequality*, for example, Zunz shifts to a more top-down framework when it moves into its discussion of the early twentieth century. See also Heather B. Barrow, *Henry Ford's Plan for the American Suburb: Dearborn and Detroit* (DeKalb: Northern Illinois University Press, 2015).

20. See, e.g., Bigott, *From Cottage to Bungalow*, which warns against relying on middle-class readings of working-class material culture.

21. Gaston Bachelard, *The Poetics of Space* (New York: Orion, 1964), originally published in French in 1958. In an interesting corollary from design discourse, the early twentieth-century architect Eileen Gray challenged modernism's emphasis on conceptual purity, arguing that "theory is not sufficient for life" and favoring spaces and furniture that engaged people experientially: see Caroline Constant, "E.1027: The Nonheroic Modernism of Eileen Gray," *Journal of the Society of Architectural Historians* 53, no. 3 (1994): 265–279.

22. Michel de Certeau, *The Practice of Everyday Life* (Berkeley: University of California Press, 2011). See also John Friedmann, *Insurgencies: Essays in Planning Theory* (New York: Routledge, 2011), 121–122.

23. Lizabeth Cohen, *Making a New Deal: Industrial Workers in Chicago, 1919–1939*, 2d ed. (Cambridge: Cambridge University Press, 2008).

24. Mario Tronti, "Marx in Detroit," in *Workers and Capital*, by Mario Tronti (New York: Verso, 2019), originally published in Italian in 1966 and 1971. See also Pier Vittorio Aureli, *The Project of Autonomy: Politics and Architecture within and against Capitalism* (New York: Princeton Architectural Press, 2008), 9, 33–34, 83.

25. Robert Fishman, *Bourgeois Utopias: The Rise and Fall of Suburbia* (New York: Basic, 1987); Kenneth T. Jackson, *Crabgrass Frontier: The Suburbanization of America* (New York: Oxford University Press, 1985). Other prominent narratives of suburbanization that preceded the rise of working-class suburban histories include Jon C. Teaford, *The Twentieth-Century American City* (Baltimore: Johns Hopkins University Press, 1993); Wright, *Building the Dream*.

26. Bigott, *From Cottage to Bungalow*; Margaret Garb, *City of American Dreams: A History of Home Ownership and Housing Reform in Chicago, 1871–1919* (Chicago: University of Chicago Press, 2005); Lewinnek, *The Working Man's Reward*; Zunz, *The Changing Face of Inequality*. See also Robert Lewis, *Manufacturing Suburbs: Building Work and Home on the Metropolitan Fringe* (Philadelphia: Temple University Press, 2004).

27. Thomas C. Hubka, *How the Working-Class Home Became Modern, 1900–1940* (Minneapolis: University of Minnesota Press, 2021); Thomas C. Hubka and Judith T. Kenny, "Examining the American Dream: Housing Standards and the Emergence of a National Housing Culture, 1900–1930," *Perspectives in Vernacular Architecture* 13, no. 1 (2006): 49–69. Hubka's interpretation is reinforced in Robert Gordon, *The Rise and Fall of American Growth: The U.S. Standard of Living since the Civil War* (Princeton, NJ: Princeton University Press, 2017), 94–128.

28. See Aggregate Architectural History Collaborative, *Governing by Design: Architecture, Economy, and Politics in the Twentieth Century* (Pittsburgh: University of Pittsburgh Press, 2012), esp. chap. 2 (Jonathan Massey, "Risk and Regulation in the Financial Architecture of American Houses"). See also Garb, *City of American Dreams*, 5.

29. N. D. B. Connolly, *A World More Concrete: Real Estate and the Remaking of Jim Crow South Florida* (Chicago: University of Chicago Press, 2014), illustrates the ways that real estate development and racial segregation have been intertwined in twentieth-century America.

30. International Labor Office, *An International Enquiry into Costs of Living*, 172–173.

31. See, e.g., Jeanna Smialek, "Rising Wages Are Good News for Workers but Keep Pressure on the Fed," *New York Times*, April 1, 2022.

CHAPTER 1

Epigraph: Gaston Bachelard, *The Poetics of Space* (New York: Orion, 1964), 27.

1. Steve Babson, *Working Detroit: The Making of a Union Town* (New York: Adama, 1984), 27–28; James Barrett and David Roediger, "Inbetween Peoples: Race, Nationality and the 'New Immigrant' Working Class," *Journal of American Ethnic History* 16, no. 3 (Spring 1997): 3–44; Sophonisba P. Breckinridge, *New Homes for Old* (New York: Harper and Brothers, 1921), 1–4, 19; David A. Gerber, *American Immigration: A Very Short Introduction* (New York: Oxford University Press, 2011), 2; David R. Roediger, *Working toward Whiteness: How America's Immigrants Became White* (New York: Basic, 2005), 5–6; Edward A. Steiner, *On the Trail of the Immigrant* (New York: F. H. Revell, 1906), 20.

2. Steiner, *On the Trail of the Immigrant*, 37–38.

3. Ibid.

4. Gerber, *American Immigration*, 10.

5. Steiner, *On the Trail of the Immigrant*, 87–88.

6. Ibid.

7. Eli Zaretsky, "Introduction," in William Thomas and Florian Znaniecki, *The Polish Peasant in Europe and America: A Classic Work of Immigration History*, edited by Eli Zaretsky (Urbana: University of Illinois Press, [1918] 1996), xi.

8. Thomas and Znaniecki, *The Polish Peasant in Europe and America*, 405.

9. Robert Rockaway, "Moving In and Moving Up: Early Twentieth-Century Detroit Jewry," *Michigan Historical Review* 41, no. 2 (Fall 2015): 59–79.

10. Ford Motor Company, *Fifty-one Human Interest Stories*, internal report no. 12, 1915, accession no. 1018, Benson Ford Research Center, Henry Ford Museum of American Innovation, Dearborn, MI (hereafter, The Henry Ford); Thomas and Znaniecki, *The Polish Peasant in Europe and America*, 1:480, 2:348–374.

11. Thomas and Znaniecki, *The Polish Peasant in Europe and America*, 5:29.

12. Ibid., 1:466–467.

13. Ibid., 1:468.

14. Ibid., 1:485.

15. Raymond E. Cole, "The Immigrant in Detroit," report to the Americanization Committee, Detroit Board of Commerce, 1915, Americanization Committee of Detroit papers, 1914–1931, Bentley Historical Library, University of Michigan, Ann Arbor, 15.

16. Ibid.

17. Elaine Latzman Moon, *Untold Tales, Unsung Heroes: An Oral History of Detroit's African American Community, 1918–1967* (Detroit: Wayne State University Press, 1994), 25.

18. Julius Combs, interview by Louis Jones, accession no. UOH001949, 2005, print transcript, Westsider Oral History Project, Walter P. Reuther Library, Wayne State University, Detroit.

19. James Gregory, *The Southern Diaspora: How the Great Migrations of Black and White Southerners Transformed America* (Chapel Hill: University of North Carolina Press, 2005), 45.

20. Moon, *Untold Tales, Unsung Heroes*, 27–29.

21. Ibid., 80–84.

22. Richard W. Thomas, *Life for Us Is What We Make It: Building Black Community in Detroit, 1915–1945* (Bloomington: Indiana University Press, 1992), 28, 38.

23. Moon, *Untold Tales, Unsung Heroes*, 92–93.

24. Olivier Zunz, *The Changing Face of Inequality: Urbanization, Industrial Development, and Immigrants in Detroit, 1880–1920* (Chicago: University of Chicago Press, 1982), 341–349. On the housing shortage, see David Allan Levine, *Internal Combustion: The Races in Detroit, 1915–1926* (Westport, CT: Greenwood, 1976), 37–42. On boarding conditions near Detroit's central business district, see Jerome Thomas, "The City of Detroit: A Study in Urban Geography" (Ph.D. diss., University of Michigan, Ann Arbor, 1928), 89–121. On crowding near Ford's plant, see Clarence Hooker, *Life in the Shadows of the Crystal Palace, 1910–1927: Ford Workers in the Model T Era* (Bowling Green, OH: Bowling Green State University Popular Press, 1997).

25. Robert Barrows explains that, despite the prominence of the New York–style tenement house in urban history literature, most early twentieth-century workers experienced variations on the detached residence: Robert Barrows, "Beyond the Tenement: Patterns of American Urban Housing 1870–1930," *Journal of Urban History* 9, no. 4 (1983): 395–420.

26. "Detroit's Housing Situation Has Become Grave Problem," *The Detroiter*, May 8, 1916, 7–8. On boarding, see Kevin Boyle and Victoria Getis, *Muddy Boots and Ragged Aprons: Images of Working-Class Detroit, 1900–1930* (Detroit: Wayne State University Press, 1997); Zunz, *The Changing Face of Inequality*, 62–63, 253–254; Thomas, "The City of Detroit," 89–121.

27. "Detroit's Housing Situation Has Become Grave Problem."

28. Many photographs of boarding conditions are kept in a private Ford Motor Company archive today, but through the efforts of the historians Victoria Getis and Kevin Boyle, a number of them have been published and made available: see Boyle and Getis, *Muddy Boots and Ragged Aprons*.

29. See Ford Motor Company, "Unhealthy Living Conditions," in *Fifty-one Human Interest Stories*, 1915. The image is published along with a Ford investigator's commentary in Boyle and Getis, *Muddy Boots and Ragged Aprons*, 68–69.

30. Ford Motor Company, "Unhealthy Living Conditions."

31. Ibid.

32. Jacob Riis, *How the Other Half Lives: Studies among the Tenements of New York* (New York: Charles Scribner's Sons, 1889).

33. Boyle and Getis, *Muddy Boots and Ragged Aprons*, 68–69.

34. The quote is from the inscription on the photograph "Russian Family Recently Emigrated to Detroit, Michigan, 1917," no. P.O. 4542, digital collections, The Henry Ford.

35. Boyle and Getis, *Muddy Boots and Ragged Aprons*, 62–63.

36. Ford Motor Company, "Kitchen of Employee's Home, 1913–1914," photograph, accession no. 1660, The Henry Ford, folder 19: Laboring Classes-Housing.

37. Ford Motor Company, *Fifty-one Human Interest Stories*, internal report, no. 38, The Henry Ford.

38. Ibid., no. 12.

39. Sanborn Map Company, *Insurance Maps of Detroit, Michigan*, vol. 4, 1922, sheets 70, 72, 81, 83, 86, University of Michigan, Ann Arbor. The bourgeois ideal is explored in Robert Fishman, *Bourgeois Utopias: The Rise and Fall of Suburbia* (New York: Basic, 1987).

40. For a view of the building, see "Young Woman's Home, Clifford and Adams Ave., Detroit, Mich.," color postcard, ca. 1917, no. 2012.020.388, Digital Archive, Detroit Historical Society, http://detroithistorical.pastperfectonline.com/archive/84CEC124-ECE3-444B-B0E1-390168172701.

41. The quotations are from Young Woman's Home Association, *Fortieth Annual Report*, 1917, 17, Young Woman's Home Association Collection Papers, accession no. 1923, Archives of Labor and Urban Affairs, Walter P. Reuther Library, Wayne State University. See also the annual reports for 1914–1920 in ibid.

CHAPTER 2

Epigraph: Henry Ford with Samuel Crowther, *My Life and Work* (London: W. Heinemann, 1923), 107.

1. Detroit's population added an extraordinary 113 percent in the 1910s, growing from 465,776 in 1910 to 993,078. This was the fastest growth among large cities in the nation. Second in decennial growth was Los Angeles, which added 81 percent in the decade. New York City still dwarfed all American cities, adding 17 percent to its population in the 1910s, to reach 5.6 million residents by 1920: Campbell Gibson, "Population of the 100 Largest Cities and Other Urban Places in the United States: 1790 to 1990," Working Paper no. POP-WP027, U.S. Bureau of the Census, June 1998, https://www.census.gov/library/working-papers/1998/demo/POP-twps0027.html.

2. C. F. Holderman, "Second Session: Discipline," in *Packard Advanced Training School Lecture Course* (Detroit: Packard Motor Car Company, 1919), 42–57; Stephen Meyer, *The Five Dollar Day: Labor Management and Social Control in the Ford Motor Company, 1908–1921* (Albany: State University of New York Press, 1981).

3. David Brody, *Workers in Industrial America: Essays on the Twentieth Century Struggle* (New York: Oxford University Press, 1980), 32–39; Meyer, *The Five Dollar Day*, 68–70.

4. On early twentieth-century nativism, see David R. Roediger, *Working toward Whiteness: How America's Immigrants Became White* (New York: Basic, 2005). For a classic example of progressive thought, see Jane Addams, *Twenty Years at Hull House* (New York: Macmillan, 1912).

5. The metaphor of the "melting pot" was popularized by Israel Zangwill's play of that name, first staged in 1908. Olivier Zunz quotes a Ford Motor Company description of the company's English School commencement ceremony in *The Changing Face of Inequality: Urbanization, Industrial Development, and Immigrants in Detroit, 1880–1920* (Chicago: University of Chicago Press, 1982), 312.

6. Detroit Board of Commerce, "Housing Conditions," *The Detroiter*, June 1913, 8.

7. "New York Evening Sun Praises Night School Work in Detroit," *The Detroiter*, November 1, 1915, 12; "Immigrant Education Expert Praises Night School Work," *The Detroiter*, December 13, 1915, 3; "Many Cities Follow Detroit's Example Regarding Foreigners," *The Detroiter*, February 14, 1916, 4.

8. National Americanization Committee, *Americanizing a City: The Campaign for the Detroit Night Schools, Conducted in August–September, 1915* (New York: National Americanization Committee and Committee for Immigrants in America, 1915), 8.

9. Charles Paull, *Americanization: A Discussion of Present Conditions with Recommendations for the Teaching of Non-Americans* (Syracuse, NY: Solvay Process Company Printing Department, 1918), 6.

10. Meyer, *The Five Dollar Day*, 156.

11. Samuel Marquis, "Address Delivered by Dean Marquis, May 17, 1916, before the Convention of the National Conference of Charities and Corrections, Y.M.C.A," 12, Samuel Marquis Papers, Speeches, Cranbrook Center for Collections and Research, Bloomfield, MI (hereafter, Marquis Papers).

12. Ford Motor Company, "Advantages of the Ford English School," in "Sociological Department Book 1914–1916," unpublished ms., folder 8: Writings, Marquis Papers.

13. "Detroit Night Schools Can Accommodate 525 More Men," *The Detroiter*, October 11, 1915, 4.

14. "Great Impetus Given Americanizing Plan," *The Detroiter*, February 7, 1916, 1, 3; "Alvan Macauley Is Member of Committee on Education," *The Detroiter*, February 28, 1916, 6.

15. David Allan Levine, *Internal Combustion: The Races in Detroit, 1915–1926* (Westport, CT: Greenwood, 1976), 27–28; Zunz, *The Changing Face of Inequality*, 313–314.

16. "Great Impetus Given Americanizing Plan."

17. "Night School Campaign Is Carried into All Sections," *The Detroiter*, September 3, 1917, 1.

18. Levine, *Internal Combustion*, 30; National Americanization Committee, *Americanizing a City*, 14.

19. Detroit Board of Commerce, "Number of Night Schools Doubled," *The Detroiter*, September 11, 1916, 2; "Over 7,000 Enroll in Evening Schools," *The Detroiter*, September 18, 1916, 1; "Evening School Map of Detroit," *The Detroiter*, September 11, 1916. On ethnic enclaves within the city, see Steve Babson, *Working Detroit: The Making of a Union Town* (New York: Adama, 1984), 26; Jerome Thomas, "The City of Detroit: A Study in Urban Geography" (Ph.D. diss., University of Michigan, Ann Arbor, 1928), fig. 6.

20. Detroit Board of Commerce and Detroit Board of Education, "Important Information about Detroit," in *Manual of American Citizenship* (Detroit: Day's Work, 2019), n.p.

21. See Stephan Thernstrom, *Poverty and Progress: Social Mobility in a Nineteenth Century City* (Cambridge, MA: Harvard University Press, 1964), 115–137; Zunz, *The Changing Face of Inequality*, 161, 170–76, 227–240. On self-building, see Richard Harris, "Self-Building in the Urban Housing Market," *Economic Geography* 67, no. 1 (1991): 1–21. See also Gail Radford, *Modern Housing for*

America: Policy Struggles in the New Deal Era (Chicago: University of Chicago Press, 1996), 9–10.

22. Packard Motor Car Company, "Standard Instruction Sheet for Cutting Off Both Sides of Piece on Oliver Cut-Off Saws, Showing Elementary Time," *Packard Advanced Training School Lecture Course*, 1. On the theory and experience of modern production see Siegfried Giedion, *Mechanization Takes Command: A Contribution to Anonymous History* (New York: Oxford University Press, 1948); David A. Hounshell, *From the American System to Mass Production, 1800–1932: The Development of Manufacturing Technology in the United States* (Baltimore: Johns Hopkins University Press, 1984); Meyer, *The Five Dollar Day*; Terry Smith, *Making the Modern: Industry, Art, and Design in America* (Chicago: University of Chicago Press, 1993). For its popular and comic representation, see Charlie Chaplin, dir., *Modern Times* (film, Charlie Chaplin Productions, 1936).

23. Meyer, *The Five Dollar Day*, 108–109.

24. Beth Tompkins Bates, *The Making of Black Detroit in the Age of Henry Ford* (Chapel Hill: University of North Carolina Press, 2012), 23–24.

25. Histories of the five-dollar day emphasize its effects on workers' behavior inside the plant: see Meyer, *The Five Dollar Day*; Joyce Shaw Peterson, *American Automobile Workers, 1900–1933* (Albany: State University of New York Press, 1987).

26. Thomas Laurence Munger, *Detroit Today: A Brief History of Detroit's Origin and Development* (Detroit: Board of Commerce, 1921), 51.

27. The full title is *Helpful Hints and Advice to Employes, to Help Them Grasp the Opportunities Which are Presented to Them by the Ford Profit-sharing Plan* (Detroit: Ford Motor Company, 1915), Benson Ford Research Center, Henry Ford Museum of American Innovation, Dearborn, MI (hereafter, The Henry Ford).

28. Samuel Marquis, largely as quoted in Martha Banta, *Taylored Lives: Narrative Productions in the Age of Taylor, Veblen, and Ford* (Chicago: University of Chicago Press, 1993), 26, with additional phrasing from Samuel Marquis, "The Ford Idea in Education," undated text, folder 7: Writings, Marquis Papers.

29. Ford Motor Company, *Helpful Hints and Advice to Employes*, 25.

30. Meyer, *The Five Dollar Day*, 114–118.

31. Marquis, as referenced in Robert Conot, *American Odyssey* (New York: William Morrow, 1974), 174.

32. Marquis, "Address Delivered by Dean Marquis," 13.

33. James Couzens, quoted in Meyer, *The Five Dollar Day*, 140.

34. U.S. Bureau of Labor Statistics, *Wages and Hours of Labor in the Automobile Industry, 1922*, Bulletin No. 348, 2–3, https://fraser.stlouisfed.org/title/3958#493008.

35. Ford Motor Company, *Helpful Hints and Advice to Employes*, 13.

36. Ibid., 21.

37. Ford Motor Company, "A Back Yard in the Tenement District," *Fifty-one Human Interest Stories*, internal report, 1915, accession no. 1018, Benson Ford Research Center, The Henry Ford.

38. Ida Tarbell, "Making Men at Ford's," book ms., 1916, 16, in Correspondence, Marquis Papers.

39. Ford Motor Company, "A Back Yard in the Tenement District."

40. Ford Motor Company, *Fifty-one Human Interest Stories*, no. 9, 1915.

41. Ibid.

42. Ford Motor Company, "Improved Living Conditions," *Fifty-one Human Interest Stories*, 1915, n.p.

43. Detroit Board of Commerce, *The Detroiter*, vol. 7, no. 21, 1916, Burton Historical Collection, Detroit Public Library.

44. Frank Vivian, interview by Owen Bombard, accession no. 65, print transcript, 1953, 39, The Henry Ford.

45. Ford Motor Company, *Helpful Hints and Advice to Employes*, 6.

46. Thomas C. Hubka and Judith T. Kenny, "Examining the American Dream: Housing Standards and the Emergence of a National Housing Culture, 1900–1930," *Perspectives in Vernacular Architecture* 13, no. 1 (2006): 49–69.

47. "Board Sets Pace in Welfare Movement," *The Detroiter*, July 24, 1916, 1–2.

48. For a summary of mortgage conditions in the period, see John Gries and James Ford, eds., *The President's Conference on Home Building and Home Ownership, Volume 2: Home Finance and Taxation* (Washington DC: National Capital Press, 1932), 1–24.

49. In 1900, 30,491 Wayne County houses were owner-occupied, and 39 percent of them were "encumbered" with mortgage debt. In 1920, 104,072 Wayne County houses were owner-occupied, and 59 percent of them were encumbered: *Twelfth Census of the United States: 1900* and *Fourteenth Census of the United States: 1920*, data queried through the demographic research tool *Social Explorer*, http://www.socialexplorer.com. The 1930 census does not address the question of encumbered ownership, but the 1940 census document *Characteristics of Housing* shows that of the 212,042 Wayne County houses that were owner-occupied, 63 percent were encumbered.

50. On building-and-loan organizations, which were prominent in Muncie, Indiana, see Jonathan Massey, "Risk and Regulation in the Financial Architecture of American Houses," in *Governing by Design: Architecture, Economy, and Politics in the Twentieth Century*, by Aggregate Architectural History Collaborative (Pittsburgh: University of Pittsburgh Press, 2012), 27. See also Robert S. Lynd and Helen Merrell Lynd, *Middletown: A Study in American Culture* (New York: Harcourt, Brace, 1929), 47, 104.

51. Nelson Young, *A Study of the Problems of the Distressed Home Owner of Detroit as Revealed by Applications to the Home Owners' Loan Corporation* (Ann Arbor: Earhart Foundation, 1934), 4.

52. George Walter Woodworth, "The Detroit Money Market, 1934–1955," *Michigan Business Studies* 5, no. 2 (1932): 190, 236–238.

53. Young, *A Study of the Problems of the Distressed Home Owner of Detroit as Revealed by Applications to the Home Owners' Loan Corporation*, 4.

54. Clement Lowell Harriss, *History and Policies of the Home Owners' Loan Corporation* (New York: National Bureau of Economic Research, 1951), 32–33; Upton Sinclair, *The Jungle* (New York: Jungle, 1906).

55. On the growth of the mortgage market, see Mason C. Doan, *American Housing Production, 1880–2000: A Concise History* (Lanham, MD: University Press of America, 1997), 28–33. See also Radford, *Modern Housing for America*, 49.

56. "Detroit Society for Savings," *Michigan Manufacturer and Financial Record*, vol. 16, 1915, 22.

57. Southern Pine Association, *Housing Plans for Cities* (New Orleans: Southern Pine Association, 1920), 26–30.

58. "House Financing Company Completes Organization; Will Start Building Soon," *The Detroiter*, June 9, 1919, 11.

59. "Now Watch the Desert Bloom," *The Detroiter*, April 7, 1919, 3.

60. "Industries Lead in Movement to Reduce Shortage of Houses," *The Detroiter*, March 17, 1919, 1–2.

61. Harry B. Warner, Secretary, Detroit Board of Commerce, letter, August 9, 1920, Detroit Board of Commerce Papers, Bentley Historical Library, University of Michigan, Ann Arbor.

62. "Home Buying in Detroit," *Municipal Journal and Public Works*, vol. 46, no. 22, 1919, 384.

63. Sam Bass Warner, *Streetcar Suburbs: The Process of Growth in Boston, 1870–1900* (Cambridge, MA: Harvard University Press, 1962), 127.

64. "Home Buying in Detroit," 384.

65. "Industries Lead in Movement to Reduce Shortage of Houses," 1.

66. Arthur Pound, *The Turning Wheel: The Story of General Motors through Twenty-five Years, 1908–1933* (Garden City, NY: Doubleday, 1934), 413.

67. See Paul C. Murphy, "The National Own Your Home Campaign," *American Contractor*, July 12, 1919. On the wartime drop in home building, see Doan, *American Housing Production*, 27–29.

68. Herbert Hoover, "Foreword," in *How to Own Your Own Home: A Handbook for Prospective Home Owners*, by John M. Gries and James S. Taylor (Washington, DC: Government Printing Office, 1923), v.

69. Gries and Taylor, *How to Own Your Own Home*, 4.

70. Ford Motor Company, *Helpful Hints and Advice to Employes*, 32–33; Ford Motor Company, *Fifty-one Human Interest Stories*, no. 19, 1915.

71. Doan, *American Housing Production*, 30–31.

72. Thomas, "The City of Detroit," 47–49.

73. Scott Martelle, *Detroit: A Biography* (Chicago: Chicago Review, 2012), 87, 92.

74. Douglas S. Massey, Jonathan Rothwell, and Thurston Domina, "The Changing Bases of Segregation in the United States," *Annals of the American Academy of Political and Social Science* 626, no. 1 (November 2009): 76–78.

75. On the racial politics around whiteness in early twentieth-century America, see Roediger, *Working toward Whiteness*.

76. Bates, *The Making of Black Detroit in the Age of Henry Ford*, 37, 61–64.

77. Levine, *Internal Combustion*, 44–59.

78. Harold Black, "Restrictive Covenants in Relation to Segregated Negro Housing in Detroit" (master's thesis, Wayne State University, Detroit, 1947); Doan, *American Housing Production*, 32.

79. Bates, *The Making of Black Detroit in the Age of Henry Ford*, 79.

80. Detroit Board of Commerce, "Remedy Must Be Found for Conditions Disclosed by Americanization Committee," *The Detroiter*, December 13, 1919, 1.

81. Ibid.; Reynolds Farley, Sheldon Danziger, and Harry J. Holzer, *Detroit Divided* (New York: Russell Sage Foundation, 2000), 28–31, 145–146; Zunz, *The Changing Face of Inequality*, 352–354, 373–378. For citywide housing costs for unskilled Ford workers, see International Labor Office, *An International Enquiry into Costs of Living: A Comparative Study of Workers' Living Costs in Detroit (USA) and Fourteen European Cities*, 2d rev. ed. (Geneva: International Labor Office, 1931), table 1.

82. "Remedy Must Be Found for Conditions Disclosed by Americanization Committee," 2.
83. Ibid.
84. Bates, *The Making of Black Detroit in the Age of Henry Ford*, 34.
85. Poverty is a more complex phenomenon than merely the lack of income: see John Friedmann, "Rethinking Poverty: The Dis/empowerment Model," in *Insurgencies: Essays in Planning Theory*, by John Friedmann (New York: Routledge, 2011), 87–108.

CHAPTER 3

Epigraph: Le Corbusier, *Toward an Architecture*, translated by Jean-Louis Cohen (Los Angeles: Getty Research Institute, 2007), 254.
1. Le Corbusier, *Toward an Architecture*, 291–307.
2. On the Russian case, see Milka Bliznakov, "Soviet Housing during the Experimental Years, 1918–1933," in *Russian Housing in the Modern Age: Design and Social History*, edited by William C. Brumfield and Blair A. Ruble (Washington, DC: Woodrow Wilson Center Press, 1993), 85–148; Greg Castilo, "Stalinist Modern: Constructivism and the Soviet Company Town," in *Architectures of Russian Identity, 1500 to the Present*, edited by James Cracraft and Daniel B. Rowland (Ithaca, NY: Cornell University Press, 2003), 135–149.
3. Mark Swenarton, *Building the New Jerusalem: Architecture, Housing and Politics 1900–1930* (Bracknell, UK: IHS BRE Press, 2008), includes important comparative work on planned housing between England and Germany, while Margaret Crawford, *Building the Workingman's Paradise: The Design of American Company Towns* (London: Verso, 1995), and Joseph Bigott, *From Cottage to Bungalow: Houses and the Working Class in Metropolitan Chicago, 1869–1929* (Chicago: University of Chicago Press, 2001), explore U.S. planned company towns and commercially built housing, respectively.
4. On rising post–World War I U.S. economic power, see Robert Allen, *Global Economic History: A Very Short Introduction* (Oxford: Oxford University Press, 2011), 7; Francis Ching, Mark Jarzombek, and Vikramaditya Prakash, *A Global History of Architecture* (Hoboken, NJ: Wiley, 2017), 659.
5. On Social Democratic politics in Germany, see Barbara Miller Lane, "Modern Architecture and Politics in Germany, 1918–1945," in *Housing and Dwelling: Perspectives on Modern Domestic Architecture*, edited by Barbara Miller Lane (New York: Routledge, 2007), 260; Anthony McElligott, "Political Culture," in *Weimar Germany*, edited by Anthony McElligott (Oxford: Oxford University Press, 2009), 29–30; Richard Pommer and Christian Otto, *Weissenhof 1927 and the Modern Movement in Architecture* (Chicago: University of Chicago Press, 1991), 18–19. On the case of England, see Swenarton, *Building the New Jerusalem*, 1–11.
6. The quote is from Edith Wood, *The Housing of the Unskilled Wage Earner: America's Next Problem* (New York: Macmillan, 1919), 1. See also Graham R. Taylor, *Satellite Cities: A Study of Industrial Suburbs* (New York: D. Appleton, 1915), 263–301.
7. Swenarton, *Building the New Jerusalem*, 1–11.
8. Ibid., 41–57.

9. Mark Swenarton, *Homes Fit for Heroes: The Politics and Architecture of Early State Housing in Britain* (Portsmouth, NH: Heinemann Educational Books, 1981), 162–177.

10. Susan R. Henderson, "A Revolution in the Woman's Sphere: Grete Lihotzky and the Frankfurt Kitchen," in Lane, *Housing and Dwelling*, 248–258; Susan R. Henderson, *Building Culture: Ernst May and the New Frankfurt Initiative, 1926–1931* (New York: Peter Lang, 2013). See also Pommer and Otto, *Weissenhof 1927 and the Modern Movement in Architecture*.

11. Henderson, "A Revolution in the Woman's Sphere," 264; Adam Tooze, *The Wages of Destruction: The Making and Breaking of the Nazi Economy* (New York: Penguin, 2006), 136–143; International Labor Office, *An International Enquiry into Costs of Living: A Comparative Study of Workers' Living Costs in Detroit (USA) and Fourteen European Cities*, 2d rev. ed. (Geneva: International Labor Office, 1931), 17–18. See also Anthony McElligott, "Introduction," in McElligott, *Weimar Germany*, 14; Pommer and Otto, *Weissenhof 1927 and the Modern Movement in Architecture*, 8.

12. Adelheid von Saldern, "'Neues Wohnen': Housing and Reform," in McElligott, *Weimar Germany*, 209–212.

13. Ibid.; Elizabeth Denby, *Europe Rehoused* (New York: W. W. Norton, 1938), 125. On flat and sloped roof forms as symbolic of modern versus traditional culture, see Pommer and Otto, *Weissenhof 1927 and the Modern Movement in Architecture*, 28.

14. Denby, *Europe Rehoused*, 251.

15. Von Saldern, "Neues Wohnen," 208.

16. Siegfried Gideon, *Walter Gropius: Work and Teamwork* (New York: Reinhold, 1954), 87, 215.

17. Walter Gropius argued that the "dwelling for the subsistence level" might be as small as forty square meters (430 square feet), which he interpreted as a "progressive development in lifestyle": von Saldern, *Neues Wohnen*, 209.

18. Denby, *Europe Rehoused*, 135.

19. Von Saldern, "Neues Wohnen," 217–223.

20. Denby, *Europe Rehoused*, 129. See also von Saldern, "Neues Wohnen," 209–212.

21. Denby, *Europe Rehoused*, 122–147.

22. Andrew Wright Crawford, "War-time Housing—A Supreme Opportunity," *Architectural Forum*, April 1918, 91. See also Janet Hutchison, "Building for Babbitt: The State and the Suburban Home Ideal," *Journal of Policy History* 9, no. 2 (1997): 184–210. On American company towns in this period, see Crawford, *Building the Workingman's Paradise*, 152–173.

23. Clarence Burton, *The City of Detroit, Michigan, 1701–1922* (Detroit: Clarke, 1922), 542–543.

24. Solvay Process Company, "Report of the Director," *Solvay Guild Yearbook 1914–1915*, Burton Historical Collection, Detroit Public Library.

25. Crawford, *Building the Workingman's Paradise*, 95–98, 152–163.

26. "Jefferson Rouge, the Development of Solvay Process Company, Detroit, Mich.," *Architectural Forum*, April 1918, 121–122.

27. Charles May, "Some Aspects of Industrial Housing: III. The Need for Maintenance Measure," *Architectural Forum*, March 1918, 75–76.

28. Ford Bryan, *Beyond the Model T: The Other Ventures of Henry Ford* (Detroit: Wayne State University Press, 1990), 76–77. Descriptions and illustrations of Fordson Village are in Thomas Brunk, *Leonard B. Willeke: Excellence in Architecture and Design* (Detroit: Wayne State University Press, 1986), 137–147; Bryan, *Beyond the Model T.*

29. A rejected offer to pursue home building for Ford is in Chester Emergency Housing Corporation to Ford Motor Company, letter, August 5, 1918, in Thomas W. Brunk, "The Work of Leonard Bernard Willeke," microfilm reel, accession no. 1605, box 1; residential specifications of the Moraine Development Company provided to Ford Motor Company, accession no. 47, box 5, both in Collections of the Henry Ford Museum of American Innovation, Dearborn, MI (hereafter, The Henry Ford). See also Bryan, *Beyond the Model T*, 75–76.

30. Ida Tarbell to Samuel Marquis, letter, May 12, 1916, Samuel Marquis Papers, Correspondence, Cranbrook Center for Collections and Research, Bloomfield, MI (hereafter, Marquis Papers).

31. Roveda's "City of the Sun" project is in accession no. 47, box 5, "Concrete Houses 1916" folder, The Henry Ford. The majority of documents in the folder relate to concrete houses, but there is no indication that Roveda's project is based in concrete construction.

32. Peter Roveda, "The City of the Sun," *American Homes and Gardens*, vol. 7, November 1910, 447.

33. Tommaso Campanella, *The City of the Sun* (N.p.: Merchant Books, [1602] 2009), 18; Ebenezer Howard, *Garden Cities of Tomorrow* (London: Swan Sonnenschein, 1902). Regarding the homeownership ideal, see Ford Motor Company, *Helpful Hints and Advice to Employes.*

34. Roveda, "The City of the Sun."

35. Brunk, *Leonard B. Willeke*, 137.

36. Brunk, *Leonard B. Willeke*, 79–135; Detroit Society of Arts and Crafts (DSAC), "List of Members 1916–17," *Eleventh Annual Report Officers and Members for 1918*, DSAC Archive, College for Creative Studies, Detroit, 29–35.

37. Solvay's Jefferson Rouge appeared on an analytical list of U.S. workers' housing precedents prepared by Willeke and reproduced in Brunk, *Leonard Willeke*, 141.

38. Crawford, *Building the Workingman's Paradise*, 95–97, 160–163. On the Pullman Strike see Jane Addams, "A Modern Lear: A Parenthetical Chapter," in Taylor, *Satellite Cities*, 68–90; Bigott, *From Cottage to Bungalow*; Crawford, *Building the Workingman's Paradise*, 37–45.

39. "General Notes on Housing," Leonard B. Willeke Papers, Bentley Historical Library, University of Michigan, Ann Arbor.

40. Crawford, *Building the Workingman's Paradise*, 165.

41. On Hoover, see Hutchison, "Building for Babbitt," 185. The housing numbers are from *Annual Report for the City of Detroit*, 1915–1930, as collected in Matthew Daley, "City of Mass Production: Building, Managing, and Living in Detroit, America's First Automobile Metropolis, 1920–1933" (Ph.D. diss., Bowling Green State University, Bowling Green, OH, 2004), 98–99. The national trend in production is illustrated in Mason C. Doan, *American Housing Production, 1880–2000: A Concise History* (Lanham, MD: University Press of America, 1997), 3–4.

42. Bryan, *Beyond the Model T*, 78–82.

43. On the Maloney Subdivision, which is called the "Ford Homes Historic District" today, see Carolyn S. Loeb, *Entrepreneurial Vernacular: Developers' Subdivisions in the 1920s* (Baltimore: Johns Hopkins University Press, 2001), 19–54.

44. Samuel Marquis to Edsel B. Ford, "The Ford Cooperative Plan," letter, June 28, 1920, Marquis Papers.

45. Beth Tompkins Bates, *The Making of Black Detroit in the Age of Henry Ford* (Chapel Hill: University of North Carolina Press, 2012), 55–58; Lizabeth Cohen, *Making a New Deal: Industrial Workers in Chicago, 1919–1939*, 2d ed. (Cambridge: Cambridge University Press, 2008), 160–161.

46. "To Close a Solvay Plant: Indefinite Shut-Down, Affecting 1,600, Announced in Detroit," *New York Times*, June 26, 1921.

47. María Arquero de Alarcón and Larissa Larson, "Mapping Delray," in *Mapping Detroit: Land, Community, and Shaping a City*, edited by June Manning Thomas (Detroit: Wayne State University Press, 2015), 121.

48. See Barry Neal Johnson, "Wastewater Treatment Comes to Detroit" (Ph.D. diss., Wayne State University, Detroit, 2010), 148; Sanborn Map Company, *Insurance Maps of Detroit, Michigan*, vol. 5, 1923 [updated to 1961], sheet 97, University of Michigan, Ann Arbor.

49. Marc Weiss, *Rise of the Community Builders: The American Real Estate Industry and Urban Land Planning* (New York: Columbia University Press, 1987); Thomas C. Hubka and Judith T. Kenny, "Examining the American Dream: Housing Standards and the Emergence of a National Housing Culture, 1900–1930," *Perspectives in Vernacular Architecture* 13, no. 1 (2006): 49–69.

50. "Form New Realty Firm: Chas. W. Burton and V. C. Gnad Will Open Subdivision," *Detroit Free Press*, April 27, 1913, 9; "The Burton Realty Company," advertisement, *Detroit News*, December 14, 1913, 32.

51. G. William Baist, *Baist's Real Estate Atlas of Surveys of Detroit and Suburbs, Michigan*, vol. 2 (Philadelphia: N.p., 1923), plan 55.

52. On the range of housebuilding practices in this period, see Richard Harris, *Unplanned Suburbs: Toronto's American Tragedy* (Baltimore: Johns Hopkins University Press, 1996), 168–199.

53. Sanborn Map Company, *Insurance Maps of Detroit, Michigan*, vol. 12, 1924, sheet 29, University of Michigan, Ann Arbor.

54. International Labor Office, *An International Enquiry into Costs of Living*, 17–19, 126, 185.

55. Ibid., 25–26.

CHAPTER 4

Epigraph: Standard Homes Company and F. M. Sibley Lumber Company, *Better Homes at Lower Cost: 101 Modern Homes Standardized* (Washington, DC: Standard Homes, 1926), n.p.

1. Mason C. Doan, *American Housing Production, 1880–2000: A Concise History* (Lanham, MD: University Press of America, 1997), 27–28.

2. Ibid., 28.

3. Detroit Board of Commerce, caption to an illustration by Tom May featuring three men at work on a residential construction site, *The Detroiter*, March 24, 1919, 3.

4. Steve Babson, *Working Detroit: The Making of a Union Town* (New York: Adama, 1984), 48, for example, attributes the homebuilding boom of the 1920s to the "mass production" of houses. A mass-producing machine operator at the Packard Motor Car Company, for example, went through motions that his or her employer had studied down to a fraction of a second. On the building site, by contrast, it was considered a modernizing practice in the early 1920s to have employees account for their day's work in five-minute increments: see "What's New: New Materials and Equipment That Keep Your Work Up to Date," *Building Age*, March 1922, 45.

5. Charles B. Ball, *Homes of Today and Citizens of Tomorrow: Address of Mr. Charles B. Ball of Chicago at the Detroit Museum of Art, April 15, 1915* (Detroit: Detroit Housing Association, 1915), 5.

6. Ibid.

7. "Ask Help to Remedy Housing Conditions," *The Detroiter*, June 12, 1916, 1.

8. Detroit Housing Association, *Right Methods in a Housing Bureau* (Detroit: Detroit Housing Association, 1915).

9. "Michigan Leads the Way," *Housing Betterment*, vol. 6, no. 2, May 1917, 3–5.

10. State of Michigan, *Housing Law of Michigan* (Act 167 of 1917) (Lansing: Fort Wayne Printing, 1924), 8, 13.

11. Ibid., 9–11.

12. Maurice Ramsey, "Some Aspects of Non-partisan Government in Detroit, 1918–1940" (Ph.D. diss., University of Michigan, Ann Arbor, 1944), 24–51.

13. Beth Tompkins Bates, *The Making of Black Detroit in the Age of Henry Ford* (Chapel Hill: University of North Carolina Press, 2012), 34–36; Ramsey, "Some Aspects of Non-partisan Government in Detroit," 85–110.

14. Campbell Gibson, "Population of the 100 Largest Cities and Other Urban Places in the United States: 1790 to 1990," Working Paper no. POP-WP027, U.S. Bureau of the Census, June 1998, https://www.census.gov/library/working-papers/1998/demo/POP-twps0027.html. On the nineteenth- and twentieth-century history of urban annexation, see Kenneth T. Jackson, *Crabgrass Frontier: The Suburbanization of America* (New York: Oxford University Press, 1985), 138–156.

15. Graeme O'Geran, *A History of the Detroit Street Railways* (Detroit: Conover, 1931), 333–387, esp. 363–364, 378–379. On the role of streetcars in urban decentralization, see Jackson, *Crabgrass Frontier*, 116–120.

16. Richard Harris, *Building a Market: The Rise of the Home Improvement Industry, 1914–1960* (Chicago: University of Chicago Press, 2012), 33–38.

17. G. W. Drennan, president, Detroit Real Estate Board, to the membership, letter, February 28, 1919, Detroit Real Estate Board, Real Estate Files, Burton Historical Collection, Detroit Public Library.

18. Janet Hutchison, "Building for Babbitt: The State and the Suburban Home Ideal," *Journal of Policy History* 9, no. 2 (1997): 187.

19. "The Government's Aid to Building: Recommend Building Code and Standardization of Sizes Will Result in More Economical Construction," *Building Age*, April 1923, 56; Gail Radford, *Modern Housing for America: Policy Struggles in the New Deal Era* (Chicago: University of Chicago Press, 1996), 51–52; Gwendolyn Wright, *Building the Dream: A Social History of Housing in America* (New York: Pantheon, 1981), 197.

20. Detroit Builders' Exhibition Inc., *Detroit's Second Annual Builders Show: Ford Exhibition Building Woodward and Grand Boulevard, February 28–March 7*, program, 1920, Burton Historical Collection, Detroit Public Library.

21. Thomas C. Hubka and Judith T. Kenny, "Examining the American Dream: Housing Standards and the Emergence of a National Housing Culture, 1900–1930," *Perspectives in Vernacular Architecture* 13, no. 1 (2006): 49. On the interwar culture of standardization, see Greg Hise, *Magnetic Los Angeles: Planning the Twentieth-Century Metropolis* (Baltimore: Johns Hopkins University Press, 1997), 56–85. Hubka and Kenny note that this standard was not limited to the single-family bungalow but was applicable to other national and regional types, such as the duplex, the New England triple-decker, and the Chicago four-family flat.

22. Standard Homes and Sibley Lumber, *Better Homes at Lower Cost*.

23. Harris, *Building a Market*, 98–124.

24. "What the Editor Thinks," *Building Age*, March 1923, 79.

25. Standard Homes and Sibley Lumber, *Better Homes at Lower Cost*, 92.

26. Virginia McAlester and Lee McAlester, *A Field Guide to American Houses* (New York: Alfred A. Knopf, 1985), 453–454.

27. Olivier Zunz describes this late-nineteenth century split between an informal housing market for workers and a formal housing market for the middle class in Detroit as the "Dual Housing Market": Olivier Zunz, *The Changing Face of Inequality: Urbanization, Industrial Development, and Immigrants in Detroit, 1880–1920* (Chicago: University of Chicago Press, 1982). On the increase of amenities from the worker's cottage type to the bungalow type, see Thomas C. Hubka, *Houses without Names: Architectural Nomenclature and the Classification of America's Common Houses* (Knoxville: University of Tennessee Press, 2013), 64–68.

28. Clifford Edward Clark, *The American Family Home, 1800–1960* (Chapel Hill: University of North Carolina Press, 1986), 131–157, 171–183. See also Hubka and Kenny, "Examining the American Dream."

29. Standard Homes and Sibley Lumber, *Better Homes at Lower Cost*, 100.

30. Hubka, *Houses without Names*, 57.

31. Hubka and Kenny, "Examining the American Dream."

32. Standard Homes and Sibley Lumber, "Important," *Better Homes at Lower Cost*."

33. Aladdin Company, *Aladdin "Built in a Day" House Catalog, 1917* (New York: Dover, 1995), 75.

34. Ibid., 89–91.

35. Data from HOLC have been digitized by the University of Richmond's Digital Scholarship Lab and are available at https://dsl.richmond.edu/panorama/redlining/#loc=5/39.1/-94.58. The ownership comparison is in "Area Description" documents—see, e.g., Detroit neighborhood areas D19, C37, and D2. The oral history referenced here is Catherine Carter Blackwell, interview by Louis Jones, accession no. UOH001949, 2005, print transcript, Westsider Oral History Project, Walter P. Reuther Library, Wayne State University, Detroit.

36. Real Estate Listing Bureau, "1376 Victoria Ave[nue]," *Real Estate Listing Bureau Bulletin*, November 18, 1926, Real Estate Files, Burton Historical Collection, Detroit Public Library.

37. Detroit Builders' Exhibition Inc., *To Those Who Build*, 8.

38. Richard Harris, *Unplanned Suburbs: Toronto's American Tragedy* (Baltimore: Johns Hopkins University Press, 1996); Nicolaides, *My Blue Heaven*.

39. Carolyn S. Loeb, *Entrepreneurial Vernacular: Developers' Subdivisions in the 1920s* (Baltimore: Johns Hopkins University Press, 2001), 63–67, 73.

40. Brightmoor Community Center, *Brightmoor: A Community in Action* (Detroit: Brightmoor Community Center, 1940), 4; Loeb, *Entrepreneurial Vernacular*, 59–60.

41. Brightmoor Community Center, *Brightmoor*, 61.

42. For example, agents with the Treppa Realty Company sold the Conant Avenue Subdivision in terms of the momentum they had established developing it. "The streets are already being prepared, cement sidewalks will also be laid soon. The foundations under two beautiful houses are being dug and 10 to 20 houses are going to be built this summer. . . . [F]ive rooms with hard floors": Treppa Realty Company Agents, "Attention: Treppa-Ciganek Conant Avenue Subdivision," advertisement, *Dziennik Polski*, May 13, 1916, translated from Polish by Justyna Zdunek-Wielgolaska. Harris describes merchant building in batches of forty houses in Toronto: see Harris, *Unplanned Suburbs*, 187.

43. Detroit Housing Corporation, "Building Propositions," advertisement, *Detroit Free Press*, September 16, 1923.

44. Harris, *Unplanned Suburbs*, 190–191.

45. Henry S. Coppin Company, *Detroit Free Press*, May 13, 1923.

46. "Home Builders Do Own Work: East Side Area Shows 1,000 Houses Under Way," *Detroit Free Press*, May 13, 1923.

47. Detroit Builders' Exhibition Inc., "List of Exhibitors," in *Detroit's Second Annual Builders Show*, n.p.

48. See Sidney Glazer, *Detroit: A Study in Urban Development* (New York: Bookman Associates, 1965), 94–95; Sam Bass Warner, *Streetcar Suburbs: The Process of Growth in Boston, 1870–1900* (Cambridge, MA: Harvard University Press, 1962), 118–127; Marc Weiss, *The Rise of the Community Builders: The American Real Estate Industry and Urban Land Planning* (New York: Columbia University Press, 1987), 1, 5–6, 20, 39.

49. Loeb, *Entrepreneurial Vernacular*; Joan M. Meister, "Civic Park: General Motors' Solution to the Housing Shortage," *A Wind Gone Down: Smoke into Steel*, edited by Michigan History Division (Lansing: Michigan Department of State, 1978), 8–11.

50. "Employers to Form Company to Build Workmen's Homes," *The Detroiter*, April 7, 1919, 1.

51. See Weiss, *The Rise of the Community Builders*. A Chicago-based home builder, in contrast to Taylor and General Motors, had produced five hundred houses over about a ten-year career, a feat noted as "almost one a week! A record to be proud of": "Homes That Holm Built: Interesting Story of How a Bricklayer's Apprentice Became a Successful Contractor Specializing in Home Building," *Building Age*, May 1922, 50–51.

52. H. R. Horton, "From Carpenter to Large Scale Speculative Builder," *Building Age*, October 1923, 58.

53. "College Park Development," *Pipp's Weekly*, April 18, 1925, 3.

54. "Sloan Brothers to Build 50 Homes," *Pipp's Weekly*, July 11, 1925, 5.

55. "Building Propositions," *Detroit Free Press*, May 5, 1923, September 16, 1923.

56. H. Colin Campbell, "Making an Early Start," *Building Age*, February 1923, 54.

57. Lawrence S. Keir, "How to Protect Work and Workers during the Winter Season," *Building Age*, November 1922, 47–48.

58. "Suggestions for Winter Work: Modern Methods of Working Provide Twelve Months' Work to the Building Year," *Building Age*, January 1922, 30.

59. A. Ashmun Kelly, "Painting in Winter-Time: And Its Difficulties," *Building Age*, November 1922, 49.

60. Noble Foster Hoggson and E. J. Russell, "Uniting the Construction Industry: Progressive Aims of American Construction Council Now Being Formed, the Raising of Standards and Efficiency Its Object," *Building Age*, June 1922, 28.

61. "Plan Now to Add Field Equipment," *Building Age*, January 1923, 80.

62. "What the Editor Thinks," *Building Age*, December 1922, 53.

63. "How Can We Best Handle the Building Boom?" *Building Age*, June 1923, 47–50.

64. "What the Editor Thinks," *Building Age*, May 1922, 53.

65. C. J. Kelsey, vice-president, Title Guarantee and Trust Company, quoted in "How Can We Best Handle the Building Boom?" 49.

66. Leo Wolman, *Growth of American Trade Unions 1880–1923* (New York: National Bureau of Economic Research, 1924), 91–95.

67. Ramsay Muir, *America the Golden: An Englishman's Notes and Comparisons* (London: Williams and Norgate, 1927), 85–86.

68. Ibid.

69. "The American Plan in Detroit," *Michigan Manufacturer and Financial Record*, vol. 26, 1920, 17–18.

70. "Lauds Detroit Building Organization," *Domestic Engineering*, vol. 100, 1922, 391–392.

71. "The Most Important Problem Now Confronting the Building Industry Is the Shortage of Men," *Building Age*, August 1923, 39

72. Samuel Hotchkiss, Hotchkiss Company, Louisville, KY, comments made at the Associated General Contractors of America conference, in "Progress in the Construction Industry," *Building Age*, March 1923, 45–46.

73. D. Knickerbacker Boyd, "Apprentices and Craftsmanship," *Building Age*, July 1923, 43–44.

74. "The Most Important Problem Now Confronting the Building Industry Is the Shortage of Men," *Building Age*, August 1923, 39.

75. H. R. Horton, "From Carpenter to Speculative Builder: Interesting Story of How Two Apprentices Became Successful Builders, Erecting Many Blocks of Homes in a Few Years," *Building Age*, October 1923, 58.

76. Burt L. Fenner of McKim, Mead and White notes the continued importance of tradespeople from abroad, despite immigration restrictions: "The Cause of Our Shortage of Men: Excerpts from Address before New York Building Congress," *Building Age*, August 1923, 41–42.

77. "What the Editor Thinks" (March 1923), 79.

78. Huber Bros. Builders, "How We Hold Our Men," *Building Age*, August 1923, 66.

79. W. M. Newton, "What One Builder Thinks about Training Our Future Workers," *Building Age*, September 1923, 56.

80. Herbert Gottfried, "The Machine and the Cottage: Building, Technology, and the Single-Family House, 1870–1910," *IA* 21, no. 2 (1995): 47–68. See also Joseph Bigott, *From Cottage to Bungalow: Houses and the Working Class in*

Metropolitan Chicago, 1869–1929 (Chicago: University of Chicago Press, 2001), 28–41.

81. Standard Homes and Sibley Lumber, "Important."
82. Standard Homes and Sibley Lumber, "Save from $200 to $1000 on Your Home by Using Plans Carefully Standardized to Avoid Waste in Materials and Labor," in *Better Homes at Lower Cost*, n.p.
83. Warner, *Streetcar Suburbs*, 118–127.
84. Weyerhaeuser Forest Products, *High Cost of Cheap Construction: A Book for Home-Builders on the Importance of Right Construction in House Building* (St. Paul, MN: Weyerhaeuser Forest Products, 1922), 17. See also David Monteyne, "Framing the American Dream," *Journal of Architectural Education* 58, no. 1 (September, 2004): 24–33.
85. Bigott, *From Cottage to Bungalow*, 30–39; F. E. Kidder, "Chapter II: Wooden Framing. Ordinary Construction," *Building Construction and Superintendence*, vol. 2, 1920, 94.
86. Harris, *Building a Market*, 102–105.
87. A. H. Scott, "Shop Framed Houses: Save Labor and Material by Fabricating and Assembling the Framing Sections at the Mill," *Building Age*, May 1922, 40–41.
88. Richard Harris, "Chicago's Other Suburbs," *Geographical Review* 84, no. 4 (October 1994): 394–410.
89. Babson, *Working Detroit*, 49.
90. Philip L. Sniffen [sic], "Do Your Trucks Live Up to Their Jobs?" *Building Age*, August 1924, 92–93.
91. P. L. Sniffin, "Truck Operation in Winter," *Building Age*, January 1923, 66–67.
92. "Plan Now to Add Field Equipment," 80.
93. American Floor Surfacing Machine Company, advertisement, *Building Age*, July 1923, 89. The quote is from *Building Trades Blue Book*, 1926, 7.

CHAPTER 5

Epigraph: H. T. Clough, "1915—Detroit's Banner Year Draws to Close," *The Detroiter*, December 20, 1915, 12.

1. Across the 1910s and 1920s, the number of automobiles registered in the United States soared fortyfold, and in this same boom period the total value of Detroit's real estate grew nearly tenfold, from $377 million to $3.394 billion: see Sidney Glazer, *Detroit: A Study in Urban Development* (New York: Bookman Associates, 1965), 91–92.
2. Detroit Real Estate Board, "History," *Detroit Realtor*, special edition for Better Homes and Building Exposition, May 20–27, 1922, n.p., Real Estate Files, Burton Historical Collection, Detroit Public Library (hereafter, Burton Collection).
3. Detroit Real Estate Board, "State Income Tax: March Diner," March 11, 1921, and "The [Detroit United Railways] Wants Fifteen Minutes," n.d., letters, Real Estate Files, Burton Collection. The Red Cross appeal was made in a letter from Board President Thad E. Leland to the membership, December 17, 1917, Burton Collection.
4. See Marc Weiss, *The Rise of the Community Builders: The American Real Estate Industry and Urban Land Planning* (New York: Columbia University

Press, 1987), 21–27; "Will Acquaint Public with 'Realtor' Ethics and Meaning of Term," *Detroit Free Press*, January 25, 1925, Real Estate Files, Burton Collection. See also "Detroit Real Estate Board: Officers and Members, Commissions and Charges," pamphlet, 1915, Detroit Real Estate Board Papers, Burton Collection.

5. Harry Culver, "Address of Harry H. Culver Delivered before Detroit Real Estate Board," *Detroit Realtor*, supp., November 1927.

6. Ralston Printing Company, *Reliability: Detroit's Real Estate Values Are Sound*, pamphlet, Facts about Detroit series, pt. 4, n.d. (ca. 1921–1929), Real Estate Files, Burton Collection.

7. The Detroit Real Estate Board writes "Detroit—Two Million in 1930," at the header of the cover page of *Detroit Realtor*, special edition for Better Homes and Building Exposition, May 20–27, 1922.

8. Hannan Real Estate Exchange, *The Hannan Bible: Being a Compilation of Inspirational Data out of the History of Detroit and Its Real Estate Development* (Detroit: Hannan Real Estate Exchange, 1928), 61.

9. Joseph Mulcahy, a former New Yorker and editor of the *Detroit Times*, quoted in *Detroit Times*, May 19, 1928, and reprinted in Hannan Real Estate Exchange, *The Hannan Bible*, 71.

10. Hannan Real Estate Exchange, *The Hannan Bible*, 67.

11. See Robert Fishman, *Urban Utopias in the Twentieth Century: Ebenezer Howard, Frank Lloyd Wright, and Le Corbusier* (Cambridge, MA: MIT Press, 1982).

12. Culver, "Address of Harry H. Culver Delivered before Detroit Real Estate Board."

13. Paul Rohr, *Am I My Dollar's Keeper?* (Detroit: Adix Realty, 1926), 25–26, Burton Collection.

14. Ibid., 30–31.

15. Ibid., 24.

16. Reprint from *Detroit News*, May 14, 1928; Harry Carman, quoted in "He Pictures Detroit Queen of Hemisphere: Columbia University Professor Says Time Is Not Far Distant When City Will Assume Crown," Hannan Real Estate Exchange, *The Hannan Bible*, 64–65.

17. Hannan Real Estate Exchange, *The Hannan Bible*, 42.

18. Ibid.

19. Ernest W. Burgess, "The Growth of the City: An Introduction to a Research Project," in *The City*, edited by Robert E. Park, Ernest W. Burgess, and Roderick D. McKenzie (Chicago: University of Chicago Press, 1925).

20. Ibid.

21. Hannan Real Estate Exchange, *The Hannan Bible*, 33.

22. Roy P. Swanson Company Real Estate, "Too Far Out," excerpt from an advertisement, 1924, Real Estate Files, Burton Collection.

23. Ibid., 76.

24. Ibid., 79.

25. John M. Gries and James S. Taylor, *How to Own Your Own Home: A Handbook for Prospective Home Owners* (Washington, DC: Government Printing Office, 1923), 1–2.

26. Olivier Zunz, *The Changing Face of Inequality: Urbanization, Industrial Development, and Immigrants in Detroit, 1880–1920* (Chicago: University of Chicago Press, 1982), 326–371.

27. Gries and Taylor, *How to Own Your Own Home*, 11.
28. Samuel A. Merchant Company, "The Elmwood Plan Should Interest Every Board Member," advertisement, *The Detroiter*, May 29, 1916, 11.
29. Burgess, "The Growth of the City."
30. Hannan Real Estate Exchange, *The Hannan Bible*, 84–85
31. Ibid., 85.
32. Ibid., 81.
33. F. S. Prikryl and Company, "High Class Workingmen's Homes," advertisement, in *Detroit Today: A Brief History of Detroit's Origin and Development*, by Thomas Laurence Munger (Detroit: Board of Commerce, 1921), 654.
34. Robert S. Lynd and Helen Merrell Lynd, *Middletown: A Study in American Culture* (New York: Harcourt Brace, 1929), 34.
35. Hannan Real Estate Exchange, *The Hannan Bible*, 24.
36. B. E. Taylor, *Your Real Opportunity to Secure a Home of Your Own*, advertising poster, 1922, B. E. Taylor, Realtor, Miscellaneous Material, Real Estate Files, Burton Collection.
37. International Labor Office, *An International Enquiry into Costs of Living: A Comparative Study of Workers' Living Costs in Detroit (USA) and Fourteen European Cities*, 2d rev. ed. (Geneva: International Labor Office, 1931), 120.
38. Rohr, *Am I My Dollar's Keeper?* 6.
39. "The Detroit Terminal Railroad." *Railway Age Gazette*, June 19, 1914, 1522–1523, http://michiganrailroads.com/images/PDFDocs/DetroitTerminalRailroad[RailwayAgeGazette061914].pdf.
40. "What the New Ford Highway Means to Detroit and to the Northwest Section," *Detroit News*, March 25, 1916, 9; Walt Clyde, "Great South and West Area of Yesterday—Today—Tomorrow," *Greater Detroit Magazine*, reprint, 1925, Real Estate Files, Burton Collection. See also Jerome Thomas, "The City of Detroit: A Study in Urban Geography" (Ph.D. diss., University of Michigan, Ann Arbor, 1928), 54–56.
41. "What the New Ford Highway Means to Detroit and to the Northwest Section," 9.
42. Gwendolyn Wright, *Building the Dream: A Social History of Housing in America* (New York: Pantheon, 1981), 96, 162.
43. Ibid.
44. Thomas, "The City of Detroit," 125.
45. A neighborhood in southwestern Detroit, not to be confused with Springwells Township or the nascent development within what would become Dearborn that is also sometimes referred to as Springwells.
46. The name Springwells appears to have been derived from Springwells Township, the west side jurisdiction from which Detroit annexed the neighborhood's territory.
47. Thomas, "The City of Detroit," 130. See also Works Progress Administration (WPA), *Sixteenth Census of the United States: 1940, Housing. Analytical Maps, Detroit, Mich[igan] Block Statistics* (Washington, DC, 1943[?]), 51, Main Branch, Detroit Public Library.
48. Sanborn Map Company, *Insurance Maps of Detroit, Michigan*, vol. 5, 1923, sheets 1–48, University of Michigan, Ann Arbor.
49. Thomas, "The City of Detroit," 125–126.
50. WPA, *Sixteenth Census of the United States*, 19.

51. The quote is from Real Estate Listing Bureau, "8737 Mason Pl[ace]," *Real Estate Listing Bureau Bulletin*, November 18, 1926. See also Thomas, "The City of Detroit," fig. 6; Zunz, *The Changing Face of Inequality*, 344–347.

52. Detroit Housing Commission, *Housing in Detroit: Reviewing the Past, Previewing the Future*, pamphlet, 1943, 6–7, Burton Collection.

53. Anne Durkin Keating, *Building Chicago: Suburban Developers and the Creation of a Divided Metropolis* (Urbana: University of Illinois Press, 2002), 124–125; Jon C. Teaford, *City and Suburb: The Political Fragmentation of Metropolitan America, 1850–1970* (Baltimore: Johns Hopkins University Press, 1979), 83–87.

54. Lambrecht, Kelly and Company, *Why Don't You Make Money by the City's Growth?* advertising pamphlet, n.d. [ca. 1920], Real Estate Files, Burton Collection.

55. Ibid.

56. Lambrecht, Kelly and Company, *James W. Fales Holden Ave. Subdivision*, advertising poster, n.d. [ca. 1920], Real Estate Files, Burton Collection.

57. National Association of Real Estate Boards (NAREB), "Article 34," in *Code of Ethics: Adopted by the NAREB at its Seventeenth Annual Convention, June 6, 1924*, 7, Burton Collection. See also David M. P. Freund, *Colored Property: State Policy and White Racial Politics in Suburban America* (Chicago: University of Chicago Press, 2007), 80; Elaine Lewinnek, *The Working Man's Reward: Chicago's Early Suburbs and the Roots of American Sprawl* (New York: Oxford University Press, 2014), 171.

58. NAREB, *Code of Ethics*, 3, 8.

59. A view of Taylor's office window appears in *Detroit—B. E. Taylor—and You*, undated advertising pamphlet, B. E. Taylor, Realtor, Miscellaneous Material, Burton Collection. See also Carolyn S. Loeb, *Entrepreneurial Vernacular: Developers' Subdivisions in the 1920s* (Baltimore: Johns Hopkins University Press, 2020), 63.

60. Loeb, *Entrepreneurial Vernacular*, 60.

61. Regarding this emerging standard, see Thomas C. Hubka and Judith T. Kenny, "Examining the American Dream: Housing Standards and the Emergence of a National Housing Culture, 1900–1930," *Perspectives in Vernacular Architecture* 13, no. 1 (2006): 49–69.

62. B. E. Taylor, *Crescent Heights: Taylor's Newest and Best Offering*, advertising poster, 1919, Real Estate Files, Burton Collection.

63. Brightmoor Community Center, *Brightmoor: A Community in Action* (Detroit: Brightmoor Community Center, 1940), 61.

64. Ibid.; Loeb, *Entrepreneurial Vernacular*, 59–60.

65. Loeb, *Entrepreneurial Vernacular*, 60.

66. Taylor, *Your Real Opportunity to Secure a Home of Your Own*; B. E. Taylor, "Our Combination Home Offering," advertising postcard excerpt, n.d. [ca. 1922], B. E. Taylor, Realtor, Miscellaneous Material, Real Estate Files, Burton Collection.

67. B. E. Taylor, *Thanksgiving Day Is Turkey Day* and *Let Santa Bring You a Turkey*, advertising posters, n.d. [ca. 1920s], B. E. Taylor, Realtor, Miscellaneous Material, Real Estate Files, Burton Collection.

68. Thomas J. Sugrue, *The Origins of the Urban Crisis: Race and Inequality in Postwar Detroit* (Princeton, NJ: Princeton University Press, 1996), 39–40.

69. WPA, *Sixteenth Census of the United States*, 1, 22.

70. Detroit City Plan Commission, *Redevelopment Study: Selection of Areas and Assignment of Priorities* (Detroit: The Commission, 1954), fig. 1.

71. Thomas, "The City of Detroit," 141. Note that a crowded district of tenements and workers' houses was developed adjacent to Ford's plant, but most of Highland Park was composed of deed-restricted subdivisions limited to fine bungalows for the middle class. On Highland Park, see Clarence Hooker, *Life in the Shadows of the Crystal Palace, 1910–1927: Ford Workers in the Model T Era* (Bowling Green, OH: Bowling Green State University Popular Press, 1997).

72. Arthur Evans Wood, *Hamtramck, Then and Now: A Sociological Study of a Polish-American Community* (New York: Bookman Associates, 1955), 19, 115.

73. Hannan Real Estate Exchange, "Great Opening of Sonk Subdivision," advertisement, *Dziennik Polski*, April 4, 1916. All quotations from *Dziennik Polski* were translated from Polish by Justyna Zdunek-Wielgolaska.

74. E. D. Preston, "Flemming Subdivision," advertisement, *Dziennik Polski*, August 1, 1914.

75. Epstein and Tighon, "Edgewood Park Subdivision," advertisement, *Dziennik Polski*, July 25, 1914.

76. Ibid.

77. B. A. Horger, "Great Lot Sale at Frederick-Roberts-McKenny Realty Co[mpany] Subdivision," advertisement, *Dziennik Polski*, July 10, 1914.

78. Lerchenfeld, "The Most Beautiful Subdivision in Hamtramck," advertisement, *Dziennik Polski*, May 20, 1914.

79. Epstein and Tighon, "Edgewood Park Subdivision."

80. Ibid.

81. Jan B. Sosnowski, "Dear Compatriots," advertisement, *Dziennik Polski*, June 20, 1914.

82. Jan B. Sosnowski, "ATTENTION FELLOW COUNTRYMEN!" advertisement, *Dziennik Polski*, n.d.

83. Jan B. Sosnowski, "ATTENTION *FELLOW COUNTRYMEN!*" advertisement, *Dziennik Polski*, May 30, 1914; "ATTENTION: FORD CO[MPANY] WORKERS!" advertisement, *Dziennik Polski*, July 4, 2014.

84. E. D. Preston, "Flemming Subdivision."

85. Teaford, *City and Suburb*, 76–104; June Manning Thomas, *Redevelopment and Race: Planning a Finer City in Postwar Detroit* (Baltimore: Johns Hopkins University Press, 1997), 31–32.

86. Thomas, "The City of Detroit," 106.

87. Walter E. Kruesi, *Hamtramck: A Survey of Social, Educational, and Civic Conditions* (Detroit: Citizens of Detroit, 1915), 9–10, Burton Collection.

CHAPTER 6

Epigraph: Jane Jacobs, *The Death and Life of Great American Cities* (New York: Random House, 1961), 204.

1. José Luis Sert, *Can Our Cities Survive? An ABC of Urban Problems, Their Analysis, Their Solutions* (Cambridge, MA: Harvard University Press, 1942), 41.

2. Michel de Certeau, *The Practice of Everyday Life* (Berkeley: University of California Press, 2011), 30. See also Gwendolyn Wright, "Prescribing the Model Home," in *Home: A Place in the World*, edited by Arien Mack (New York: New York University Press, 1993), 223.

3. Thomas C. Hubka and Judith T. Kenny, "The Worker's Cottage in Milwaukee's Polish Community: Housing and the Process of Americanization, 1870–1920," *Perspectives in Vernacular Architecture* 8 (2000): 33–52, references Harriman's story. See Karl Edwin Harriman, *The Homebuilders* (Philadelphia: G. W. Jacobs, 1903).

4. For other portrayals of the lives of immigrants in urban America, see ibid.; Harold Waldo, *Stash of the Marsh Country* (New York: G. H. Doran, 1921); Anzia Yezierska, *Salome of the Tenements* (New York: Boni and Liveright, 1923).

5. Thomas S. Gladsky, *Princes, Peasants, and Other Polish Selves: Ethnicity in American Literature* (Amherst: University of Massachusetts Press, 1992), 53; Harriman, *The Homebuilders*, 29.

6. Harriman, *The Homebuilders*, 44.

7. Ibid., 62.

8. Mary Douglas, "The Idea of a Home: A Kind of Space," in *Housing and Dwelling: A Reader on Modern Domestic Architecture*, edited by Barbara Miller Lane (New York: Routledge, 2007), 62–63.

9. Gaston Bachelard, *The Poetics of Space* (New York: Orion, 1964), 5–16, 79–80.

10. Harriman, *The Homebuilders*, 161.

11. Ibid., 183.

12. *Detroit News*, quoted in Richard Bak, *Detroit, 1900–1930* (Charleston, SC: Arcadia, 1999).

13. Walter E. Kruesi, *Hamtramck: A Survey of Social, Educational, and Civic Conditions* (Detroit: Citizens of Detroit, 1915), 7.

14. Jacobs, *The Death and Life of Great American Cities*, 29–54. In this influential chapter Jacobs argues that the density of "eyes upon the street" facilitated by the urbanism of her Greenwich Village neighborhood made it safe.

15. Felix Seldon, interview by Louis Jones, accession no. UOH001949, 2005, print transcript, Westsider Oral History Project, Walter P. Reuther Library, Wayne State University, Detroit (hereafter, Westsider Project).

16. Horace Jefferson, interview by Louis Jones, accession no. UOH001949, 2005, print transcript, Westsider Project.

17. The referenced photograph is no. 2011.051.039, Digital Archive, Detroit Historical Society. Very few homes on the Diplocks' block had auto garages in 1916, but most had acquired one by 1929: Sanborn Map Company, *Fire Insurance Maps of Detroit*, vol. 8, sheet 53, 1916, vol. 11, sheet 75, 1929. Neighbors' professions are listed in *Polk's Detroit City Directory* (Detroit: R. L. Polk, 1924). The Ford survey is cited in Joyce Shaw Peterson, *American Automobile Workers, 1900–1933* (Albany: State University of New York Press, 1987), 81.

18. International Labor Office, *An International Enquiry into Costs of Living: A Comparative Study of Workers' Living Costs in Detroit (USA) and Fourteen European Cities*, 2d rev. ed. (Geneva: International Labor Office, 1931), 187.

19. Robert S. Lynd and Helen Merrell Lynd, *Middletown: A Study in American Culture* (New York: Harcourt Brace, 1929), 100.

20. Jefferson interview.

21. Jean Ernst Mayfield, interview by Louis Jones, accession no. UOH001949, 2005, print transcript, Westsider Project.

22. Jefferson interview.

23. Candace Volz, "The Modern Look of the Early Twentieth Century House," in *American Home Life, 1880–1930: A Social History of Spaces and Services*, edited by Jessica H. Foy and Thomas J. Schlereth (Knoxville: University of Tennessee Press, 1992), 31–33.

24. Edgar A. Guest, "At the Door" (excerpt), in Guest, *A Heap o' Livin'* (Chicago: Reilly and Britton, 1917), 132.

25. Lynd and Lynd, *Middletown*, 148.

26. Julius Combs, interview by Louis Jones, accession no. UOH001949, 2005, print transcript, Westsider Project.

27. Lynd and Lynd, *Middletown*, 28–29, 49–51.

28. Ruth Schwartz Cowan, *More Work for Mother: The Ironies of Household Technology from the Open Hearth to the Microwave* (New York: Basic, 1983), 152; Alice Kessler-Harris, *Out to Work: A History of Wage-Earning Women in the United States* (New York: Oxford University Press, 1982), 229; Alice Kessler-Harris, *Women Have Always Worked: A Historical Overview* (Old Westbury, NY: Feminist Press, 1981), 69; Linda McDowell, *Gender, Identity and Place: Understanding Feminist Geographies* (Cambridge: Polity, 1999), 71–81; U.S. Bureau of Labor Statistics, *Wages and Hours of Labor in the Automobile Industry, 1922*, Bulletin no. 348, October 1923, 2–3. The quote is from Lynd and Lynd, *Middletown*, 28–29.

29. International Labor Office, *An International Enquiry into Costs of Living*, 186–193.

30. Lynd and Lynd, *Middletown*, 62–63.

31. International Labor Office, *An International Enquiry into Costs of Living*, 157.

32. See, e.g., Brushaber, "The Influence of Home Atmosphere Cannot Be Overestimated," advertisement, and (for the quote), Weil and Company, "Michigan's Largest Furniture Store," advertisement, in *Marriage Record and Hints on Housekeeping: An Indispensable Household Guide* (Detroit: B. B. Schermerhorn, 1920).

33. Ramsay Muir, *America the Golden: An Englishman's Notes and Comparisons* (London: Williams and Norgate, 1927), 83.

34. International Labor Office, *An International Enquiry into Costs of Living*, 187.

35. People's Outfitting, "Clearing Sale Soon to Be Over," advertisement, *Dziennik Polski*, May 15, 1914.

36. International Labor Office, *An International Enquiry into Costs of Living*, 159, 194.

37. Volz, "The Modern Look of the Early Twentieth Century House," 37.

38. Donna Braden, "'The Family That Plays Together Stays Together," in Foy and Schlereth, *American Home Life*, 156.

39. Lizabeth Cohen, "Encountering Mass Culture at the Grassroots: The Experience of Chicago Workers in the 1920s," *American Quarterly* 41, no. 1 (March 1989): 8–9.

40. James Gregory, *The Southern Diaspora: How the Great Migrations of Black and White Southerners Transformed America* (Chapel Hill: University of North Carolina Press, 2005), 7.

41. Douglas, "The Idea of a Home," 65. See also Thomas C. Hubka and Judith T. Kenny, "Examining the American Dream: Housing Standards and the Emer-

gence of a National Housing Culture, 1900–1930," *Perspectives in Vernacular Architecture* 13, no. 1 (2006): 56–57.

42. Stephen Meyer, *The Five Dollar Day: Labor Management and Social Control in the Ford Motor Company, 1908–1921* (Albany: State University of New York Press, 1981), 95–121.

43. Lynd and Lynd, *Middletown*, 53.

44. Karin Calvert, "Children in the House," in Foy and Schlereth, *American Home Life*, 87. This was also a period when workers' children began to receive extended school education and enjoyed delayed entry into the workforce.

45. Seldon interview.

46. See, e.g., *Helpful Hints and Advice to Employes*, Benson Ford Research Center, Henry Ford Museum of American Innovation, Dearborn, MI, 12.

47. Edgar A. Guest, "When Father Shook the Stove," in Guest, *A Heap o' Livin'*, 154–155.

48. Seldon interview.

49. Edgar A. Guest, "Home" (excerpt), in Guest, *A Heap o' Livin'*, 29. See also Edgar A. Guest, "Home and the Baby," in Guest, *Just Folks* (Chicago: Reilly and Lee, 1919), 173–174.

50. Jeffrey Mirel, "The Politics of Educational Retrenchment in Detroit 1929–1935," in *Urban Education in the United States: A Historical Reader*, edited by John L. Rury (New York: Palgrave Macmillan, 2005), 180–181.

51. Clifford Edward Clark, *The American Family Home, 1800–1960* (Chapel Hill: University of North Carolina Press, 1986), 157–162; Cowan, *More Work for Mother*, 178.

52. *Outline for the Teaching of Home Making* (Detroit: Merrill-Palmer Institute, 1922), 4.

53. Ibid., 26.

54. International Labor Office, *An International Enquiry into Costs of Living*, 126, 185.

55. This photograph and research on the family who lived at 23 Elsa in 1914 appear in Kevin Boyle and Victoria Getis, *Muddy Boots and Ragged Aprons: Images of Working-Class Detroit, 1900–1930* (Detroit: Wayne State University Press, 1997), 34–37.

56. Clark, *The American Family Home*, 132.

57. Edgar A. Guest, "The Old Wooden Tub," in Guest, *The Path to Home* (Chicago: Reilly and Lee, 1919), 128–129.

58. International Labor Office, *An International Enquiry into Costs of Living*, 126, 185; NuBone Corsets, advertisement, in *Marriage Record and Hints on Housekeeping*, 66.

59. David Allan Levine, *Internal Combustion: The Races in Detroit, 1915–1926* (Westport, CT: Greenwood, 1976), 44–59.

60. Paul B. Shirley, in Elaine Latzman Moon, *Untold Tales, Unsung Heroes: An Oral History of Detroit's African American Community, 1918–1967* (Detroit: Wayne State University Press, 1994), 48–49.

61. Forrester B. Washington, "Environment" and "Social Classes among the Negroes of Detroit," in Washington, *The Negro in Detroit: A Survey of the Conditions of a Negro Group in a Northern Industrial Center during the War Prosperity Period* (Detroit: Associated Charities of Detroit, 1920), n.p.

62. Ibid.

63. Jefferson interview.
64. Frank Angelo, in Moon, *Untold Tales, Unsung Heroes*, 41.
65. Ibid., 60–66.
66. Jefferson and Mayfield interviews.
67. Kessler-Harris, *Women Have Always Worked*, 62–99; Forrester B. Washington, "Industrial Status of Colored Women in Detroit Today," in Washington, *The Negro in Detroit*, n.p.
68. Catherine Carter Blackwell, interview by Louis Jones, accession no. UOH001949, 2005, print transcript, Westsider Project. See also Combs, Jefferson, Mayfield, and Seldon interviews.
69. Combs interview.
70. bell hooks, "Homeplace (A Site of Resistance)," in Lane, *Housing and Dwelling*, 68–73. See also McDowell, *Gender, Identity and Place*, 89.
71. Cyril Arthur Player, "Detroit: Essence of America," *New Republic*, August 3, 1927, 27.

CHAPTER 7

Epigraph: bell hooks, "Homeplace (A Site of Resistance)," in hooks, *Yearning: Race, Gender, and Cultural Politics* (Boston: South End, 1990), 42.
1. The *Free Press* referred to the west side district, where several mob attacks had occurred in a matter of weeks, as "storm centers" and the "storm area": "Stop Rioting, Smith Pleads with Citizens," *Detroit Free Press*, July 12, 1925, 1.
2. Dianne Harris, *Little White Houses: How the Postwar Home Constructed Race in America* (Minneapolis: University of Minnesota Press, 2013), 2.
3. Reynolds Farley, Sheldon Danziger, and Harry J. Holzer, *Detroit Divided* (New York: Russell Sage Foundation, 2000), 144. Kevin Boyle, *Arc of Justice: A Saga of Race, Civil Rights, and Murder in the Jazz Age* (New York: Henry Holt, 2004), esp. 168–169, explores the events at the Sweet residence and the subsequent trial in great detail. See also David Allan Levine, *Internal Combustion: The Races in Detroit, 1915–1926* (Westport, CT: Greenwood, 1976); Richard W. Thomas, *Life for Us Is What We Make It: Building Black Community in Detroit, 1915–1945* (Bloomington: Indiana University Press, 1992), 137–140.
4. Cameron McWhirther, *Red Summer: The Summer of 1919 and the Awakening of Black America* (New York: Henry Holt, 2011).
5. Ibid., 147.
6. See John T. McGreevy, *Parish Boundaries: The Catholic Encounter with Race in the Twentieth-Century Urban North* (Chicago: University of Chicago Press, 1996), 4. McGreevy points out that racial violence centered on housing more so than on other issues in the urban North.
7. William M. Tuttle, "Contested Neighborhoods and Racial Violence: Prelude to the Chicago Riot of 1919," *Journal of Negro History* 55, no. 4 (October 1970): 266–288.
8. "Stop Rioting, Smith Pleads with Citizens."
9. On earlier race-based residential violence, see Levine, *Internal Combustion*, 45–46.
10. Recall Olivier Zunz's observation that Blacks "lived history in reverse" in early twentieth-century Detroit. As "new immigrants" were invited into whiteness and enjoyed increasing residential mobility, African Americans suffered increasing

segregation: see Olivier Zunz, *The Changing Face of Inequality: Urbanization, Industrial Development, and Immigrants in Detroit, 1880–1920* (Chicago: University of Chicago Press, 1982), 352–354, 373–378.

11. Writers' Program, Work Projects Administration (WPA), *Cosmopolitan Education: A History of Hamtramck High School* (Detroit: Federal Works Agency, WPA, 1940), 30.

12. Forrester B. Washington, "The Effect on Realty Values of Negro Invasion," in Washington, *The Negro in Detroit: A Survey of the Conditions of a Negro Group in a Northern Industrial Center during the War Prosperity Period* (Detroit: Associated Charities of Detroit, 1920), n.p.

13. N. D. B. Connolly, *A World More Concrete: Real Estate and the Remaking of Jim Crow South Florida* (Chicago: University of Chicago Press, 2014), 6.

14. The historian Kevin Boyle has shown that the threat of real estate depreciation weighed on the minds of heavily mortgaged white homeowners on the east side of Detroit, as word spread that the family of the Black physician Ossian Sweet was preparing to move into the neighborhood: Boyle, *Arc of Justice*, 134, 147–149.

15. Forrester B. Washington, "Housing (Section V)," in Washington, *The Negro in Detroit*, n.p. See also Gunnar Myrdal, *An American Dilemma: The Negro Problem and Modern Democracy* (New York: Harper, 1944), 623. George Galster discusses panic selling and describes homeowners' investments in neighborhoods as "fraught with an unusual amount of uncertainty," given the many changes beyond any one investor's control that could affect an area's perceived values: George Galster, "On the Nature of Neighbourhood," *Urban Studies* 38, no. 12 (2001): 2111–2124.

16. Boyle reflects on how depreciating values increased the risk that heavily encumbered workers would default—especially on shorter-term loans—when they came up for payment or renewal and the value of the home itself was, as we now call it, "underwater": Boyle, *Arc of Justice*, 149–150.

17. Harold Black, "Restrictive Covenants in Relation to Segregated Negro Housing in Detroit" (master's thesis, Wayne State University, Detroit, 1947).

18. Ibid., 58–59.

19. Ibid., 13–23.

20. The deterioration of this neighborhood's housing stock is explored in John Gries and James Ford, eds., *Negro Housing: Report of the Committee on Negro Housing* (Washington, DC: President's Conference on Home Building and Home Ownership, 1932), 127–128.

21. On the diversity and internal tensions within Detroit's and the east side's Black communities, see Victoria W. Wolcott, *Remaking Respectability: African American Women in Interwar Detroit* (Chapel Hill: University of North Carolina Press, 2001). On the geography of immigrant populations in the late 1920s, see Jerome Thomas, "The City of Detroit: A Study in Urban Geography" (Ph.D. diss., University of Michigan, Ann Arbor, 1928), fig. 7, 101–102.

22. "Stop Rioting, Smith Pleads with Citizens." Boyle cites the Improvement Association's questions: see Boyle, *Arc of Justice*, 131.

23. Gries and Ford, *Negro Housing*, 35.

24. David M. P. Freund, *Colored Property: State Policy and White Racial Politics in Suburban America* (Chicago: University of Chicago Press, 2007), 10–13.

25. Thomas, "The City of Detroit," 101–102.

26. An employee in Ford's employment office during the 1910s, for example,

relays—in a story that seems to illustrate the lewd imagination of its teller more than the lived experience of the boardinghouse—that the Sociological Department found a boardinghouse with eighteen male residents where "each man had a contract to have the landlady as their wife every 18 days," a condition to which the interviewed employee believed the Sociological Department had put a stop: A. G. Bondie, interview by Owen Bombard, accession no. 65, 1958, print transcript, Collections of the Henry Ford Museum of American Innovation, Dearborn, MI, 14.

27. Myrdal, *An American Dilemma*, 591.

28. Black, "Restrictive Covenants in Relation to Segregated Negro Housing in Detroit." The quote is from a letter of appeal from a white neighborhood association in far southwestern Detroit to the local police station in 1945.

29. H. W. Evans, "The Attitude of the Knights of the Ku Klux Klan toward the Jew," *Papers Read at the Meeting of Grand Dragons at their First Annual Meeting Held at Ashville, North Carolina, July 1923*, Ku Klux Klan Files, Burton Historical Collection, Detroit Public Library (hereafter, Burton Collection).

30. Ku Klux Klan, *The K.K.K. Katechism: Pertinent Questions, Pointed Answers*, pamphlet, 1924, Burton Collection, 34.

31. McGreevy, *Parish Boundaries*, 29–38.

32. Kenneth T. Jackson, *The Ku Klux Klan in the City, 1915–1930* (New York: Oxford University Press, 1967), xi–xii.

33. Levine, *Internal Combustion*, 136.

34. Jackson, *The Ku Klux Klan in the City*, 128–129.

35. Reprinted from *The Nation*, September 14, 1921: Albert de Silver, *The Ku Klux Klan*, American Civil Liberties Union, (New York 1921), Burton Collection, 2. The author of the pamphlet, a critic of the Klan, used this quote to illustrate the Klan's absurdly grandiose claims.

36. Imperial Commander of the Women of the Ku Klux Klan, "American Women," *Kourier Magazine*, April 1925, 11–15.

37. On the Detroit chapter's growth, see Jackson, *The Ku Klux Klan in the City*, 128–133. On the culture of fear that fed the organization in the 1920s, see ibid., 235–249.

38. Ibid., 130–136.

39. "Elaborate Program on Seven Mile Road," *Fiery Cross: Michigan State Edition*, November 30, 1923, 1, 8. At an earlier event, also on Seven Mile and perhaps at the same site, an "electric cross" was used: Jackson, *The Ku Klux Klan in the City*, 131.

40. "Elaborate Program on Seven Mile Road."

41. Jackson, *The Ku Klux Klan in the City*, 136.

42. "Do You Want Klan Rule?" *Pipp's Weekly*, October 17, 1925, 1–4; "Smith's Record," *Pipp's Weekly*, October 24, 1925, 1–6.

43. See Boyle, *Arc of Justice*, 151–169; Farley et al., *Detroit Divided*, 144–149; Levine, *Internal Combustion*, 151–198; Thomas, *Life for Us Is What We Make It*, 135–143. Each addresses Detroit's neighborhood violence of 1925.

44. WestSiders, *Remembering Detroit's Old Westside, 1920–1950: A Pictorial History of the WestSiders* (Detroit: WestSiders, 1997).

45. See Wolcott, *Remaking Respectability*, 134–136. Wolcott describes the west side as "middle-class," though the presence of working-class households in the district is illustrated by the many oral histories of the area's early twentieth-century children that reference their parents' industrial work.

46. Ibid.; Boyle, *Arc of Justice*, 151.
47. WestSiders, *Remembering Detroit's Old Westside*, 103.
48. Ibid., 104; Boyle, *Arc of Justice*, 151.
49. "Smith Blames Klan Politics for Race Rows," *Detroit Free Press*, September 13, 1925.
50. Jackson, *The Ku Klux Klan in the City*, 137.
51. On the anxieties of white immigrants who felt that their modest social gains were being threatened by racial integration, see ibid., 240–245; McGreevy, *Parish Boundaries*, 34.
52. David R. Roediger, *Working toward Whiteness: How America's Immigrants Became White* (New York: Basic, 2005), 32.
53. Marcet Haldeman-Julius, *Clarence Darrow's Two Great Trials: Reports of the Scopes Anti-evolution Case and the Dr. Sweet Negro Trial* (Girard, KS: Haldeman-Julius, 1927), 29, 40.
54. Ibid., 40.
55. Citizens Research Council of Michigan, *Population (1930 Census) and Other Social Data for Detroit by Census Tracts* (Detroit: Bureau of Governmental Research, 1937), 8, tract 119.
56. WestSiders, *Remembering Detroit's Old Westside*, 103.
57. Ibid.
58. Ibid. The emphasis is Fleta Mathis's.
59. "Negroes Saved from Big Mob by City Police," *Detroit Free Press*, April 10, 1925.
60. This is a reference to the title of Dianne Harris's *Little White Houses*, a phrase that succinctly captures the interwoven construction of race and domestic space.
61. From Fleta Mathis's recollection, published in WestSiders, *Remembering Detroit's Old Westside*, 103.
62. Ibid.
63. Thomas notes that in the early twentieth century, carrying concealed weapons was a more common part of Black and white southern culture than of northern culture: Thomas, *Life for Us Is What We Make It*, 114.
64. Farley et al., *Detroit Divided*, 145.
65. Ibid., 136–137. See also Boyle, *Arc of Justice*, 152–155; Levine, *Internal Combustion*, 153–154.
66. Haldeman-Julius, *Clarence Darrow's Two Great Trials*, 40.
67. Ibid., 60–61.
68. "Negroes Saved from Big Mob by City Police."
69. Levine, *Internal Combustion*, 153–154.
70. Based on four persons per residence—the rough average according to the city's 1930 census—and an average of seventy-five residences per block, as observed in the Northfield Avenue context.
71. With a conventional nine square feet of standing room per person, this stretch of Northfield's 39,000 square feet could accommodate only 4,330 rioters.
72. "Negroes Saved from Big Mob by City Police."
73. hooks, "Homeplace (A Site of Resistance)," 41–49.
74. See the floor plan presented in Chapter 4.
75. Boyle, *Arc of Justice*, 151; WestSiders, *Remembering Detroit's Old Westside*, 104.
76. WestSiders, *Remembering Detroit's Old Westside*.

CHAPTER 8

Epigraph: Upton Sinclair, *The Jungle* (New York: Jungle, 1906), 176–177.

1. Upton Sinclair, *The Flivver King: A Story of Ford-America* (Detroit: United Automobile Workers of America, 1937), 32–33.
2. Ibid., 41, 77, 89–90.
3. Ibid., 90.
4. Sidney Fine, *Frank Murphy: Volume 1, The Detroit Years* (Ann Arbor: University of Michigan Press, 1975), 257–258. See also Steve Babson, *Working Detroit: The Making of a Union Town* (New York: Adama, 1984), 56–57; Irving Bernstein, *The Lean Years: A History of the American Worker, 1920–1933* (Chicago: Haymarket, 2010), 300.
5. Ramsay Muir, "Detroitism," in *America the Golden: An Englishman's Notes and Comparisons*, by Ramsay Muir (London: Williams and Norgate, 1927), 81–87.
6. Ibid., 81, 83–84. Automobile production began to slow down in 1926–1927, though following Ford's release of the Model A, the industry saw a record high production year in 1929 before falling again: see Joyce Shaw Peterson, *American Automobile Workers, 1900–1933* (Albany: State University of New York Press, 1987), 130. Mason Doan illustrates that the robust American homebuilding market of 1923–1926 had declined considerably by 1928–1929: Mason C. Doan, *American Housing Production, 1880–2000: A Concise History* (Lanham, MD: University Press of America, 1997), 4, 27–36.
7. Reprint of "Detroitism" from *Pipp's Weekly* (n.d., 1929), apparently distributed by the Detroit Real Estate Board, filed in Detroit Real Estate Board 1922 folder (anachronistically), Burton Historical Collection, Detroit Public Library (hereafter, Burton Collection). The title of the article borrows the neologism "Detroitism" from the British historian Ramsay Muir, who had coined it two years earlier in his travelogue *America the Golden*.
8. "City to Handle All Job Calls," *Detroit News*, October 4, 1930.
9. Howard Beebe, interview by Owen Bombard, accession no. 65, 1954, print transcript, Collections of the Henry Ford Museum of American Innovation, Dearborn, MI.
10. Miles L. Colean, *American Housing, Problems and Prospects* (New York: Twentieth Century Fund, 1944), 226, 258.
11. Ibid.
12. Nelson Young, *A Study of the Problems of the Distressed Home Owner of Detroit as Revealed by Applications to the Home Owners' Loan Corporation: Report to the Earhart Foundation* (Ann Arbor: Earhart Foundation, 1934), 5, 31.
13. Lowell Harriss, *History and Policies of the Home Owners' Loan Corporation* (New York: National Bureau of Economic Research, 1951), 20, 32–38.
14. Doan, *American Housing Production*, 34; Young, *A Study of the Problems of the Distressed Home Owner of Detroit as Revealed by Applications to the Home Owners' Loan Corporation*, 9–12, 25–26.
15. Bernstein, *The Lean Years*, 288; Fine, *Frank Murphy*, 266.
16. Fine, *Frank Murphy*, 259.
17. "City to Handle All Job Calls"; "J. N. Duncan in Charge at Job Headquarters," *Detroit News*, October 1, 1930.
18. "City Sand Men Carry Cards," *Detroit News*, January 3, 1931.

19. "Sale of Sand Is Increasing," *Detroit News*, December 29, 1930; "Sale of Sand to Aid Jobless," *Detroit News*, December 23, 1930.
20. Fine, *Frank Murphy*, 306–307.
21. Frank Murphy, quoted in "Some Bums Depart," *Detroit Saturday Night*, March 21, 1931. This quote appears in part in Fine, *Frank Murphy*, 259.
22. "Some Bums Depart."
23. Fine, *Frank Murphy*, 277.
24. Murphy, quoted in ibid., 271.
25. Peterson, *American Automobile Workers*, 135.
26. "He Wants a Job," *Detroit News*, October 3, 1930.
27. Ibid.
28. "Cold Crowds City Shelters," *Detroit News*, November 29, 1930.
29. Peterson, *American Automobile Workers*, 135.
30. "Torch Applied to Shantytown," *Detroit Free Press*, December 23, 1930.
31. Ibid.
32. Ibid.
33. Fine, *Frank Murphy*, 284.
34. "City Gardening Plan Launched," *Detroit News*, March 7, 1931; "Clubs Back Job Garden Plan," *Detroit Times*, March 21, 1931; Peterson, *American Automobile Workers*, 136–137.
35. "Mayor Forms Garden Group," *Detroit Times*, March 24, 1931.
36. "City Gardens Sought by 850," *Detroit News*, March 20, 1931.
37. Detroit Thrift Gardens Committee, "Report of the Detroit Thrift Gardens Which Helped to Feed 4,369 Families in 1931," Unemployed File, Burton Collection, 5–7, 15.
38. Detroit Thrift Gardens Committee, *Detroit Thrift Gardens: Model Layout for Vegetable Garden, Revised for 1933*, pamphlet, Unemployed File, Burton Collection. Regarding the overseers' schedule, see "Assign 6,000 Garden Plots," *Detroit Times*, April 28, 1931.
39. "Sons of Eleven Nations Toil Joyously in Thrift Gardens," *Detroit News*, May 13, 1931.
40. Ibid.
41. "Leaders Divide on Five-Day Week," *Detroit News*, November 11, 1930.
42. Ibid.
43. Ibid.; Bernstein, *The Lean Years*, 306.
44. Peterson, *American Automobile Workers*, 131.
45. The Unemployed Council calculated this by examining a sample of thirty-two thousand unemployed workers living in Detroit: Fine, *Frank Murphy*, 309–310.
46. Peterson, *American Automobile Workers*, 137.
47. Bernstein, *The Lean Years*, 426; "Idle Protest to the Mayor," *Detroit News*, October 25, 1930.
48. Babson, *Working Detroit*, 57.
49. Sinclair, *The Flivver King*, 58, 85–87.
50. On the breadth of participation in the Unemployed Councils, see Christopher Johnson, *Maurice Sugar: Law, Labor, and the Left in Detroit, 1912–1950* (Detroit: Wayne State University Press, 1988), 117.
51. "Idle Protest to the Mayor."
52. Ibid.

53. Ibid. On criticism of Murphy, see "Detroit Gibed as Sap Town," *Detroit Free Press*, March 20, 1931; "Some Bums Depart."
54. "Greater Help Asked of City," *Detroit News*, October 26, 1931.
55. "Greater Help Asked of City," *Detroit News*, February 26, 1931.
56. Babson, *Working Detroit*, 56.
57. Ibid., 57.
58. Fine, *Frank Murphy*, 247–250, and Peterson, *American Automobile Workers*, 131–135, cite the committee's report, "The Effect upon Detroit of the Three Years of the Depression."
59. Bernstein, *The Lean Years*, 428.
60. Babson, *Working Detroit*, 57–58; Johnson, *Maurice Sugar*, 117–118.
61. Maurice Sugar, *The Ford Hunger March* (Berkeley: Meiklejohn Civil Liberties Institute, 1980), 33.
62. Babson, *Working Detroit*, 59; Johnson, *Maurice Sugar*, 120; Sugar, *The Ford Hunger March*, 32–36.
63. Sugar, *The Ford Hunger March*, 34–36.
64. Ibid.; Babson, *Working Detroit*, 59; Johnson, *Maurice Sugar*, 121.
65. Henry Ford, as quoted in the epigraph to Chapter 2.
66. Sugar, *The Ford Hunger March*, 32. Average coal use is per International Labor Office, *An International Enquiry into Costs of Living: A Comparative Study of Workers' Living Costs in Detroit (USA) and Fourteen European Cities*, 2d rev. ed. (Geneva: International Labor Office, 1931), 185–186.
67. Johnson, *Maurice Sugar*, 122.
68. Bernstein, *The Lean Years*, 508–511; Young, *A Study of the Problems of the Distressed Home Owner of Detroit as Revealed by Applications to the Home Owners' Loan Corporation*, 1.
69. On the UAW's sit-down strike against General Motors in Flint, Michigan, see Sydney Fine, *Sit Down* (Ann Arbor: University of Michigan Press, 1969). On the labor movement in 1930s Detroit, see Johnson, *Maurice Sugar*.

CONCLUSION

Epigraph: Italo Calvino, *Invisible Cities* (New York: Harcourt Brace Jovanovich, 1974), 11.

1. See Kenneth T. Jackson, *Crabgrass Frontier: The Suburbanization of America* (New York: Oxford University Press, 1985); Thomas J. Sugrue, *The Origins of the Urban Crisis: Race and Inequality in Postwar Detroit* (Princeton, NJ: Princeton University Press, 1996); June Manning Thomas, *Redevelopment and Race: Planning a Finer City in Postwar Detroit* (Baltimore: Johns Hopkins University Press, 1997). On the case of Chicago, see Arnold Hirsch, *Making the Second Ghetto: Race and Housing in Chicago, 1940–1960* (New York: Cambridge University Press, 1983).
2. Bernadette Atuahene and Christopher Berry, "Taxed Out: Illegal Property Tax Assessments and the Epidemic of Tax Foreclosures in Detroit," *UC Irvine Law Review* 9, no. 4 (May 2019): 847–886; Julie Cassidy, "Detroit: The Evolution of a Housing Crisis," Michigan League for Public Policy, Lansing, May 2019, https://mlpp.org/detroit-the-evolution-of-a-housing-crisis.
3. Aaron Mondry, "Rising Rents, Falling Wages: Detroit's Poor Face a Housing Crisis," *Bridge Detroit*, August 21, 2018; Candice Williams, "Detroit Officials Brace for Affordable Housing Losses," *Detroit News*, December 10, 2018.

4. Thomas Piketty, *Capital in the Twenty-first Century* (Cambridge, MA: Harvard University Press, 2018), 31.

5. Jenny Schuetz, "Housing Trade-offs: Affordability Not the Only Stressor for the Middle Class," *Up Front* (blog), May 8, 2019, https://www.brookings.edu/blog/up-front/2019/05/08/housing-trade-offs-affordability-not-the-only-stressor-for-the-middle-class.

6. Reinhold Martin, Leah Meisterlin, and Anna Kenoff, *The Buell Hypothesis: Rehousing the American Dream* (New York: Temple Hoyne Buell Center, Columbia University, 2011); Brent Ryan, *Design after Decline: How America Rebuilds Shrinking Cities* (Philadelphia: University of Pennsylvania Press, 2012).

INDEX

Page numbers in italics refer to illustrations.

Adora phonographs, *133*, 134
Aggregate Architectural History Collaborative, 12
Akron, OH, 31
Aladdin Company, 80, 82, 94
Allied Chemical. *See* Solvay Process Company
Allwood, NJ, 62, 69
Amazon.com, Inc., 16
American Blower Company, 47
American Construction Council, 90
American Federation of Labor, 91
American Floor Surfacing Machine Company, 95
American Homes and Gardens, 66
American Institute of Architects, 91
Americanization, 13, 30–37, 40, 52–53, 113, 154
American Red Cross, 98
annexation, 4, 78, 112–113, 120
Architectural Forum, 63–64, 70
Associated Building Employers of Detroit, 91
Associated Charities (Detroit), 148
Associated Industries (Detroit), 91
Atterbury, Grosvenor, 65
automobiles: planning for, 66–67; production of, 4, 89, 97, 100, 203, 207, 219; purchase of, 8, 10, 128; use, 120, 153, 159
Auto Workers Union (AWU), 178

Bachelard, Gaston, 11, 19, 126
Ball, Charles, 77
Bates, Beth Tompkins, 51
Bauhaus (Dessau), 56, 59
Berlin, Germany, 13, 56, 59, *60*, *61*, 65, 74
Bethlehem Steel Corporation, 173
Bigott, Joseph, 12, 81
Black, Harold, 149
Black Bottom neighborhood, 49–51, *50*, 139, *140*, 149
Black migrants and workers: employment discrimination against, 5, 30, 49; Great Migration of, 22–23, 29, 48–49; houses of, 24, 114–115, *116*, 129–130, 139–141, *140*; segregation of, 6, 23, 42, 111–112, 139, 149, 169, 187; violence against, 14–15, 145–162. *See also* Black Bottom neighborhood; Eight Mile-Wyoming neighborhood; Westside neighborhood
Blair, Frank, 77
boarding, 24–28, 39, 68, 155, 164, 217
Bolshevism, 32
Boston, MA, 91

Bowles, Charles, 154, 156
Boyd, David Knickerbacker, 92
Boyle, Kevin, 27, 193
Brightmoor development, 8, 85–86, 87–88, *111*, 112–114, 120, 133, *134*
Brighton Mills, 62, 69
British Housing and Town Planning Act (1919), 57
Broadacre City, 100
Bruchfeldstrasse housing estate, 58
Building Age, 80, 87–92, 133
bungalows: construction of, 13, 87–88; design features of, 6–7, *7*, 71, 72, 79–86, *84–86*, 133; semi-bungalows among, 42, *43*, 82, *84–85*
Burgess, Ernest, 101–105, *102*
Burton, Charles, 71; Burton's Michigan Avenue Subdivision, *63*, 70, *71–73*, 87

Cadillac Motor Car Company, 45
Calvino, Italo, 183
Campanella, Tommaso, 66
capitalism, 3, 10–12, 56, 181, 186
Carman, Harry, 101
Certeau, Michel de, 11, 27, 124
Chaplin, Charlie, 1
Chicago, IL, 6, 14, 37, 77, 82, 91, 147
Chicago School (of sociology), 101
children of workers: care of, 14, 81, 128–135, 141; in reform discourse, 26, 40, 42, 77, 104, 141
Christians, 5, 21, 27, 29, 112; Catholicism among, 73, 135–136; Protestantism among, 77, 115, 148, 160; tensions between denominations of, 152, 156
cleanliness ideal, 40, 42, 83, 138
Clough, H. T., 97
Clyde, Walt, 108, *109*
Cohen, Lizabeth, 11, 133
Colean, Miles, 165–166
College Park neighborhood, 89
Columbia University, 101
Commerce Department (U.S.), 78–79; *How to Own Your Home* pamphlet by, 47–48, 103–104
communism, 15, 174, 181; Unemployed Councils, 174–176, *175*. See also Ford Hunger March
Congrès Internationaux d'Architecture Moderne (CIAM), 9
Connolly, Nathan Daniel Beau, 12, 148
consumer credit, 7–8, 132–133, 165
coronavirus, 16

cottages, 37, 81, *82*, 125, *150*
Couzens, James, 39, 78
Croster Lumber and Fuel, 80
cult of domesticity, 108
Culver, Harry, 98

Dearborn, MI, 15, 120, 173, 178–179
deed restrictions. See restrictive covenants
Delray neighborhood, 62, 74, 110–111, 171
democracy, 2, 61. See social democracy
Democratic Party, 180
Denby, Elizabeth, 59–60
Department of Labor (U.S.), 78
Detroit, MI: City Council, 77–78; growth of, 4, 31, 78, 97–100, 194; Health Department, 77; maps of, *56*, *110*; municipal bankruptcy of, 185; municipal schools of, 36, 137; municipal transit and utilities of, 78, 89, 112, 117; Thrift Gardens program of, 169–173, *171*, *172*; Unemployment Committee, 166–169, 173–176
Detroit Board of Commerce, 22, 33–34, 45, 75, 77–78, 170; Americanization Committee, 49–51; Committee on Education, 35; *The Detroiter*, 31, *32*, 34, 46–47; Free Information Bureau for Aliens, 35–36; *Manual of American Citizenship*, 37
Detroit Federation of Labor, 173
Detroit Free Press, 87–88, 145, 158–159, 168
Detroit House Finance Corporation, 46–47
Detroit Housing Association, 77, 88
Detroitism, 4, 165
Detroit News, 108, 127, 167–168, 170, 176
Detroit Public Health League, 76–77
Detroit Real Estate Board (DREB), 78, 97–99, 170
Detroit Saturday Night, 168
Detroit Seamless Steel Tube Company, 111
Detroit Society for Savings, 46–47
Detroit Urban League, 23, 49
Diplock, Frank, 128
Dodge Brothers Company, 31
Douglas, Mary, 126, 134
dreams, 1–2, 79, 125, 139, 187
duplexes (two-flats), 155, *160*; construction of, 13, 93; design features of, 71, 72, 79–88, 83, *84–85*, 161; as income property, 83
Dziennik Polski (Polish Daily News), 117–119, *118*, 133

East St. Louis, IL, 147
Eight Mile-Wyoming neighborhood, *111*, 112, 114–115, *116*
Ellis Island, 20–21
England, 13, 56–57. *See also* Roehampton estate
Entre Nous club, 155
eugenics, 150
eviction and foreclosure, 15, 48, 163–164, 173–179, *176–177*, 186

Farley, Reynolds, 146, 158
Federal Housing Authority, 115
Ferndale, MI, 42
Fishman, Robert, 12
Fletcher, John, *146*, 159
Ford, Edsel, 66
Ford, Henry, 10, 31, 70, 108, 178
Ford Hunger March, 177–181, *179–180*
Fordism, 4, 10
Ford Motor Company, 124, 164; corporate welfare, 38; Depression-era policies of, 165, 170, 173; English School, 33–34, *35–36*; Five Dollar Day, 23, 38–40, 52, 68, 70; Ford Hunger March violence, 15, 177–181; Fordson Village, 62, *63*, 65–66, *67–69*, 71, 186; *Helpful Hints and Advice to Employes* manual by, 38, 40–41, 52; Highland Park Plant, 24, 39, 108, 111, 121; moving assembly line and mass production at, 4, 89, 203; River Rouge plant, 108, *109–110*, 111; Sociological Department investigations, 24–27, *25*, 38–42, *40*, 119, 135, *136*, 151, 167, 217; working schedules within, 132, 134. *See also* Ford Hunger March
foreclosure. *See* eviction and foreclosure
Forest Hills Gardens, 65
Frankfurt, Germany, 6, 58
Frankfurt Kitchen, 58
Freund, David, 112
Fritz, M. Kelly, 23
F. S. Prikryl and Company, 106

Gamble House, 81
Garb, Margaret, 12
garden cities, 57–58, 62, 66
Gary, IN, 48
Gemmer Manufacturing Company, 47
General Electric, 173
General Motors, 164, 168, 173; Modern Housing Corporation subsidiary of, 47, 88

Germany, 6, 13, 55, *56*, 66; centers of modernism, 58; Weimar Constitution of, 57. *See also* Bauhaus (Dessau); Bruchfeldstrasse housing estate; Haselhorst housing estate
Getis, Victoria, 27, 193
Goddard, Paulette, 1
Goodyear Heights, OH, 62–63
Gray, Eileen, 191
Great Depression, 15, 164–181
Great Recession, 16, 185–186
Greene and Greene, 81
Greenwich Village neighborhood, 123
Gregory, James, 23
Gropius, Walter, 59
Grosse Pointe Park, MI, *110*
Guest, Edgar, 130

Haldeman-Julius, Marcet, 159
Hamtramck, MI, 4, 31, *110*, 111, 119–120, 127
Hannan, William, 99, 101
Hannan Real Estate Exchange, 99–100, 106–107
Harriman, Karl: *The Homebuilders*, short story collection by, 124–126
Harris, Dianne, 145
Harris, Richard, 8, 12, 79, 83, 95
Harvard Bureau of Vocational Guidance, 34
Haselhorst housing estate, 56, 59, *60*, *61*, 65, 74
Haymaker, K. V., 78
Highland Park, MI, *4*, 31, 106, *110*, 120, 173
Hodur, Francis, 73
home economics, 136–138
homeownership: challenges in achieving, 7, 45–46, 131, 148, 185; expansion of, 7–8; financing of, 45–48, 114, 117; promotion of, 14, 37–39, 47–48, 66–68, 106–107, 117–118, *118*
Home Owners Loan Corporation (HOLC), 8, 83, 166, 180, 184–185
hooks, bell, 145
Hoover, Herbert, 47–48, 69–70, 78, 103, 168–169, 184
housebuilding, 13, 75–76, 78; light wood framing in, 93, *94*; modernization of practices in, 87–95; as speculative development, 14, 71–74, 87–89, 108, 111; standards for, 79; stock plans for, 79, *80*

housing: affordability of, 5, 51, 105, 114, 118; demolition and abandonment of, 15–16, 120, 183, 186; modern features in, 6–8, 41, 58, 64, 68, 105, 125–126, 137–138; outfitting and maintenance of, 128–129, 130–138, 141; production quantities of, 2, 4, 70, 76; as a social right, 3, 174–177, 184. See also cleanliness ideal; cult of domesticity; eviction and foreclosure; housebuilding; planned housing estates; privacy ideal; segregation
Housing Association (Detroit), 25
Housing Commission (Michigan), 25
Housing Law of Michigan (1917), 77
Howard, Ebenezer, 57, 66. See also garden cities
Hubka, Thomas, 12, 79, 82
Hyde Park neighborhood, 147

immigrants, 13, 157; "new immigrants" among, 20, 29–30, 33, 49, 92, 111, 152; points of origin of, 19–20, 27, 29, 52, 62, 111, 157; present-day, 184. See also Polish immigrants and workers; Russian immigrants and workers
International Labor Office (ILO), 8, 15, 74, 123

Jackson, Kenneth, 12
Jacobs, Jane, 9–10, 123, 128
Jefferson Rouge development, 62, 63, 64, 66–67, 70, 71
Jews, 9, 20–22, 49, 112, 141, 156
Jim Crow, 23. See also segregation

Keating, Ann Durkin, 111
Keaton, Buster, 94
Kelly, Ashmun, 90
Kenny, Judith, 79, 82
Kenoff, Anna, 186
Kermode, Bob, 128
Kistler Industrial Village, 62–63
Kostruba, Joe, 41
Ku Klux Klan, 152–157, *152–154*

Ladies' Home Journal, 81
Lambrecht, Kelly and Company, 111
Lawrence, MA, 31
Le Corbusier, 55
Lee, Oscar, 23
Levine, David, 152
Lewinnek, Elaine, 7, 12, 112
Lewis, Eugene W., 33, 46

life insurance, 107
Lincoln Park, MI, 83
Loeb, Carolyn, 113
London, England, 13, 56; London County Council Architect's Department, 57. See also Roehampton estate
Los Angeles, CA, 6, 12, 85, 98
Louisville, KY, 92
Lovett, John, 173
Low-Income Housing Tax Credit (LIHTC) subsidies, 185
Lynd, Helen and Robert, 106, 123, 130

Maloney Subdivision, 70
Mann and MacNeille, 63, 64, 66
Marquis, Samuel, 34, 38, 70
marriage, 39
Martel, Frank, 173
Martin, Reinhold, 186
Marx, Oscar B., 34
Marxism, 10
Mathis, Fleta and Aldine, 155–162, *156*
May, Charles, 64
May, Ernst, 58
McGreevey, John, 152
Meisterlin, Leah, 186
Merchant, Samuel A., 104
Merrill-Palmer Motherhood and Home Training School, 137–138
Meyer, Steven, 37–38
Miami, FL, 12
Michigan Manufacturers Association, 173
modernism, 6, 58–59, 75–76
Modern Times (film), 1
Moscow, Russia, 6, 174–175
Muir, Ramsay, 165
Muncie, IN, 106, 130–131
Murphy, Frank, 15, 164–169, 179–180
Muslims, 27
Myrdal, Gunnar, 151

National Americanization Committee, 33
National Association for the Advancement of Colored People (NAACP), 164
National Association of Real Estate Boards (NAREB), 78, 98
National Association of Realtors, 14
National Lamp Works, 45
New Deal, 3, 184
Newton, W. M., 92
New York, NY, 22, 24, 26, 33, 63, 77, 100, 123. See also Forest Hills Gardens; Greenwich Village neighborhood
Nichols, Jesse Clyde, 70, 88

Nicolaides, Becky, 8, 12, 83
Nolen, John, 62, 69

One Week (film), 94
Our Savior on Golgotha Church, 73
Own Your Own Home campaign, 3, 78

Packard Motor Car Company, 34–35, 203
Paige Detroit Motor Car Company, 111
Panama-Pacific Exposition, 42
Paradise Valley, 149
Paull, Charles, 34
Pierce-Arrow Motor Car Company, 45
Pipp's Weekly, 89, 153–156, *154*, 165
planned housing estates, 57–70, 184
Polish immigrants and workers, 20–22, 36, 122, 124–128, 141, 147; houses of, 7, 117–120. See also *Dziennik Polski* (Polish Daily News); Hamtramck, MI
Polish National Catholic Church, 73
Portland Cement Association, 89
Preston, E. D., 117
privacy ideal, 7, 24, 77, 82–83, *84*, 164
Progressive Era, 25, 33, 41, 77
Pullman, IL, 68

rail lines, 78, 108, *110*
Raymond, Philip, 175
real estate agents, 97–107, 111, 117–120, 148, 165. See also Detroit Real Estate Board (DREB); National Association of Real Estate Boards (NAREB); National Association of Realtors; Own Your Own Home campaign; restrictive covenants
Reid, Katherine E., 23
renting: challenges of, 48, 68, 107, 149, 160; costs of, 75; property for, 83, 87, 103; rates of, 8. See also boarding
restrictive covenants, 49, 111–114, 117, 148–149. See also *Shelley v. Kraemer*
Riis, Jacob, 24, 26
River Rouge, MI, *110*
Roediger, David, 20
Roehampton estate, 56–63, *56*, *60*, *61*, 67, 74
Rohr, Paul, 100–101, 107
Roosevelt, Franklin Delano, 180–181
Rosenberg, Samuel, 88
Roveda, Peter: City of the Sun proposal by, 65, 66
Russia, 6, 55, 174–175; Russian Revolution, 31

Russian immigrants and workers, 21–22, 26, 29, 36
Ryan, Brent, 186

Sanborn Fire Insurance Maps, 27, *28*, 73, 160
Schütte-Lihotzky, Margarete, 58
scientific management, 37
Sears, Roebuck and Company, 80, 94
segregation, 5–6, 48–52, 103–104, 145–162, 187. See also restrictive covenants
Seldon, Felix, 135
Sert, José Luis, 9, 123
Shelley v. Kraemer, 148. See also restrictive covenants
shrinking cities, 15
Sibley Lumber Company, 75, 81–83, *84*, 93, 134
Sinclair, Upton: *The Flivver King* by, 163–164, 174; *The Jungle* by, 46, 163
Sloan Brothers Development Company, 89
Smith, John, 147, 156
social contract, 2–5, 55, 97, 112, 124, 142, 163–181, 183; racial dynamics of, 51, 146–147; of today, 16, 187
social democracy, 57
Solvay Process Company, 47, 62, 70. See also Jefferson Rouge development
Sosnowski, Jan B., 119
southerners, 22–23, 134, 155, 158
Springwells neighborhood, 109–111, 113, 168, 178
Starbucks Corporation, 16
Steiner, Edward, 20–21
St. Hedwig Church, 127
Stieglitz, Alfred, 20
St. Lawrence Seaway, 101
Studebaker Company, 79, 168
Sugrue, Thomas, 114
Swanson, Roy, 103
Sweet, Ossian, 15, 146, 155, 159
Sweetest Heart of Mary Catholic Church, 119
Syracuse, NY, 92

Tarbell, Ida, 41, 65
Taylor, Burt Eddy, 88, *105*, 107. See also Brightmoor development
Teaford, Jon, 111
Thomas, Jerome, 120, 121
Thomas, Richard, 23
Thomas, William, 21
Timken-Detroit Axle Company, 33, 46
Toronto, Canada, 12, 85

Törten housing estate, 59
Tronti, Mario, 12
Turner, Alexander, *146*, 159

Union Trust Bank, 77
United Auto Workers Union (UAW), 163, *177*
Unwin, Raymond, 57–58
urban renewal, 10, 184–185

Vandervoort, Joe, 168, *169*
Veiller, Lawrence, 77
von Saldern, Adelheid, 58

Warner, Sam Bass, 93
Washington, DC, 147
Washington, Forrester, 140, 148
Waterworks Park Improvement Association, 149
Wayne County, MI, 101
Welfare Managers' Association (Detroit), 24
Westside neighborhood, *129*, 135, 140–141, 155–162
whiteness, 17, 49, 145–146, 151–152, 158, 161
Wilder, Kate, 94
Willeke, Leonard, 66–70

women, 28–29, *132*, 138–139, 151–153, 176; employment and discrimination against, 5, 39–40, 131, 141
Wood, Albert, 70
Woodmere Cemetery, 110
workers: challenges of ageing for, 14, 106–107, 126, 166; range of jobs among, 5, 14, 23, 29, 40, 83, 90–91, 96; schedules of, 38, 89, 130–136; skilled vs. unskilled among, 8, 91, 95, 128; social divisions among, 121; unemployment of, 5, 15, 48, 163–181; unionization and strikes by, 3, 31, 68, 91, 164, 180; wages of, 4–5, 16, 31–32, 38, 40, 90–92, 131, 165, *175*, 185. *See also* Black migrants and workers; Christians; Jews; Muslims; Polish immigrants and workers; Russian immigrants and workers; southerners; women
Works Progress Administration (WPA), 115
World War I, 22, 33, 48, 62, 119
Wright, Frank Lloyd, 100

Young Woman's Home Association, 28–29

Zangwill, Israel, 195
Zaretsky, Eli, 21
zoning, 111, 185–186
Zunz, Olivier, 7, 12, 49, 104

Michael McCulloch is Associate Professor of Architecture at Kendall College of Art and Design of Ferris State University.

Kristin M. Szylvian, *The Mutual Housing Experiment: New Deal Communities for the Urban Middle Class*

Kathryn Wilson, *Ethnic Renewal in Philadelphia's Chinatown: Space, Place, and Struggle*

Robert Gioielli, *Environmental Activism and the Urban Crisis: Baltimore, St. Louis, Chicago*

Robert B. Fairbanks, *The War on Slums in the Southwest: Public Housing and Slum Clearance in Texas, Arizona, and New Mexico, 1936–1965*

Carlton Wade Basmajian, *Atlanta Unbound: Enabling Sprawl through Policy and Planning*

Scott Larson, *"Building Like Moses with Jacobs in Mind": Contemporary Planning in New York City*

Gary Rivlin, *Fire on the Prairie: Harold Washington, Chicago Politics, and the Roots of the Obama Presidency*

William Issel, *Church and State in the City: Catholics and Politics in Twentieth-Century San Francisco*

Jerome Hodos, *Second Cities: Globalization and Local Politics in Manchester and Philadelphia*

Julia L. Foulkes, *To the City: Urban Photographs of the New Deal*

William Issel, *For Both Cross and Flag: Catholic Action, Anti-Catholicism, and National Security Politics in World War II San Francisco*

Lisa Hoffman, *Patriotic Professionalism in Urban China: Fostering Talent*

John D. Fairfield, *The Public and Its Possibilities: Triumphs and Tragedies in the American City*

Andrew Hurley, *Beyond Preservation: Using Public History to Revitalize Inner Cities*

www.ingramcontent.com/pod-product-compliance
Lightning Source LLC
Chambersburg PA
CBHW060949230426
43665CB00015B/2129